RICHARD F. MEHL MFCC
4380 KATELLA AVE.
LOS ALAMITOS, CA 90720
(310) 598-8255

LOVE IS A CHOICE

D0962982

Other Books in the Series
The Lies We Believe, Dr. Chris Thurman
Worry-Free Living, Dr. Frank Minirth,
Dr. Paul Meier, Don Hawkins

LOVE IS A CHOICE

Dr. Robert Hemfelt,
Dr. Frank Minirth,
Dr. Paul Meier

THOMAS NELSON PUBLISHERS
Nashville

❖ *A Janet Thoma Book* ❖

❖ *A Janet Thoma Book* ❖

Clients' names and details of their stories have been changed and
intermingled to protect their identities.

Copyright © 1989 by Robert Hemfelt, Frank Minirth,
Paul Meier

All rights reserved. Written permission must be secured from the
publisher to use or reproduce any part of this book, except for
brief quotations in critical reviews or articles.

Published in Nashville, Tennessee, by Thomas Nelson, Inc. and
distributed in Canada by Lawson Falle, Ltd., Cambridge, Ontario.

Printed in the United States of America.

23 24 25 26 27 28 29 30

Scripture quotations are from THE NEW KING JAMES VERSION of the
Bible. Copyright © 1979, 1980, 1982, Thomas Nelson, Inc., Publishers.

Library of Congress Cataloging-in-Publication Data

Love is a choice : recovery for codependent relationships / Robert
Hemfelt . . . [et al.].
    p.   cm.
Includes bibliographical references.

    1. Co-dependence (Psychology) 2. Codependents—Rehabilitation.
I. Hemfelt, Robert.   ISBN 0-8407-3189-2
RC569.5.C63L68   1989
616.86—dc20
                      89-37906
                      CIP

CONTENTS

Acknowledgments

The authors are thankful for those whose contributions and assistance have made the publication of *Love Is a Choice* possible. We are especially grateful for the encouragement and work of Don Hawkins and for our wives, Susan Hemfelt, Mary Alice Minirth, and Jan Meier. We are also grateful to Sandy Dengler, who, with her composition skills, helped to transform years of notes and case studies into enjoyable reading; Janet Thoma, for her editorial and administrative expertise; Bruce Barbour, for his endless encouragement and support; Susan Salmon, for her editorial assistance; Vicky Warren and Kathy Short, for their tireless work, typing, revising, and proofing the copy; Kevin Kinback, for his research assistance.

PART ONE:

What Codependency Is

CHAPTER ONE

The Thread That Runs So True

Gladys Jordan perched on the edge of the chair with her feet squarely under her, as if she were ready to bolt. Her gnarled fingers laced in and out of each other, paused to draw a strand of graying hair out of her eyes, then resumed their anxious movement. Her fact sheet said she was fifty-three. She looked sixty-five.

In the chair beside her, her husband, John, crossed his arms and sat back with a scowl. A stocky, powerful man, he was by no means fat, but he'd been eating well. Fifty-four years of sun crinkled up his eyes and tanned his skin. A contractor by trade, he enjoyed a spotless reputation for always coming in under bid and on time.

"I'm here because Gladys wanted me to come," he announced. "I don't think a psychologist can help. It's too late."

John Jordan didn't soften.

Here at the Minirth-Meier Clinic, we understand from years of experience the unspoken objections behind John Jordan's guarded attitude, so we admitted that to him. "You may well feel that being here today is wrong," we said. "Seeking help from a psychologist or psychiatrist says that you're too weak to straighten things out yourself; perhaps you have no common sense, because that's all psychology is. After all, healthy people control their attitudes and emotions at all times. Are we close?"

"That's right."

"John, I understand you built your contracting firm from scratch."

"Started right out of high school, with a used pickup."

"How many trucks do you run now?"

"Seven pickups, two dumps, a couple vans, a front-end loader, and a blade." There was an edge of pride in John's voice—justifiable, healthy pride.

"I see. Too bad you're not stronger. If you were strong enough, you wouldn't need all those expensive tools. You could carry the loads yourself, level sites with a shovel . . ."

John's face was a beauty to behold. His expression shifted from confusion to realization (the aha! light-bulb-going-on look) to a sly twinkle. That twinkle was the first feeble sign that his hostility might be softening a bit, but the twinkle faded quickly. "I see your point. Counseling is a tool, but it still ends up the same. If I could just sit down and talk sense into myself, or if my faith were greater—we wouldn't be here."

"That's not so. You don't move mountains with a word; you use a grader, not because your faith is lacking but because it's the way it's done here on earth. We want to help you and your wife move a mountain.

"Gladys. Thirty-one years of marriage, three children—two boys and a girl. I assume they're out on their own now. What are they doing?" we asked.

Her voice rasped, as tight and jittery as her body. "John Junior got his BA in business and started a dry-cleaning business. He says it takes a lot of time and work, but he's doing very well. Marsha is an ER nurse at St. Joseph's Emergency Room. She likes lots of action, you know? She deals well with pressure. And James is . . ." She licked her lips. "He's had some problems, but he's in detox now and he'll do just fine."

"John, we understand your faith is very important to both of you. Divorce is not an option, right? You may have considered murder, but not divorce."

The corners of the contractor's mouth turned up, more a grimace than a smile. "You got that right." The non-smile melted away and at last a true softening crept in his voice.

"Talk about incompatibility. Irreconcilable differences. That's us, constantly. Marriage is supposed to be made in heaven. Ours sure wasn't! If divorce were an option—if we had the choice—one of us would have walked out years ago."

Gladys's features tightened. *If we had the choice.* She didn't have to use the word *trapped.* It was etched on her sad face.

Her hands had not ceased moving since she sat down. "John doesn't listen. He doesn't even try to hear what I say. It's so frustrating trying to get through a brick wall."

John countered, "She's not talking about communication. Communication is discussing good as well as bad. Everything she says is critical. In her eyes I can't do or say anything right. Whatever I provide, she wants more or different. It's never the right thing, never good enough."

There was no joy in the Jordans' marriage and their lives. The din of their constant friction had drowned out the quiet peace of a happy life. Here, on chairs positioned six feet apart, sat the ultimate tragedy: two good, sincere people wanting only to love each other, and they could not.

Through the Jordans' lives—perhaps through yours as well—runs a common thread causing untold misery and unhappiness. It tugs and pulls at their subconscious. It affects their judgment and robs them of choice, even as they falsely believe they are choosing intelligently and well. We at the Minirth-Meier Clinic, and others, have labeled that strand "codependency."

CODEPENDENCY

In its broadest sense, *codependency* can be defined as *an addiction to people, behaviors, or things*. Codependency is the fallacy of trying to control interior feelings by controlling people, things, and events on the outside. To the codependent, control or the lack of it is central to every aspect of life.

The codependent may be addicted to another person. In this interpersonal codependency, the codependent has become so elaborately enmeshed in the other person that the sense of self—personal identity—is severely restricted, crowded out by that other person's identity and problems.

Additionally, codependents can be like vacuum cleaners

gone wild, drawing to themselves not just another person, but also chemicals (alcohol or drugs, primarily) or things—money, food, sexuality, work. They struggle relentlessly to fill the great emotional vacuum within themselves. Our patients have described it as "walking around feeling like the hole in the center of the doughnut. There is something missing inside me."

SUPPORT GROUPS

Codependency was first recognized several decades ago as counselors endeavored to help alcoholics and their families. In the vanguard of this modern movement was Alcoholics Anonymous. The founders of AA observed several things about alcoholics: they were deeply embittered toward God, they were rebellious (independent), and at the same time they were childishly dependent upon those around them.

Although the first AA workers themselves knew God intimately, they felt that in some way they had to sidestep this bitterness toward God by using the phrase "God as I understand him" in their now-famous twelve steps. Their intention was to focus on the need for outside help. The alcoholic addiction was fought inch by inch, day by day through application of the steps and attendance at meetings with fellow alcoholics.

AA was successful in rescuing alcoholics, but there was serious fallout—the families were coming apart within a year after the alcoholics dried out. Workers realized that just as the alcoholic was dependent upon his or her alcohol, the family very frequently had become just as dependent upon the alcoholism. They had adjusted not only their whole lives but also their whole way of perceiving life to accommodate the alcoholic. They enabled him/her to keep the habit up; they denied; they ignored; they circumvented. To the kids especially, this warped life with an alcoholic parent was "normal." It was all they knew. The alcoholic was dependent upon the alcohol. The family was *codependent* upon alcoholism along with the alcoholic. Thus was born the term.

Al-Anon and Alateen were developed not to aid the alcoholic but those close to him. The program was designed to restructure the codependent's way of seeing the world—of unwarping him or her, if you will—to facilitate adjustment to a brand new family dynamic.

The concept of dependency and codependency is no longer limited to alcohol; it takes in the rest of the chemical spectrum—coke, pot, tobacco, heroin, and beyond. The "beyond" includes nearly any obsessive compulsion, a thing or a behavior carried to excess. Eating disorders (for example, anorexia, bulimia), sex addiction, rageaholism, workaholism, the compulsion to spend and spend, an extremely rigid and legalistic approach to living, the compulsion to wash one's hands fifty-five times a day—these and other addictions have been placed in the same class as alcoholism. These disorders and others affect the family and close associates—the *codependents*—who may suffer as severely as the dependent or more so.

The concept of codependency embraces the alcoholic also. The word *codependent* literally means "dependent with." People sometimes think of the spouse of the alcoholic as being the only codependent. Not so. The alcoholic himself or herself is actively codependent. His/her dependency is with a thing—alcohol. The spouse is dependent upon a person, the alcoholic, and upon the nature of the relationship as the spouse helps and enables the alcoholic. The two are equally dependent upon each other—codependent.

THE ULTIMATE TRAGEDY

Another tragedy with which we will deal in later chapters is the problem of the multigenerational nature. The serious dysfunction in a founding family will be absorbed by the children's families and then their children's families, a ripple of misery extending farther and farther down through the years. The dependency or dysfunction may change: an alcoholic father may sire, for instance, a workaholic son who sires a compulsive daughter who spends her way to bankruptcy. But it's there. It's almost always there, wreaking its damage.

At the clinic we treat many codependents—people with obsessive-compulsive behavior, their spouses and children, and children of dysfunctional families. Statisticians estimate that at least fifteen million Americans are alcoholic or drug dependent. We believe each alcoholic severely impacts at least four other significant people such as spouses, children, and coworkers. Potentially sixty million codependents suffer from the addiction of those fifteen million Americans. In addition, it is estimated that about twenty-eight million Americans are the adult children of alcoholics and still suffer from the codependency they experienced in their childhood.

And that's just alcohol. These figures do not address codependency generated by addictions and compulsions other than chemical abuse; they are, therefore, extremely conservative. The actual numbers of all codependents are much, much higher.

Epidemic. There's no other way to describe it. When roughly one hundred million Americans across two concurrent generations suffer problems of codependency, we are embattled by an epidemic of staggering degree. The unhappiness, despair and wasted life lie beyond comprehension.

Thousands of the patients at Minirth-Meier clinics throughout the country are codependents, and each of us counsels them, either as a psychiatrist (Dr. Frank Minirth and Dr. Paul Meier) or psychologist (Dr. Robert Hemfelt). The goal of counsel is twofold: to ease the immediate problems caused by codependency, and to prevent damage in the future, both to the codependents and to the generations following.

You stand a one-in-four chance of suffering from problems caused by codependency. What problems? Divorce and relationship difficulties, substance abuse, compulsive behaviors you can't seem to control, anger beyond reason, depression, and more. These are massive problems, recurring problems, problems that undermine your happiness and make life dismal.

What about you? Is codependency at the root of your unhappiness? And more importantly, if so, can it be somehow expunged to ease the misery?

There are two important reasons why you should examine your life and correct problems of codependency if they exist. One is to improve your own life, making it more manageable and controlled and avoiding serious mistakes. The other reason is the children, both yours and those around you. The impact of codependency, remember, is multigenerational.

Problems in this generation warp the next and condemn those following unless the cycle is broken. One of the most moving comments heard at the Minirth-Meier Clinic came from a young woman in therapy: "I'm not sure I'll ever fully achieve peace and happiness, but I've saved my children from this pain."

The Jordans needed the guiding hand of a trained counselor to unravel their tangled marital knot. We showed them what we as impartial observers could see. In this book we will walk you through that same process. In Part Two we will explore the causes of codependency: unmet emotional needs, lost childhood, and the compulsion to fix the dysfunctional family. You'll see how we brought the Jordans each to terms with the past. They analyzed it, raged about it, grieved over it, made peace with it. As you watch the Jordans deal with these issues, weigh their situation against your own personal circumstances.

In Part Three we'll look at the factors that lock codependents, like the Jordans, in a perpetual cycle of pain: the snowball effect of addiction, their denial, and their anger. Most of the thoughts and factors influencing the codependent's life are either buried, ignored, or unrecognized. We'll uncover them.

Next, in Part Four, we'll help you look at how codependency influences your relationships and how you can halt the destructive tapes playing in your mind.

Finally we'll take you stage by stage through the sometimes painful, sometimes exhilarating, steps to recovery. Discoveries of driving forces you never realized you had will emerge as you inventory your past. Anger will boil. Grief will work its healing. New choices and new directions will take you farther than you ever dreamed. It won't be easy.

Today the Jordans do not float airily through an idyllic existence. Their healing is much more profound and practical. John is still a workaholic, but he's aware of it now and compensates. Gladys understands better her place in the marriage. Most important, they know the ways in which the past drove them, and they are learning to circumvent those driving forces that once ruled so cruelly. For the first time in their lives, John and Gladys are tasting real happiness.

Much depends upon your desire to free yourself from the

ghosts of your own past. The children in your life will benefit, perhaps immeasurably. Your own happiness and your ability to genuinely love hinge on the decisions you make now.

Let's begin by looking at the ten traits of a codependent.

CHAPTER TWO

The Way Codependency Works

He was a depression-era kid, seven years old in 1929 when the stocks took their fatal plunge. "See?" his old man said. "Never put faith in money, Jerry, boy." His father, Phil Braley, didn't either. Whatever Phil Braley earned was spent within twenty-four hours. Same with his wife, Maude. Phil was never actually out of work, as were so many then. He remained fairly steadily employed as a delivery truck driver. Maude kept a little garden in her Los Angeles backyard and sometimes took in laundry. But no matter how much money she made, she never had any. Her wages disappeared as fast as Phil's.

From age nine on, only son Jerry Braley was never without a paying job. One of his best-paying jobs didn't last long; a covert cell of anarchists hired him to stuff political pamphlets under people's front doors after dark. The group was arrested and Jerry went on to more mundane jobs—sweeping floors, delivering papers and phone books, hawking oranges door-to-door.

Whenever he passed the Western Auto store, he'd check out the bikes. At first he wanted the red flyer with the mock tank on the crossbars and the pinstriping on the fenders. Then he didn't care whether it had any extras. Eventually, he didn't care what color it was. He wanted a bike. Any bike. He hungered. He yearned. And yet, for all the years he worked, he never accumulated enough money to buy a bike. His money always went to something the family needed when Dad was between paydays.

In high school Jerry was very competitive and excelled in athletics. At home he excelled in keeping creditors at bay. The family shopped at two local grocery stores and had accounts past due at both. Jerry would try one. If they refused to let him run up the bill further, he'd reshelve his purchases, highly embarrassed, and try the other store.

His family never owned a house or phone. Jerry was so ashamed of their rentals that when he got a ride home from school he'd get dropped off two blocks away. He painfully feared that someone would learn where he really lived.

Jill's family coped with the insecurity and tight money of the depression in just the opposite way. She, too, was seven when the market crashed. Her father, too, managed to remain employed throughout the depression, for he was a splendid carpenter. There the similarity ended. Phil Braley was a genial, laid-back, easygoing guy, ever ready to lend you a buck if he had it. Jill's father, Peter Winthrop, a tense and thundering rageaholic, hoarded every dime. Jill's family, like Jerry's, did without but not because of spendthrift ways. Just the opposite; money that should have gone for family needs went into the savings account instead. Belt-tightening eased and the country moved into war and prosperity. Phil Braley still never had a dime, and Peter Winthrop still hoarded every dime. Economic circumstances changed; the two families didn't.

Jerry grew into a handsome man, mature and poised. He was a little late starting a family, because he served in Korea and spent several years building a brokerage. During the war, Jill rose from clerk to director of the Los Angeles County Public Safety office. "A born manager," her superiors called her.

When Jill and Jerry met, it was love at first sight. Handsome bachelor wedded dark, slim beauty. As the years passed, Jerry amassed a chain of grocery stores and a major interest in a local bank. He's now worth in excess of fifty-five million. No Scrooge, he's an affable people-lover who spends well and frequently. He knows where to put his charity dollars and whom to trust. He knows how to live well.

Jill changed, too, her friends say. She always had responded to frightening or problematic situations by tightening control and screaming a lot. But instead of mellowing, she just kept getting worse. A compulsive cleaner, she hollered whenever Jerry or their only child, Bill, disturbed her tidiness by the mere act of living in the house. She criticized happy old Jerry every time he spent a dime, which was often. And her constant, extreme dieting was starting to threaten her health.

Jill and Jerry came into our clinic recently, not for themselves but for their son. Bill, at thirty-six, was the pride and the bane of their existence.

Jerry wagged his head sadly. "We gave the boy everything we could. If he wanted something, it was his. The best schools, the best home . . . everything. It's as if he has turned on us; and yet he hasn't. All I know is, something has to be done, and he's not about to do it himself. We're here hoping you can tell us how to reach him; how to get him straightened out before he ruins his life and our grandkids' lives."

"Tell us about Bill."

Jill grimaced, a tight prune face. "He majored in business administration in college. Jerry planned to give him the reins of the corporation someday, after he built up the necessary experience. A month before he was supposed to graduate from Yale he went into the Peace Corps or whatever they call it now. Lived like some bum in South America. I forget which country he went to."

Jerry chimed in, "But he only lasted a couple of months over there. He came home, went back to school, and took an interest in the business. A year later he flew to Boston with a woman . . . lived with her about eight months."

Jill's lips tightened into a thin white line. "She was, ah, of a different background . . . different socioeconomic status. She was everything you hope and pray your son will never run into. We can't imagine what possessed him to get involved with her. It's the worst, most horrible thing he could ever do."

"Then he met Karen," Jerry continued. "Sweet girl, goes to our church. Really a very nice girl. They have three children and a lovely home. The children go to a private school, a very good school. You'd think he would be content at last."

"He works for your company?"

"Yes. He's senior vice president. I'm grooming him to take it over."

If Jerry was proud of him, why did the voice sound so sad? "Why did you come see us, exactly?"

Jill looked like a storm at sea. Everything about her demeanor was bleak. "He's a . . . I guess you'd call him a sexaholic. Runs around on Karen constantly, with some of the most repulsive women you'd ever meet. I hesitate to call him depraved, but that's very close to it."

"And he gambles." Jerry sounded so weary. "Compulsive gambler. Dogs, ponies, Superbowl—his own bookie. Has a free suite whenever he wants it at three different hotels in Vegas. We're not talking penny-ante poker here. We're talking the big baccarat tables upstairs. I mean he *gambles*."

"Let's discuss the use of alcohol in your family."

"Nothing to discuss." Jerry brightened. "Neither my parents nor Jill's used it. Jill and I are both teetotalers. And to the best of my knowledge, Bill never drinks."

"Are you familiar with the term *codependency?*"

Jill fumed, wide-eyed. "Absolutely not! Unthinkable! That's a problem with alcoholics. My son is many things, but he is no drunkard! Nor has he ever been near one. Don't you dare so much as mention it!"

Despite Jill's bitter responses, her son, Bill, she, and her husband, as well, demonstrate the classic symptoms of extreme codependency. Although it has been unrecognized for a long time, it has become a disease of today. Codependency is emerging as *the* problem in part because today's lifestyle, attitudes, and goals magnify codependent tendencies. For generations the problem has been brewing, building. Now, fed by modern living, it's exploding.

Counselors are beginning to deal effectively with codependency. We have identified specific traits of codependents. As we go through these traits, see if they sound familiar.

1. *A codependent is driven by one or more compulsions*. The behavior may not always be labeled "bad"; in fact, some compulsions, such as workaholism, are valued in certain segments of society. Whether valued or repulsive, it's there.

Some common compulsions are alcohol, drugs, physical abuse of others, eating disorders, sexual addictions. Others are more subtle but no less driving: a need to count things, the need to arrange things geometrically or in a line, compulsive hand-washing.

Your answer to the question, What do you seek most in life? may reveal some compulsion. Are you in pursuit of money, prestige, power? If so, like Jerry Braley, you may be addicted to money or material things. Material gifts were Jerry's way of expressing love. He never spent time with Bill. He simply was never there for the boy. He spent his time making money and spent the money lavishly on Bill. It's the way he would have wished to be treated in his own impoverished childhood.

Mr. Jordan's problem was workaholism, an addiction just as powerful as alcoholism or drug abuse. "I'm a self-made man," John proclaimed, "building a two-hundred-thousand-gross business with a pickup truck and a lot of guts. It takes a six-day workweek and late hours to accomplish what I accomplished."

Is there some habit or repetitive pattern (anything from foot-tapping to marrying the wrong people time after time) that dominates your life?

2. *The codependent is bound and tormented by the way things were in the dysfunctional family of origin.* The ghosts of our past—our nurturing years and the child-hoods of our parents and their parents on back—wrap their eerie fingers around our present. Sometimes they whisper and sometimes they shout. The din can be helpful or damaging.

Jerry's poignant hunger in his youth—the bike he could never afford, the money that always disappeared, the constant need to earn, the shame and embarrassment—left a single indelible message: "It's not enough." The ghosts of his past scream, "There is never enough! Make more! Spend more! Money is the measure." Today his fifty-five million is not enough. He must earn more. The ghost of that red bicycle in the Western Auto store still speaks, even though Jerry could now buy the whole Western Auto chain.

Jill is a controller. She spent a frayed childhood trying to avert her father's rages. Today, not surprisingly, she controls with harsh criticism and rage. Her ghosts, too, cry, "It's not enough!" In the past she was severely censured for every cent spent. Today she can't stand to see money spent. It must be saved. Hoarded. Hear the ghosts?

The ghosts of the past were extraordinarily destructive in the relationship of John and Gladys Jordan. Mrs. Jordan's father was an alcoholic. As she grew up she could never trust him to be there when she needed him. He didn't listen to her; indeed, in his alcoholic stupors he was unable to comprehend. Her heart learned from her yesterdays that "All fathers are dulled and unheeding," regardless what her eyes and head today might see.

Mr. Jordan's father was an obsessive authoritarian for whom nothing was ever quite good enough. No matter what efforts little John made, Papa could see ample room for improvement. The only comment was criticism. Now whenever Gladys Jordan voiced a need or concern, John heard only the message, "What you're doing is not enough."

See the pattern?

Mr. Jordan, in fact, listened carefully to his wife and genuinely tried to understand. To the detached observer her accusation was unwarranted. Still, what she heard and saw was her original father, the man of the house. She could not get past that ghost to see the real man she married.

Mr. Jordan had just as severe a problem. The ghost of his past turned everything Gladys said into criticism. In truth, because of this tendency of his, she avoided criticizing him, even in healthy ways. The ghosts of their pasts managed to shout down reality.

Were we to deal only with the Jordans' surface problems—the lack of communication and the misperceptions—they could be in counseling for a hundred years and never budge off dead center. The ghosts must first be silenced.

Every person has these ghosts to some extent. In a healthy personality they are virtually silent, providing nothing more than a helpful little peep now and then. In the strongly codependent personality, they warp reality.

How loudly or how often do you hear your mom or dad's

voices today? Does a phrase such as "you never do anything right" echo in your mind?

3. *The codependent's self-esteem (and maturity, frequently) is very low.* Gladys Jordan could have justifiably mentioned her husband's shortcomings. She might have challenged his boasts of success with, "Self-made man, maybe. But where were you when the kids were croupy? Your son's graduation night, you were mixing cement to finish a job on schedule. You're so busy making yourself, you never have time for the kids or me." But she didn't and she wouldn't, because her self-image was so poor she had neither the courage nor the desire to speak up.

Was Bill Braley a senior vice president in his father's company because he was good or because he was the son? Everything he knew about himself came out of his parents; he was never his own man. In his youth he heard lips say "money isn't important" even as his parents weighed everything by its monetary value and argued bitterly over whether to spend or save. Even his image emerged confused and torn between polar extremes.

How contented with yourself are you? Do you defend yourself from unfair criticism? Do you feel as if you have no friends? What does that tell you about your self-esteem?

4. *A codependent is certain his or her happiness hinges on others.* A codependent's happiness depends almost totally on what others do and think. Jerry and Jill came to us not to improve their own happiness but because of their son's behavior should his peccadillos and his scandals become common knowledge. Jerry did the best he knew how to buy love; it was the only way he knew. Jill was not happy if she were not in complete control of herself and everyone around her. Such control was impossible; she was never happy.

John and Gladys were typically codependent as well. Mrs. Jordan believed, "If only he would listen to me, I could be happy. Our marriage would work then."

Mr. Jordan felt, "If she'd get off my back I'd love her more and make this marriage better."

Have you heard these words:

"If he/she would only change, I would be happy."

"If he/she will just express approval of me and my actions, I'll be happy."

"The only reason he/she is doing that is to destroy my peace of mind. He/she wants to hurt me and it's working."

Do you need that perfect marital mate to make your life complete?

5. Conversely, a codependent feels inordinately responsible for others. Parents are quite properly responsible for dependent children. That's not an issue here. Rather, the codependent feels acutely and personally responsible for just about everyone's happiness, feelings, thoughts, actions—even the ability to stay out of trouble.

"If I don't intervene, he/she will err grievously."

"I am causing his/her misery; if I work hard enough at being better, he/she will be happy."

"I don't want to handle this job/project, but _____ asked me, so I will. What I want is not as important as what _____ wants."

6. The codependent's relationship with a spouse or Significant Other Person (SOP) is marred by a damaging, unstable lack of balance between dependence and independence. No one shows that unstable extreme better than Bill Braley. In college, still completely financially dependent upon his parents, he felt a trap closing. He fled to South America, an act of desperate defiance. Extreme independence. And yet, so dependent was he upon home, he was back in months. Again that wildly independent escape to Boston . . . and within months, the yo-yo string was wrapping up, pulling him home. His career, the payment of his mortgage and his children's school bills—all that is still dependent in large part on his father. And now he is rebelling again, furiously independent, by flying in the face of all his parents hold dear with his gambling and sexual exploits.

The opposite of codependency (and this cannot be said too often) is not independence. The dependent and codependent in a situation involving addiction are *too* independent; they're spitting in the world's eye, defying reason, common sense, and moral opinion even as they are dependent.

The opposite of codependency is *interdependence*. Each of us is born with a God-given need for relationships with others and a God-given gift to strike a healthy balance in those relationships between dependence and independence. Healthy interdependent persons can be dependent enough to open themselves up and be vulnerable. At the same time they hold a unique self-concept, which needs no other person to complete.

The best reason to attend a county fair is to see the six-up and eight-up draft horse teams—the great shires, Belgians, and Clydesdales. It's worth the price of admission just to feel the ground shake as they canter. The horses of a given team look very much alike, for they are matched for color and conformation. But inside, each horse has a distinct, clearly defined personality with sharp dislikes and preferences. Each is unique. Those horses are carefully chosen for their interdependence. In harness each pulls his own weight, each does his own thing, but he does it synchronously with the others. He works fully independently, and yet he is fully dependent upon the moves and the work of his teammates. Just as the well-matched team of horses functions in concert, so do the relationships of a healthy, noncodependent adult—including that amazing creature, the human adult in love.

7. *The codependent is a master of denial and repression.* Codependency comes out of a dysfunctional family of origin. And yet the codependent quite sincerely defends that family. If the codependent remembers details of childhood at all, frequently those details are isolated or were not as memory would have them. Codependents usually cannot see things as they are, will not evaluate circumstances as being as bad as they are, pretend bad things aren't happening, find introspection too painful.

In talking about her father, Gladys Jordan repeatedly added, "But he was actually a wonderful person down inside." John Jordan praised his father, insisting, "If my father weren't the way he was, I would not have developed the determination to be so successful. I owe him a lot."

8. *The codependent worries about things he or she can't change and may well try to change them.* They are frustrated, trying to control things and persons that are beyond their control and always will be. We discuss at length the relationship of negative self-concept and worry, or anxiety, in our book *Worry-Free Living*. People with a negative self-concept often expect to fail because they believe they are failures. When they view the future, they see disappointment, defeat. If reality proves them correct—if they do experience defeat—their frustration leads to even lower self-esteem. The embattled Jordans tried, to no avail, to achieve peace for thirty-one years. "See? I tried to do it and couldn't. I'm weak. Ineffectual. Worthless. I'm what I thought I was all along."

9. *Foremost, a codependent's life is punctuated by extremes*. Personal relationships are marked by extreme ups and downs, hots and colds. Lovers' quarrels recapitulate World War II and the loving moments make Bacchus look dull. Jill's father snuggled his daughter one moment and flew into a rage at her the next. He wasn't on booze or drugs; that's the way he was, and he couldn't help it.

Hoarding and spending, bankruptcy (possibly repeated), rage and tenderness, love and war—life hardly ever remains on an even keel for long. The perfect Mr./Ms. Right romance ends in messy divorce. This extreme polarization in the codependent's actions and relationships is one of the strongest hallmarks.

The codependent's attitudes about authority are usually extreme as well. The same person who is cloyingly self-abasing in the presence of the boss at work may exercise excessive authority at home. The codependent may deeply fear certain authorities and snub others. Again, there is no healthy balance, no sense of self-determination. It's another function of the polarizing nature of the codependent's life and attitudes.

10. *Lastly, a codependent is continually looking for the something that is lacking or missing in life*. We mentioned in chapter 1 that patients sometimes describe their state as "Walking around feeling like I have a huge hole, like the center of a doughnut, inside of me. There's something missing inside."

Codependents are restless and discontent regardless of external circumstance. Jerry Braley bought more and more of everything. He never had enough. Jill could never save enough. She could never exercise enough control. The crash diets so dangerous to her health were functions of that insatiable desire for total control. She couldn't control Jerry's money habits; she couldn't control Bill's self-destructive and shameful behavior. She could control her food intake, but it didn't fill the hole. And whatever Bill Braley's sexual excesses, he soon wanted more—that hadn't been enough. His gambling sated nothing; it, too, made him hungry for more.

These ten traits (see page 28) lock codependents into three responses that influence every day of their lives.

• Our concept of family and adulthood is shaped by our childhood, and *we are bound* (or condemned, some would say) *to repeat the family experience we remember.*

• In addition to repeating the childhood experience, *we let it shape most of our choices and even the way we perceive things.*

• *Logical and rational thought cannot alter the first two items.* The adult child of an alcoholic swears, "I will never *ever* marry a drinker and subject my family to the suffering I endured." That child will almost invariably pick an alcoholic or similarly dysfunctional mate despite all the good intentions, despite the hard knowledge of what dysfunction is like. Reason and logic seem to fly right out the window, banished by the seductive siren's song of the past.

The child may begin with the same premise, as did Gladys Jordan: "I will *never* marry a drinker"; and she may pick someone who seems the exact opposite, only to find some other addiction barring happiness. John did not touch alcohol, but he was every bit as powerfully addicted to work. Gladys was in a codependent relationship all the same.

It is important here to see that Gladys made her marriage choice not with her reasoning mind (though she thought she did) but as a reaction to her own father's alcoholism. And that alcoholism stirred unwelcome ghosts throughout her married life.

There was no alcohol whatever in the Braley family. And yet harsh, driving codependency raged like wildfire from one generation through the next.

THE TEN TRAITS OF A CODEPENDENT

1. The codependent is driven by one or more compulsions.

2. The codependent is bound and often tormented by the way things were in the dysfunctional family of origin.

3. The codependent's self-esteem (and, frequently, maturity) is very low.

4. A codependent is certain his or her happiness hinges on others.

5. Conversely, a codependent feels inordinately responsible for others.

6. The codependent's relationship with a spouse or Significant Other Person (SOP) is marred by a damaging, unstable lack of balance between dependence and independence.

7. The codependent is a master of denial and repression.

8. The codependent worries about things he or she can't change and may well try to change them.

9. A codependent's life is punctuated by extremes.

10. A codependent is constantly looking for the something that is missing or lacking in life.

TIME WILL NOT MEND CODEPENDENCY

The codependent will not improve with time. It will not get better tomorrow. It will get worse. Happiness and contentment, so elusive now, will fade ever farther even if external circumstances improve. Can it be fatal? Yes. Codependency is never written as the cause of death on a death certificate. But extreme codependency can lead to severe depression and suicide. Physical health deteriorates, permitting illnesses that would otherwise not be a problem. Many of codependency's compulsions and addictions, such as alcoholism, drug abuse, and eating disorders, are life-threatening. Rage and physical abuse can endanger the lives of innocents.

There are steps to take that will help you reverse your descent into misery, but you must take them. They won't just happen. Much depends upon your desire to free yourself from the ghosts of your own past, the causes of codependency which we will discuss in Part Two.

PART TWO:

The Causes of Codependency

CHAPTER THREE

Unmet Emotional Needs

LOVE HUNGER

Narcissus, classic Greek legend tells us, was a very beautiful, and very aloof, young man. Lovely nymphs threw themselves at him, but he spurned them all. He never fell in love until the day he saw his reflection in a quiet pool. Instantly he became infatuated with that splendid specimen—himself.

Completely enamored of the image, Narcissus pined at the poolside, and of course his love went unrequited. When he spoke there was no response. Whenever he reached down and touched the gorgeous reflection it fled, scattered by surface ripples. Eventually, he wasted away to death. The nymphs wanted to burn his body, but it vanished. In its place grew our familiar garden flower, native to the eastern Mediterranean, which we call by his name.

To most people today the term *narcissism* carries some un-pleasant connotations. Narcissism is an inordinate love of self, a life view that is completely self-centered. But some profes-sionals use the concept without that negative connotation to describe that inborn narcissistic, or love hunger, which we all possess.

This love hunger, in contrast to narcissism, is a very positive drive, the God-given need to love and be loved that is born into every human infant. It is a legitimate need that must be met from cradle to grave. If children are deprived of love—if that primal need for love is not met—they carry the scars for life.

Meeting the need to be loved is critically important even when babies are too young to exercise abstract understanding. You cannot merely tell a baby "I love you" as you stroll past the crib. You must convey love in nonverbal ways the infant innately understands. Cuddling, cooing, and talking to the baby are as important as warmth and food. This is why hospitals recruit volunteers or schedule staff to simply sit and rock newborns, even preemies sprouting cobwebs of IVs. Infants can literally die if deprived of love.

LOVE TANKS

At the Minirth-Meier Clinic, we illustrate your love hunger by drawing a heart-shaped love tank (love tanks, as you may guess, are reservoirs for love). Imagine being a newborn child possessing a heart-shaped love tank deep inside yourself. Were the tank to have a gas gauge, it would be nudging empty at the beginning.

Now picture above that tank two other tanks, your biological parents. Over the course of years they fill your tank from their own tanks. Fifteen or twenty years later, as you wean yourself from the original family and go forth to build a family of your own, your tank is pretty well filled. Now an adult, you're primed and ready to fill the tanks of your own children who in turn will be able to fill the tanks of their children. Thus in a normal, functional family, love is transmitted from generation to generation, poured down from parents to children (see the illustration on page 35).

In a family of eight, the parents can still adequately fill all the little love tanks from their own, as much as parents of one or two children. The analogy is not quantitative in that sense, but it is quantitative in other senses.

What if one of the parents is not available for some reason? The child has, at best, half a reservoir to draw from and usually less.

Consider Gladys Jordan's family of origin. Her father was an alcoholic. His love tank, almost certainly low to start with, drained further and further as his alcoholism progressed. He had less and less to offer his child as he became increasingly self-involved. She would ask for things, including quite necessary things, and he would not get around to providing them. Promises he made were constantly broken. Oftentimes, in his drunken stupors he didn't hear her at all. He was not available emotionally, and at times physically, to fill her love tank.

But surely little Gladys could draw from Mom, right? No. Mom was preoccupied with Dad, either keeping his alcoholism a family secret or trying to help Dad shape up. It was Mom who held the family together, kept the shaky finances afloat, agonized over the tragedy they were all living through. She grew increasingly angry, depressed, disappointed with life. Although she truly loved Gladys and wanted the best for her, functionally she was no more available on a consistent basis than was Dad. Gladys came out of her family of origin with her love tank still near empty. She became a codependent adult.

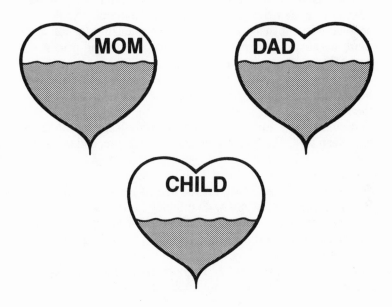

Even if the love flow does not stop, it may be severely restricted. In Mr. Jordan's case, both parents loved little John deep in their hearts and sincerely desired to give him their full measure of affection. But Papa was maddeningly perfectionistic.

"Of course he loves you, Johnny. That's just the way he is," Mama would say, and down inside she, too, hated that nagging perfectionism. Johnny heard the word *love* on his mother's lips but with his unconscious childhood radar he could pick up the resentment. And he received only criticism from his father's lips. The parents were caught up in so much pain, the family so stressed by friction and dissatisfaction, that the love flow nearly stopped in spite of their feelings and best intentions. John Jordan grew up with the unnatural hunger for love that is typical of the codependent adult.

Charles and Sandy Dumont, typical of hundreds of couples we've counseled, visit our office. They are fairly affluent and comfortable externally. Strangers watching them drive by in their BMW would say they were a family who had it made. Internally, Sandy can't stand the aloof and distant man her husband has become. Charles, owner of a chain of computer stores, despises the way his wife puts monetary values on absolutely everything. He doesn't enjoy talking to her anymore because she constantly brings up costs and prices. In seventeen years of marriage they've agreed on only one thing: "We've been in emotional pain for years. Our marriage is a fiasco. But we're taking care of Junior. He's the pride and joy of the family."

A counselor could only respond with the caution, "I know you mean well, but Junior is in just as much pain and travail as you are.

"You've heard it said that when a mother carrying a fetus drinks, she drinks for two, for the baby is drinking also. True. But it doesn't end at birth. The family is, in a sense, an expanded womb. Any significant and unrelieved pain, tension, and difficulty the parents feel is imparted to the children, usually to a great extent."

When Charles and Sandy Dumont experience chronic unhappiness, little Junior Dumont will surely suffer and pay.

In order to keep the parents' tanks filled, there must be a consistently nurturing relationship between them. At the clinic we sketch a bond between your parents' tanks. In a normal, functional family, that bond is mutual love and respect— genuine friendship, if you will, between Mom and Dad.

In the ideal love-tank sketch a huge heart tank hovers above the parents' and child's—God. Our love is flawed; His is perfect. Ours has limits; His does not. Ours depends upon the response we receive; He acts in our best interests whether we requite His love or not. We cannot make each other happy; He

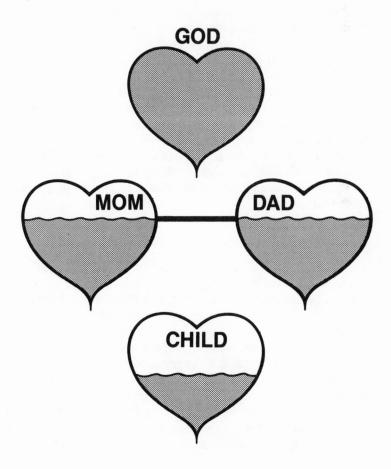

can. He is the ultimate source of nurturing. Under the best-case scenario the parents receive His love freely and with full tanks send it freely on to the child (see illustration, page 37).

So what if the parents are at odds, you say, as long as they can adequately love the child? The point is, unless they are keeping each other's tanks replenished, they *cannot* adequately pass a filled tank to their child. In fact, parental friction often engenders a particularly sad situation. Without realizing it, one or both parents may reverse the flow. To meet their own innate needs they draw from the child's tank what little he or she has, leaving the child with less than nothing.

If we were to coin another definition for codependency, we might say, "It's the condition when the love tanks are running on empty."

Doctor Hemfelt still remembers a tree from his childhood. It had started out as a normal tree. But at some point in its growth it was struck by lightning. The bolt ripped its trunk and felled it, but the tree survived. It continued to grow, as trees do, the roots reaching downward and the top expanding upward from its new and nearly prostrated position. The tree's position, its attitude, was permanently offset, skewed by that lightning strike. Similarly, codependency skews a person's attitude. The codependent's whole way of looking at things is thrown off kilter.

THE FOUR-TIER RELATIONSHIP CAKE

Another illustration we use frequently at the clinic is an allusion probably most appealing near mealtimes. We draw a big four-layer cake (page 39). In a sense you are that cake, because this is the way codependency operates deep within you.

The top layer consists of the symptoms you can see. Addictions, including the non-substance abuses such as workaholism, rageaholism, behavioral compulsions, and many other symptoms form the surface layer. In John Jordan's case, it was his extreme willingness to spend time and energy on his business goals rather than his family—classic workaholism presented in today's society as a desirable attitude.

The next layer down (the second layer) is the relationship

level. Like the tree struck by lightning, the person finds that all relationships are skewed or distorted by what happened before. But what is the lightning that causes this?

The third layer, the lightning, the cause most commonly fingered as the culprit, is some form of abuse. At the clinic we use a much wider definition for abuse than the ones you read about in the daily paper. We'll devote the next full chapter to these sometimes silent forms of abuse because they are fundamentally important. These various forms and methods of abuse, building the third layer of your cake, underlie the twisted personal relationships and surface symptoms of co-dependency. But there is a deeper foundation still.

The fourth layer, the very bottom, is that hunger for love that is as much a part of us as breathing. It cannot be satisfied by substitutes; it must be met. A person with significant un-met emotional needs walks about as a half-person, constantly seeking another person to provide the missing half. This half-ness, this less-than-wholeness, incidentally, is the root of many tragic problems in marriage, like the Jordans' and the Dumonts.'

Patients may express this hunger when they describe their marriage relationship in this way: "We're like two half people trying to come together to make a whole." This condition is far from new. We can even see codependency in a classic literary character from Merrie Olde England, although no one identi-fied the condition that long ago.

RUNNING ON EMPTY

His name is Ebenezer Scrooge. You probably know him from Dickens's beloved *A Christmas Carol*. Let's pretend he's sitting in Robert Hemfelt's office, for old Scrooge is a classic example of the codependent personality. He scowls defiantly, his body folded into a sort of perpetual huddle—huddled over his desk, huddled over his ledgers, huddled now in this padded leather chair. He's certainly not out to impress anyone with his appearance. The elbows on his heavy wool frock coat are worn clear through. You would think a man with his wealth would employ a washerwoman a little more frequently. The stark, aquiline face reminds you a bit of Frederic March. He balances his beaver hat on one knee and drums impatiently with his fingers. This isn't going to be an easy interview.

"There is no reason I should be here," he opens. "I'm an exacting man, but honest. I pay my bills and taxes. I practice common thrift, which any man can do with a little discipline. If everyone else took care of his own matters as honestly as I and quit meddling, there would be no need for jails and poor-houses. You should be talking to wastrels and criminals, not me."

"Ah, Mr. Scrooge, but you are the one who interests me. I understand your mother died at your birth."

"It happens, Dr. Hemfelt, as you well know. And it was no fault of mine. I didn't choose to be born."

"But your father blamed you. He farmed you out, so to speak, in boarding schools and apprenticeships. Is that correct?"

"His blame was irrational, but his course of action benefited me immensely. I learned sound financial skills from a mentor, whom I would not have known had I stayed home with my father. What you, with your psychological mumbo jumbo, might construe as misfortune was in fact a great boon to me."

"You never married."

"Do you realize what a financial drain even a quiescent wife causes?"

"But there is no love in your life. No warmth."

"Bah! What guarantee does marriage make for love? What if I inadvertently married a virago? Misery! Or a frail woman—all women are frail. Doctor bills, the undertaker, and I no better off than if it had never been. You let romantic fantasy blind you to the reality of life."

"Have you never yearned for a comforting touch or a kind word? For simple affection?"

Mr. Scrooge stands erect. He plops his hat on his head and gives it a firming pat. "No, my good man, those are the things of childhood. My life is in perfect order, and I'm content with it. Go find yourself some scoundrel to straighten out, or some simpleton who lets his heart rule his head. Good day."

He crosses to the door and walks out into the waning light of a winter afternoon. Nothing short of the supernatural will save that man from the cold misery of his bitter existence. He is certainly in no frame of mind to choose love!

Poor old Ebenezer Scrooge. There is no substitute for a mother's love, and he never knew his mother. When his father blamed little Ebenezer for her death, how was the child to know the father was wrong? If Papa said it, it must be true. In little Eb's young mind, skewed by the dual lightning strikes of his mother's involuntary abandonment and his father's rejection, he was utterly unlovable. Talk about running on empty! The adult Ebenezer filled his tank with pounds sterling, for pounds sterling are nonjudgmental. They are manageable. He never learned the tank was designed as a reservoir for love, not lucre. Ebenezer Scrooge is a classic codependent.

ADDICTION TO MONEY

Money. Lucre. Mammon. Moolah. Bread. The readies. Cash. Greenery. Bucks (moans a man with a pile of bills in a one-panel cartoon: "I wish the buck stopped here!"). Build a list of all the multifarious names for the coin of our realm. Amazing.

How we handle money is a strong reflection of how we feel about ourselves and how we deal with relationships. Moreover money is almost always a central issue in recovery from co-dependency. Financial affairs are a very sensitive barometer of codependency because money has a lot to do with two basic elements of our existence: discipline and nurturance.

Money is probably our single most powerful nurturance symbol. If Peter wishes to reward Paul, Peter does not hand Paul a potato or a carrot that Paul could literally take in as nurturance. Peter slips Paul a few bucks. Paul then converts that reward into whatever sort of nurturance he wishes—food, shelter, clothing. Money is the standard bonus for good work or windfall success. It is pay for work, and a workman often measures his worth by the size of his paycheck. It is almost always an appropriate gift.

Almost without exception, deep codependent disturbances exercise themselves in financial affairs. This strong link of money with codependency may take many forms, some of them diametrically opposed.

Old Ebenezer Scrooge hoarded money and loathed spending a penny. That's a frequent manifestation of codependency.

In marked contrast stood Roy Ware, a government employee we counseled. Roy was a sucker for gadgets. These weren't just miracle potato peelers as seen on TV ($8.98 if you want it, $10.98 if you don't. Act now! Operators are standing by). He bought the Green Machine—a combination rototiller, power hoe, sidewalk edger, circular saw, weed cutter, and pruning saw—even though his whole lawn covered less than a hundred square yards and there wasn't a tree on the place. He didn't just buy a video camcorder; he got the top-of-the-line model with advanced editing and titling capabilities. He has two VCR's (one has VHS and the other has the old disk system), a microwave that thinks, several cordless phones, a personal computer, a digitally controlled sprinkler system, and a scanner that catches police and fire radio chatter. He holds four major credit cards and every one of them is pegged out to the max.

Scrooge's penny-pinching is considered a blight on commerce. Retailers welcome Roy with open arms. Both extremes derive from the same unmet emotional needs we've been discussing throughout.

Money may well become its own form of addiction. You can plug money into the addiction cycle just as effectively as alcohol or drugs. The same addiction elements pertain—shoot up by either spending or hoarding, feel that momentary false sense of control, see the wrong effects, experience guilt for not handling the money better, assuage the guilt by shooting up again. Around and around it goes.

THE PROBLEM OF DENIAL

If the effects of codependency are so glaringly obvious, why bother with counseling? After all, surely the sufferer need simply identify the problem and take steps to resolve it. John Jordan would be the first to agree that we're talking about common sense here.

There is in all this an ogre, a bugaboo. Denial. Ask the average person if she/he had a happy childhood and he/she will hasten to say "Yes!"

"And were your parents good to you?"

"They were wonderful people."

One of two things is going on here: (a) the person's parents really were neat people deserving of their children's praise or (b) the person had an absolutely rotten, abused childhood and his/her love tank is on empty.

Codependents with significant unmet emotional needs are

masters of denial. It comes built in. For their whole lives, these people have been living a lie—pretending, wishing, yearning that their lives were lovely when in reality they were unbearably painful emotionally and perhaps physically. They can't stop lying now. If reality sinks in, the wracking past will surface with all its open sores, its pockets of pus and filth. Codependents spent a lifetime burying that mess. Denial, therefore, becomes a major hurdle to healing. In fact, healing cannot begin until denial is dealt with properly.

Denial cowers behind many different masks. Quite commonly pain, though not forgotten, is carefully and deliberately buried. Consider the case of Beryl Mason, who came to us in extremity, her life in pieces.

Just looking at her you wouldn't dream that her life was anything short of spectacular, for she was a popular actress, a face known to many millions around the world. She was one of the very few persons on earth who might claim rightly, "I have it all." Yet celebrities are people, neither more nor less human than we.

The woman who entered our office lounge had put aside the special stage presence that separates the well-known from the unknown. The elegance remained, though—that natural grace which the very attractive exhibit without trying. She had deliberately shed both glamour and makeup to stand before us a tortured, weary, and miserable lady. She was past the fresh bloom of youth and happiness had so far eluded her. If life would offer no more than material abundance, it was not worth living. Why could she not love and be loved? Why could she never—*never*—feel at peace?

Now here she sat in our most comfortable interview room. Her overstuffed chair whispered, "Get comfortable and let 'er rip!" Nervously puffing a foreign cigarette in a holder long enough to shoot pool with, she laid out the sad litany of her life.

"My first husband—what a cad! Dr. Meier, he looked so good on the outside. In private he was a vicious, wife-beating thug. My second was considered the catch of Hollywood. Some catch. A shark in an Italian suit."

Paul Meier settled back and folded his hands. "All five husbands were like that? Attractive on the outside and rotten in private?"

"All five. The fifth—what a piece of work! The worst of the lot. He was attentive at first without smothering, know what I mean? Treated me really well. Two months into the marriage it was like he turned a page inside his head and started a new chapter. Booze, coke, grass, the whole enchilada. Knocked me around when he was half-tanked and in a stupor the rest of the time. The cleaning lady was so scared of him she wouldn't come in if he was home."

"Now you're wary of all men."

"Yes and no. It's crazy. I keep getting burned but it's like I can't help myself. I keep sticking my stupid hand back in the fire. You'd think after two or three disasters I'd learn. All I want is a nice, normal man who cares about me. Is that too much to ask?"

"And you're certain you can't be happy unless you're married?"

She thought about that a moment. "No, that's not it. I don't *need* a good man. I *want* a good man. So I'm not a flaming feminist. Is that so bad?"

"It's a good attitude. Have you any other problems where you can't help yourself?"

"Oh good gravy, yes! You should hear my business manager whine whenever I get near a shop. He calls it a spending compulsion. So I like nice things. Is that a crime? And I have trouble off and on with booze and tranquilizers. Not when I'm working, but there are months between jobs sometimes."

There was no holding back now. This was her last desperate try for help and she went for it. During the next hour she told Dr. Meier everything she could about the crossed stars of her life. Not even her soggy, rumpled little Shar Pei would obey the way she wanted. She trotted out symptom after classic symptom. Her life was a vividly colored magnification of the codependency problems many of us encounter.

During a lull as she was lighting up again, Paul took a wild shot he was pretty sure would hit close to center. "When did your father sexually abuse you? Early teens?"

You should have seen the eyes go wide and the mouth drop open. She snapped from eager cooperation to livid rage. "I've never told a soul about that my whole life! Never! Not even Mom! How could you suggest such a thing!" And out she stormed. She had not blotted it from memory but she'd been denying it for years. She'd kept the dirty secret totally swept under the mat. No one knew—no one except her memory.

So what really happened to Beryl Mason? The relationships in her family of origin always had been rocky; she and her siblings did not get the loving attention they needed. During the actual period of abuse, when her love tank should have been receiving nurturing from her father's, the valve was tightly closed. Pain, humiliation, guilt, betrayal—all that and more had blocked off the flow and poisoned her own tank. Beryl lost that part of her childhood as literally as if those important years had been cut out of her lifetime with some cosmic knife.

Her love hunger, the bottom layer of her cake, had not been met; her tank was empty; and the abuses of the third layer guaranteed that the top two layers would not sit straight. Now she had just left in a huff, not the least bit ready to deal with any aspect of her problems. She would keep her secrets buried because digging them up was too painful to contemplate.

Some persons don't just bury their painful memories; they banish them. Unfortunately, because the pain is pervasive, the whole block of experience must be banished. Some of our clients who were patently abused in childhood lose all recollection of that part of their lives, and they may emotionally resist addressing those memories that do remain.

HOPE FOR THE FUTURE

Can a person like Beryl be helped? If Scrooge had ended up at our clinic instead of out in the ether with a trio of spooks, how much could we have done for him? Can anyone—can you—break through the wall of denial by reading a book?

Yes. It can be done, but the process is immensely painful. Then why do it, if suffering results, and the cure feels worse than the disease? In Beryl's case, as in the Jordans', without intervention and help life would never get better. It would deteriorate further and further, the misery becoming ever more wrenching. The wounds of the past continue festering. The warping effect of codependency keeps us from seeing reality clearly; we make the same errors, the same mistakes over and over, all the while believing what we think we see and not what is. Beryl went through five episodes of marriage before it dawned upon her that her perception was faulty.

Fixing up the top layer so that it looks good is mere cosmetic adjustment. It doesn't help the deeper problems. Doctoring the second layer (her daily relationships with other people) with Band-Aids isn't going to improve the cake at all. Only when the foundation layers (the lightning strike that caused her pain and her fundamental need for love) are uncovered and repaired will the cake be at all appealing. If these people's lives, and yours, are to improve in quality, this repair must be done. In *A Christmas Carol* Scrooge's greatest joy the next morning was learning that the opportunity to relish life had not passed him by.

Beryl's story has a happy ending. She cooled down after a day or two, decided that if the doctor could pull that out of the air he might offer something, and returned. As does every patient seeking hospital treatment, she underwent a complete physical to rule out possible medical causes for any of her problems. She entered the hospital as much for privacy as for cure and worked diligently with us. We pieced together her sorry childhood, every bit of it, and her disastrous relationships. We examined the whats and whys. Over the weeks she dealt with each item. She hurt terribly during the process, but she emerged whole. Beryl finally learned to relate to both men and women without having to marry the men and then be abused by them.

"I never realized happiness and peace came in the same package. I never knew how sick I was until I got well," Beryl said.

Beryl's problems were rooted in the third layer of her cake. We will explore the nature of that layer next, for it is a foundation upon which both Beryl's relationships and presenting symptoms and yours are based.

It's not easy to shore up a foundation that was bad to start with and has been deteriorating your whole life. Once you set your mind to the task you must see it through. "Pursuit of happiness" is not a hollow phrase on a yellowed piece of parchment. It is your birthright! Happiness and love lie within your grasp.

CHAPTER FOUR

Lost Childhood

Ann's father worked a sixty-five-hour week serving a sales territory that covered three states. Her mother was into things—causes, Eastern religions, a parade of temporary enthusiasms. But Ann knew the real persons her parents were beneath the surface.

Her father had been raised in the postwar gospel that the husband worked hard to support his family while the wife made a happy home for him. He loved his family enough to break his back for their good. He lavished his love in ways appropriate to his day, his role, and his culture.

Understandably, Mom had grown restless trying to fit into the traditional mold, for she was not a June Cleaver cookies-and-milk person. At heart she was a free spirit, full of fun and curiosity. It's natural she would take up new ideas every now and then; she was a bright and articulate woman who saw the female revolution going on all around her, and she was somehow not included. She loved as deeply as any mother.

Now Ann was in the clinic to lick some unhealthy dietary habits early, before they got too big to handle. She wasn't about to let something like that gain the upper hand in her life. Like her mother, Ann was articulate, smart, and beautiful, with flashing dark eyes and gleaming black hair. Like her father she was ambitious and no stranger to hard work. Recently she had been named loan officer of the bank branch where she had started as a teller. Unlike her mother, she had caught the feminist movement, and now she was riding it to the top. She was unaware that it had become her enemy.

She settled into her chair. "I'm not sure I need a whole lot of help. It's just this eating business that seems to be getting out of control. Daddy was skinny, you know? It's inherited."

"You speak very affectionately of your father."

"He was good to us. He gave a hundred and ten percent."

"How often did he, say, take you to the zoo? To the park?"

"He didn't have time for that kind of thing."

" A Sunday picnic? A little softball with your brothers?"

"Too tired. Look, he worked hard. We wouldn't ask him to."

"Your two brothers. How are they doing?"

"Jerry, the younger one, has an assembly-line job. It suits him, actually. He's a real earthy person. Burger and beer, no pretentions. He's a lot of fun to be with, though."

"Likes his beer?"

"Yes. In fact, that's exactly how his wife says it. 'He sure likes his beer.' Mark—my older brother—took the tri-state region next to Dad's and turned it from a hundred-thousand route into a two-million-dollar operation. Dad's really proud."

"Must take a lot of time and hard work to be so successful."

"I bet he puts in more hours than Dad does."

"What about special times with your mother? Did *she* take you places? Just sit around and talk girl-talk?"

Ann pondered that one a moment. "No, not really. Now and then she'd—what's the word? Pontificate. She'd pontificate on some cause or idea that caught her fancy. Not girl-talk."

"But you don't go overboard on anything."

"No, except this eating thing, and I'll have that under control soon." She tossed her head slightly; the black hair floated. "I'm just ordinary. Go to work, go home, and watch TV."

"Favorite shows?"

" 'Leave It to Beaver' on cable. And 'Dobie Gillis.' They stripped Dobie Gillis a year ago on 56. Ever see that show? Really stupid, but fun. I understand its creator, Max Schulman, died not long ago."

"Stripped Dobie Gillis?"

"You know—syndicated. Daytime Monday through Friday."

"I see. Uh . . . How many television sets do you own, Ann?"

"Umm . . ." She counted mentally. "Five."

"But Ann. You live in a one-bedroom condo!"

The remainder of the interview and those following uncovered revealing information about this extraordinary young woman who called herself ordinary. Besides her obsession with television, she was an exercise junkie who could tell you the calorie content in a three-ounce serving of okra. Young and beautiful, she had undergone plastic surgery four times. She was still dissatisfied. Now she was considering changing her name.

Ann was painfully, obviously, codependent. Her compulsivity? Food, but not just food. Like most codependents, Ann had more than one addiction. The others: her workaholism, her television addiction, exercise compulsion, and scalpel slavery.

Facts of her original family life were even more revealing. Her mother would have liked her a lot more if she weren't so delicately feminine-looking, and she told her so. Ann could not once remember ever sitting in her father's lap.

THE MANY FACES OF ABUSE

"Unmet emotional needs," the bottom layer of our four-tier cake, is such a diffuse, abstract concept. It would mean something totally different to Ann than to the child of an alcoholic or a violently abusive parent. Yet the subtle lacks of her own childhood were just as damaging as a more obvious victim's. No court of law could properly say that her childhood was abusive, but we're not discussing legal parameters here. Ann was abused.

Let's look more closely at the third layer in the cake—the various kinds of abuse to which a growing child may be subject. Some are obvious, some very subtle. All lead to an impoverished love tank.

As we go down through these categories of abuse, weigh them against your own childhood memories. No parent is perfect. Even the best parent in ignorance or frustration is going to blow it royally now and then. That's human. The difference between an occasional misstep and damaging abuse is degree and consistency. A temporary constriction may slow the love flow but it quickly resumes. Persistent abuse dries it up.

Remember, too, that "parents" in this sense may mean more than just biological parents. Foster parents or adoptive parents qualify. A powerful mentor such as another family member, a coach, a teacher, or spiritual leader may rate as a parent because of the enormous influence wielded in your life. At the clinic we may deal with five or six "parents" in a client's situation. All helped shape the person either for good or for ill.

These various forms of abuse are in something of a descending order of obviousness. In the most obvious, active abuse, law officers can see, evaluate, and intervene. Passive abuse is not nearly so easy to recognize. As we continue down the list, the abuse becomes harder and harder to identify. Only the damaging effects remain obvious. It takes a lot of digging, therefore, for our clients to recognize some of these more subtle forms and deal with them.

Understand, these forms of abuse do not cause one hundred percent irreversible damage; there is some hope even without treatment. Jacob's son Joseph (he of the coat-of-many-colors fame) in the book of Genesis was perhaps the ultimate victim of abuse. His mother died during his childhood; his father doted on him overprotectively; his brothers hated him and said so. They sold him into slavery and he suffered for years. And yet, when the tables turned he was strong enough to forgive his brothers and welcome his father.

Still, for most people, these things must be dealt with. There is a healing process. One of the first steps in that process is to identify the nature of the third layer of the cake, the factor or factors that prevented the patient's love tanks from being filled adequately.

ACTIVE ABUSE

These are physical out-in-front abuses, easy to see. Beating. Battering. Sexual molestation of any degree up to and including intercourse. They are not only morally wrong but illegal in nearly all venues.

Active and destructive, but not necessarily illegal, are such manifestations as extreme anger or rage—verbal violence. Shrieks and the irate laying of blame (whether deserved or not, usually it's not) leave scars and bruises that will be felt but not seen. The child who is beaten down emotionally or verbally is being actively abused.

One television commercial helps parents realize how depreciating verbal abuse can be. The camera focuses on a large adult mouth. All one sees during the course of the ad is that overwhelming mouth, and all one hears is the adult voice saying, "You make me sick!" "Can't you do anything right?" "If only it weren't for you, I'd be happy." Anyone who watches that commercial feels the pain of verbal abuse.

Next, picture a child attempting some project or action. The parent physically reaches out, redirects the child, perhaps takes over the project to do it himself: "Here; you're not doing it well enough. Let me." Now imagine the effect on the child. Such intervention, even when well-meaning, is active abuse, affecting the child the same way as do more obvious forms.

If active physical abuse lurks in your past, you must deal with it. At this point you need do no more than simply see that it existed. That is the important first step to wholeness.

You may well say truthfully, "My parents never did *that*." But you're not off the hook. There are other, more pervasive, silent abuses which are every bit as damaging. The factors needed to fill your love tank in childhood, things provided by the parents such as time, attention, and affection are missing.

PASSIVE ABUSE

One or both parents are so preoccupied they are not available to the child emotionally, physically, or both. Unfortunately, many very damaging forms of passive abuse are never identified as such. The ones universally recognized, the ones with the really bad press, are alcoholism and substance abuse. Others may be praised and idealized in certain quarters—workaholism, for example. Industry is a virtue; to some, work is a form of worship. Abuse? cries the adult child. No way!

We counseled a client named Bob about possible abuse in his childhood. Bob was shocked and downright offended that we should consider his workaholic father abusive. "How dare you say I was abused! You have no idea how hard my father worked for us!"

"Agreed, he worked hard. Now let's talk about the time, attention, affection—the involvement a parent must invest in his child."

"Yes, but . . ."

"You needed that affection, that affirmation. Denying you—"

"Yes, but . . ."

"We're not assigning fault in any way. We're establishing exactly how your childhood was. He wasn't there for you emotionally when you needed him."

"But . . . but . . ." It took a long time for the light to dawn. Whether Bob's father intentionally neglected his son or not, the neglect had occurred. It was not a question of fault; it was a question of did-it-happen-or-not? It had happened.

There are other forms of passive abuse. Unintentional or unavoidable though they may be, the effects remain the same.

Abandonment is abusive, and make no mistake, divorce, however amicable, is abandonment. The long absences of a father in military service is abandonment. So is premature death of a parent. The abandonment may be necessary, as with the military man. It may be unintentional or unavoidable, as for example, an accidental death. But to the child's subconscious, wherein resides the love tank, it is abandonment nonetheless.

At the clinic we will ask an adoptee, "Have you ever wondered about your biological parents?" A healthy answer is "Yes" or "Sometimes." When the adoptee vehemently denies interest—"No! Never!"—a warning flag goes up. Quite probably the adoptee has not dealt with the abandonment.

The parent who constantly brushes the child aside commits passive abuse. We find not too infrequently that such abuse can be very hard to remember or define. Dad comes home from work and puts his feet up to watch the evening news. "Not

now, son." "No, Junior, I'm too tired now." "Later maybe."
"Hey, can't you see I'm watching the news? Do that somewhere else." "You kids play outside or something." The child
will probably not remember the constant snubs because to the
child, that's Dad. That's normal.

Mom returns from work, her hair appointment, the school
committee meeting, tennis lessons, or the fitness center and
starts supper. "No." "Get out from underfoot, will you?" "If
you want something to do, fold the laundry." "No, you can't
help me; you'll just make a mess." "You're too little to do it
right. Go play." "I don't want you in the kitchen while I'm
making dinner."

A parent who is nonemotional—a Star Trek Mr. Spock type
of cerebral person—is not going to fill the child's love tanks
simply because children react at a spontaneous, visceral level;
the child and the adult aren't speaking the same language.

Consider passive verbal abuse. The child is never shouted
at or condemned, but then, neither is he or she praised. No
encouragement. No joy. No support. A woman we are counseling lived at home her first twenty years. Her father was never
harsh, but not once in that time did he ever use her name.

It is startling to us how many people enter our clinic saying,
"In my family we never touched or hugged." In passive rather
than active sexual abuse, no inappropriate touching occurs,
but neither does any appropriate contact. No embrace, no
holding, no roughhousing or even tamehousing. No sexual discussion, preparation, or teaching.

A lack of love between the parents is another form of passive
abuse. For instance, a serious breakdown in the sexual relationship of the parents, though not openly manifest, may tele-
graph itself to the child. "I always knew something was wrong
with Mom and Dad, but not what. That certainly could not
have affected me. I was ignorant of it." Yes, it could. It does.
Part of the sexual education of the child is intuitive, the unspoken feeling that Mom and Dad are, or are not, at peace with
each other sexually.

The parent with compulsions or perfectionism may not
force it on the child, but the child is watching as Mom weekly

cleans the bathroom tile with a toothbrush and Dad mows the lawn every three days. The message is there, expressed non-verbally.

If you have lived around a parent who is chronically depressed, you were in an abusive situation. A parent who is excessively legalistic or ritualistic imparts an abusive message. Instead of grace, love, acceptance, the child "hears" estrangement, alienation. Performance only.

Think back to your growing-up days. Remember that "normal childhood" means nothing to the person doing the recalling. Children do not weigh their home life against an outside set of standards. Their home life sets the standards. Whatever they are growing up with is "normal." They assume *home* and *family* are whatever their own home and family teach them.

A client of ours illustrated it this way: "In our home my dad always held his hands out over the food while he blessed it. Somehow it wasn't edible until he did that. I was startled when I dined the first time with my fiancee's family and they all joined hands around the table for the blessing. I know it's just a little detail, but it made me realize that 'normal' is relative."

So forget about "normal." In your childhood, did your parents hug you and each other? Can you specifically recall bringing some problem to either of them *and being heard?* Did you sit on laps, get rocked, tell about your day at school on a regular basis? Did they take you along to places? Did you all do things together? In other words, as you look back, can you remember your parents being there for you on a regular basis? If such memories are sketchy at best, or simply not there, make a note (yes, a real, written-down note) and move on.

EMOTIONAL INCEST

We keep seeking some other fancy term for this. *Incest* in one way brings up the wrong connotations. But in a greater way, the word's connotations are exactly right. Emotional incest has of itself nothing to do with sexual matters, although in extreme cases it can lead to incest of a sexual sort. Rather, it is an extreme role reversal.

In incest as we usually think of it—that is, some form of active sexual abuse by a parent—the child becomes a surrogate adult in a sense, a sexual substitute for a parent. In emotional incest, too, the child is called upon to be parent to the parent.

This role reversal called emotional incest is even more subtle and elusive, harder to identify and isolate, than passive abuse. Denial is much more intense here too. In fact, one reason we use the powerful term *emotional incest* is to get attention. Its impact helps the person identify that this is something very serious. It may not be the same thing as sexual incest, but it does involve distortion, a transgression of appropriate family roles.

Here is where a loving relationship between parent and child has somehow been turned upside down. In the parent's mind (and rarely consciously considered) is the thought, "I don't care much for my spouse, but I have this child, whom I love more than life itself." What that statement so often means is, "My spouse isn't giving me the love I crave (because both our tanks are near empty) but I can get it from my child." The half person is going to that little person for completion.

An example is Stephanie. Her mom, chronically depressed, had nearly ceased functioning as a wife and mother. Mom slept in, stayed in her bathrobe all day, took pills. By the age of eight Stephanie was making breakfast. Her first stop when she got home from school was to look in on Mom in the bedroom and help if needed. She might start dinner. Stephanie had for practical purposes become Mommy. Without knowing it, Dad came to depend heavily on Steph not just for the nuts and bolts of housekeeping but for emotional support as well. Both parents siphoned off from Steph's tanks nurturance she should have been receiving.

In extreme cases of emotional incest, where the unnatural bond intensifies sufficiently, physical incest can occur. But physical incest need not occur before the emotional incest becomes very damaging.

Previously we asked, "Were your parents available for you?" Now we ask, "Were you frequently available for your parents?" Don't say "Yes, but . . ." We're not assigning fault of any sort; we're merely establishing the circumstances of your youth. Whether deliberately or because of some situation, were you an emotional bolster and support to your parent(s)?

UNFINISHED BUSINESS

A client who recovered from this problem gave us a lovely illustration. In her family is a quilt in progress, which the women have been passing down from generation to generation. Each generation makes a couple new squares. The quilt has been growing since the mid-1800s. Unfinished business, like that quilt, is a desire or strong opinion of the parents that is transmitted to the children.

The classic play *Death of a Salesman* is the quintessential paean to unfinished business. Willy Loman, two-bit huckster, ultimately failed. But he can yet succeed through the success of his sons. Ultimately it's not their own lives the sons are called upon to play out but the father's. Biff's resistance provides great dramatic power, indicating how strong this source of problems can be.

Unfinished business is Mom's or Dad's business that was never completed. One or both may have some area of their lives in which they've always felt discontent. Perhaps Dad feels frustrated and sexually unfulfilled in his marriage. As he views his marriage and his life he gets this tremendous sense of uselessness, of lack. Let's say, for instance, that he's chronically angry with his wife, perhaps with women in general. Unless he makes peace with that (and it requires God's help to deal with the big unfinished pieces in our lives), without intending to do so he may well hand that frustration down to his sons and daughters.

Death of a Salesman is a classic work because of its structure and language. It is great stage literature. But it also speaks to perhaps the most common piece of unfinished business we see, a thread that runs deep in many families, the hunger for success. Dad didn't make it to the top, but success is still within Junior's grasp. The parent vicariously achieves when the child achieves.

This was also an important subtheme in the powerful film *The Turning Point.* Two ballerinas in a dance company took divergent roads. Anne Bancroft's character stayed on stage to pursue fame; Shirley MacLaine's character left public performance for marriage and motherhood. Said she, "You got sixteen curtain calls; I got pregnant." Now Shirley's daughter, with Anne as mentor, is poised on the brink of fame. Both Shirley and Anne have the prospect of ending unfinished business—one, the motherhood she never knew; the other, the fame she never enjoyed. Other universal themes and conundrums wind through the film as well, but the unfinished business theme shines prominently.

This silent abuse shows up frequently in clinical work. *Death of a Salesman* is blatant. In real life, unfinished business may be hidden. For example, Peter sought relief from his constant deep depression. Peter had always yearned to attend seminary, and now here he was doing splendidly with seminary training. God had called him to the ministry and all was going swimmingly—so why the intense depression?

In desperation his counselors called in other family members, seeking different perspectives. The father confessed, "I wanted very much to go to seminary. I applied and was turned down." Humiliated, he and his wife kept the episode an absolute secret. Yet the son had intuitively picked up on that bit of unfinished business. Through counseling the son realized he was not answering God's call; he was hearing that ghost from his father's past. He left seminary and his depression evaporated.

Incidentally, Peter is serving quite happily in his local church as a deacon. He is, if you will, doing his own thing, which turned out to be what God had in mind all along.

Commonly this unfinished business problem may surface during mid-life. Men particularly, but also women, may have been spending their early productive years chasing a goal, be it money, success, family. Then somewhere in introspection he or she says, "Wait a minute! I don't enjoy doing this. This is empty." The momentum behind the compulsion seems to run out, like a rocket running out of fuel. "Why am I on this treadmill?" Thus there can be a healthy aspect to a mid-life crisis. The person realizes at last that he or she is living out someone else's unfinished business.

For the person with Christian convictions, there are important theological considerations here. If I want to operate in God's will, it is essential that I not be working under the handicap or encumbrance of Mom's or Dad's unfinished dream.

Reverberations may extend into the child's mating choices as well. If Mom is embittered toward men in general and Dad specifically, or Dad is angry with women in general and Mom in particular, try as the parents may to hide it, the child will pick up on it. This is sometimes the reason a young man or woman goes out and makes what seems like a terrible marriage choice. The whole family sits there scratching heads, and saying, "What can the kid be thinking of?" A part of the choice is Mom and Dad's unfinished anger. The child lives out the parent's expectations that the opposite sex is rotten. The child is externalizing a battle internalized by Mom or Dad.

NEGATIVE EXISTENTIAL MESSAGES

The fifth category of abuse, and perhaps the most subtly insidious, are the messages the child picks up from the parents about himself and the world around him, both overt and covert. Who am I? Can I trust anyone? What is the nature of life? Who is God? How worthy am I? The child's life view grows out of messages both spoken and unspoken.

Abusive messages may be verbal. Instead of simply correcting her child's behavior, Mom angrily bursts out with, "I wish you had never been born! You're no good." In other words, character assassination. The child has no independent frame of reference with which to weigh the statement. If Mom says it, it must be so. The child has no rational defense mechanisms; he can't say, "Poor Mom. She must be having personal problems not related to me." No. In the child's eyes it *all* relates to him. The most important person in the world just gave him a message and he took it in raw and unedited. Such messages hit a defenseless child with tremendous force.

A child's instinctive radar puts the most sophisticated *Star Wars* gizmo to shame. A child picks up meaning and nuance when the parents themselves fail to realize the message is being broadcast. Tell the child you love him all you want; if he was unplanned and you still regret his birth, he'll know it.

An autocratic or rigidly authoritarian household also engenders codependency. Abuse results when the parent's way of thinking is the only permissible way of thinking; when the parent's view is the only acceptable view; when the child has no avenue for question or analytical thought, let alone experimentation.

Children leave home by stages. Mentally, emotionally, and physically, they venture forth from the nest, often before their flight feathers are grown. That's normal and healthy. The rigid parent who expects the child to fall obediently into lockstep had better brace for an explosion. Even if the explosion be muted, damage will occur.

Healthy authority versus authoritarianism. Strong spiritual leadership versus rigid tunnel vision. Where is the line? As you reflect on the past, you may not be able to see the line, let alone evaluate which side of it your original family sat on. Keep this possible source of problems in mind as you read on. If fair evaluation eludes you now, it may emerge later.

Often in the clinic or on our radio call-in program, "The Minirth-Meier Clinic," as we enumerate these forms of abuse a patient or caller will say, "Bingo! I had all of them in my home." One form of abuse may breed another; several may grow concurrently.

CHILDHOOD LOST

We have learned through long experience that consistent abuse in these areas does more than lead to problems identified as codependency. Significant portions of childhood in which abuse occurs are quite literally lost.

Charles can remember nothing about his seventh- and eighth-grade experiences—not even the school he attended. During those two years an uncle who moved in next door sexually molested him.

Jennifer knows her father was preoccupied with a major legal battle when she was ten, but she cannot remember being ten.

Loss stemming from abuse disrupts the symmetry of the cake, drains the tank, generates severe problems. Ann, the food-and-TV addict, had a great deal of difficulty identifying her childhood as abused. After all, her parents meant well; they were such good people. Her father's abuse was absolutely unintentional. He loved Ann so much he was willing to work long and hard. Most admirably did he fulfill the role society decreed for him, family provider and head. He faithfully did what the day required of him. Her mother's agile mind saw a multitude of truths and beauties. They distracted and consumed her because that is what those heady days offered a woman. Her neglect and lack of communication were not intentional. But it was there. Both parents, and Ann as well, were certain they were doing just fine at child-raising. Identifying the realities of her childhood was essential to Ann's recovery, as it is to yours. Without that identification neither Ann nor you can learn to choose love.

How could Ann's TV addiction or scalpel slavery or eating compulsions come from passive abuse? Might your own present misery have its roots in the past? We've looked at the third layer of the cake, abuse in its multifarious forms. Now let's see how that translates into present-day problems.

CHAPTER
FIVE

The Repetition Compulsion

How exactly did John and Gladys Jordan root out the ghosts that destroyed their contentment? It wasn't easy.

Several weeks later they came filing reluctantly into the office for their next visit. They sat as they had sat before, John squirming around in his chair, Gladys's fingers still playing odd little games with each other in her lap. On this visit her tight, drawn face didn't look a day younger.

We began. "On your last visit, Gladys, we talked about your father and the influence he worked on you . . . the fact that he never listened, was never there for you. I suggested then that you've applied your father's obtuseness to John—the role you learned to expect of the father—even though John is not obtuse. Have you been thinking about that?"

"Well, yes." She licked her lips. "Frankly, I don't see that it has anything to do with this. Daddy wasn't the least bit like John. John doesn't smoke or drink, he's a good Christian man—Daddy wasn't. The only similarity is that neither one of them can listen. They don't really *hear*. Doctor, you don't understand what I'm trying to tell you."

Since counselors are trained to hear and listen exactly, that said something about Gladys's problem.

"John, do you think because your father was so extremely

critical and nonaccepting that you've been oversensitized in a way—you hear criticism where none is intended?"

John snorted. "Easy for you to say. You don't live with Gladys."

"Then I take it that you don't buy my analysis."

"I'd love to, but it just isn't the way things are. They make all these jokes about nagging wives. It's not funny."

"That we agree on."

Any impartial little mouse in the corner who listens in on a typical day at the Jordans' would see right away that the analysis was correct. It was obvious. The only two people in the world who could not see the solution were the Jordans themselves. Why?

FACTORS BEHIND THE COMPULSION

THE HOMING INSTINCT

In 1960 Sheila Burnford gave us the classic animal tale, *The Incredible Journey*. Although the story is fictional, it was based on anecdotal tales of actual incidents. Two dogs and a cat, boarding out while their family is on an extended vacation, respond to the overpowering urge to return home. That relentless homing instinct drives them inexorably westward across nearly three hundred miles of Canadian outland. Danger, discomfort, and disaster fail to deter them. They must know home again.

Many long years after salmon fingerlings have descended the streams of their origin to live in the ocean, the call of home brings them back, to the very stream, up the very branch. Over the very shoal where its life began, each salmon spawns and dies.

Human beings wag their heads in amazement at the mysterious homing skills of birds and animals, unaware that Man the Wanderer also possesses a homing instinct, but it manifests itself in a very different way.

John wagged his head at those examples. "Homing instinct? Don't bet on it. Gladys could get lost on her way to the mall."

"And if you didn't have me beside you with the map, navigating, you couldn't find Dallas," she replied.

"We're *in* Dallas."

"I know."

The homing instinct in human beings is not geographic. It operates totally within the distant vistas of our minds. Rather than seek out physically the place of our birth and childhood, we seek to reconstruct it in our present lives. Thomas Wolfe said, "You can't go home again."

We don't have to. We bring the home to us. We all possess a primal need to recreate the familiar, the original family situation, *even if the familiar, the situation, is destructive and painful.* This is one of the most baffling things a codependent will have to come to terms with.

Codependents characteristically have an excess load of guilt and magical thinking. These two factors (among others) play an important role in this perpetuation of the original family, as codependents feel the intense need to replicate the past even more so than most of us. It is said that twenty percent of our decisions come from the conscious, reasoning mind. The rest come from deep within. And the depths within the codependent have been skewed like that lightning-struck tree.

MAGICAL THINKING

Magical thinking might also be called wishful thinking and can perhaps be best explained by illustration. Consider the case of Louise, whose parents were both alcoholics. Her brother, two years older, kept the family together. Louise just wanted to get out. She did well in school, skipped eighth grade, graduated a year early and immediately enrolled in a nursing program, where she became a star pupil.

Yet after two years into St. Joseph's four-year program, she was a patient in our hospital. She sat listlessly in a chair beside her bed. Tired. More than anything else she seemed so very tired. She wore her rich brown hair pulled back tightly into a ponytail, making her gaunt face look even thinner. She was five feet seven with long, graceful hands and darting eyes. She weighed ninety-nine pounds.

"Dr. Minirth," she began, "I don't think I belong here. You might as well know that up front."

"I'm glad you're being candid. Candor puts us right on the fast track." Frank took a seat near the corner, the better to put himself at a comfortable distance from her. "How do you feel?"

The darting eyes rested a moment on him and danced away to other things. "Do you really want to know?"

"Please."

"In four days I gained three pounds here. If my nursing supervisor didn't insist I come here I'd be gone."

"You weighed ninety-six pounds at check-in. How close is that to your ideal weight?"

"Pretty close. Ideally, I'd lose another ten, but it's close." She smiled mirthlessly. "The last ten are always the hardest, they say."

"As a student nurse you've surely learned about anorexia."

Her eyes paused and flared to life. "Of course I know what anorexia is," she snapped. "My supervisor's wrong; that's not the case with me. I watch my weight. I stay fit. That's good sense, not disease. She's wrong." She shrugged. "But until you run me through the tests and tell her she's wrong, I'm stuck here."

"I received a call from her today. She praises your industry highly. She admires your devotion—says you seem so eager to help others."

"Yes, I guess so."

Frank watched her quietly for a minute. "Louise? Why did you go into nursing? Really?"

The eyes weren't darting anymore. They held his momentarily, then drifted downward. Her head dipped slightly. "To get away from home. You know about Mom and Dad. Heavy drinkers. Dad lost his job six months before I graduated and Mom never worked. No money. It's tough to get into St. Joseph's nursing program but once you're there, they provide dorm and meals and an allowance. It was the only way I could afford an education, unless I joined the army. I figured this would get me farther faster."

"Your parents must be proud of you."

"Dad is. Mom's upset. She thinks I should live at home and go to the community college."

"Does upsetting your mom bother you?"

"Everything I've ever done upsets her. She wants me home to keep house, that's all. I figure when I'm a nurse I'll make enough money and I can hire her a housekeeper. Then the job will get done right. When I was in high school I couldn't handle all that and school, too."

"Extracurricular activities?"

"No. Dad used to say I ought to go out for basketball, but five-seven isn't that tall these days." She leaned forward and her pallid lips formed a tight thin line. She took a deep breath. "You know . . . Mom drove Dad to drink. He's said so. If it just weren't for her, he'd be such a wonderful person."

You can already piece together the cause of Louise's lost childhood: both parents alcoholic and thus unavailable; an apparent victim of emotional incest as she took on a job far beyond her years; the negative messages her mother sent so consistently. Poorly nurtured, the little child within Louise never had a chance to grow. Her love tank was empty.

Now how does a child deal with the world? Consider a newborn, so completely egocentric. I am hungry. I am uncomfortable. I want. I need. I cry. Food comes. Warmth comes. Comfort comes. I asked and I received. I am the reason I was fed and cared for. This is all natural. God assumed love of self when He said, "Love thy neighbor as thyself."

The infant's world constantly expands, its horizons ever pushing outward, as it grows. Still, no matter how selfless we become, a bit of us feels or wishes that the world did indeed revolve around us, as once it seemed to. When Galileo locked horns with the geocentrists, the battle was far more than the positions of stars and planets: *I, and by extension all mankind, exist at the center of all things*. It's in our bones.

The magic extends beyond infancy. Even when the child sees that the world spreads out far beyond its knowledge, that self-focus remains. To the child, and incidentally to certain cultures today, the world is literally in the mind of the beholder—the elements of the world are perceived as important only as they affect the child. Conversely, surely the child can influence the world around itself, and if the child fails to change what should be changed, it must somehow be the child's fault. Magic wands are not the sole property of fairy godmothers. The child thinks: *If I do such-and-so, this-and-that will happen. If I am perfect, Mommy will love me. If I do everything exactly right, Daddy will notice me.*

A child doesn't guess that perhaps Mommy or Daddy have problems all their own that stem from sources beyond the child's knowledge. His only emotional bond is with them; logically, theirs is bound into him. In the child's eyes, anything Mommy and Daddy feel is necessarily generated by the child. "If Mommy is unhappy it must be because of me." "If I weren't a pain in the neck, Daddy wouldn't drink so much."

"If I do *X* then *Y* will happen." Magical thinking. Codependent thinking.

In actuality, of course, children exercise very little control over anything. Usually, not even the family dog obeys the five-year-old. Their only hope for control lies in the unseen world, the primordial desire to wish something into being.

Parents plan a divorce and their child believes, *If I can just behave perfectly, this won't happen.* Daddy is a workaholic and the child thinks, *If I become more fun to be with, Daddy will stay home.* Magical thinking is childlike, and small children are masters of it. So are lost children, even when they're adults.

Major actresses possess slim, beautiful figures. In every magazine and fashion layout tall, lean models strut. Most fashions are created for the slim. "Fitness! No fat!" cries our culture. In the dark corridors of Louise's mind lurks the obsession, *If I can just get thin enough, I'll be happy and everyone will love me.* With it dwells: *I know I can fix the past if I try hard enough.* One of the fixes: *Mom will finally find something to like about me if I can somehow become lovable enough and successful enough.* And the most hideous and dangerous of all lurking thoughts: *Dad's character and happiness are shaped by others; therefore mine are, too.* Magical thinking. Louise's whole life is riddled with it.

With this magical thinking comes guilt. Guilt and magical thinking feed upon each other.

That feeling of responsibility for what happens ("If I do

things exactly right, I can magically force a happy ending to this unpleasant situation") has a very ugly flip side: "If it doesn't turn out all right, it's my fault for not trying harder." So what happens? No matter how hard the child tries, the unpleasant situation ends tragically. The divorce occurs anyway. Despite the child's best efforts, Dad the workaholic doesn't come home. When the child's magic fails, guilt takes over.

"If I had only tried harder, it would have worked out well. I failed."

"I'm the reason Mom and Dad fight. I can prove it—I hear them argue about me. It's all my fault."

THE SELF-MADE GUILT TRIP

None of those assumptions is true, of course. The child has no power, magical or otherwise, to control what his or her parents think and do. No human being, the child included, can single-handedly make or destroy the happiness of another. The child has very little influence on his or her parents at the emotional level, particularly if (as is usually the case) they are codependent with deep-seated problems of their own. Of course it's not logical; our primal feelings are not generated by logic.

Guilt was a powerful driving force in the hidden journeys of Beryl Mason's mind. When towering father-figure Dad came on to her sexually, it had to be in response to something she did. Why else would he approach her like that? In her very depths she sensed it was terribly, terribly wrong. What she did not feel was that the wrong was wholly his. Her adult moral values were just forming at that age. This whole situation was beyond her scope. Fantasy took over. *It must be my fault!*

Everyone incurs guilt naturally and justifiably, often without trying. You don't have to argue the validity of original sin to find genuine guilt in even a small child. And true guilt can be resolved. The normal transgressions of childhood are obvious; they can be forgiven. False guilt is not obvious and is, therefore, rarely suspected. It galls. It eats. Years later, unnoticed, unforgiven, it surfaces in unpredictable ways.

Beryl Mason in her adulthood still had not resolved the ugly tragedy of her childhood. The guilt and other factors surfaced as self-flagellation. She kept linking up with men her innermost being believed she deserved, men who treated her as shabbily as Dad had in that dark, musty past.

THE REPETITION COMPULSION

Now combine magical thinking and false guilt with the innate need to recreate the original family situation. If the original family was painful (even if the child doesn't specifically remember it as being painful), that pain must be replicated, for several reasons.

Reason number one: *If the original situation can be drummed back into existence, this time around I can fix it. I can cure the pain. I know I can!* Magical thinking.

The codependent possesses a powerful need to go back and fix what was wrong. We all do that to an extent, with things physical as well as things social. "If I had it to do over . . ." is so common. Of itself, it's a good thing. We learn from our mistakes and fix what we can. But codependents, as always, carry it to the extreme. They *must* fix it. They *must* correct the original problem, cure the original pain.

Reason number two: *Because I was responsible for that rotten original family, I must be punished. I deserve pain.* Social workers, including us here at the clinic, find so much opportunity to say, "You're asking for these problems! You're deliberately putting yourself in situations that will bring nothing but pain." We try not to say that out loud; we let the patient realize it on his or her own.

Besides the hidden desire to make atonement for the false guilt, the codependent may actually be hooked on misery. A major symptom of codependency is addiction, and the codependent may well be addicted to emotional pain. No matter how miserable, at least it's *home*. It's familiar. It is comfortable in a painful way.

Reason number three: Finally, then, *there's that yearning for the familiar, the secure*. The codependent's original family may not have been secure in reality, but it was the codependent's childhood haven—the only security that little person knew. Even moreso than the healthy adult, the codependent seeks the refuge of the familiar.

Add that homing instinct to magical thinking and guilt, and you begin to see why adult children of dysfunctional families almost always end up in dysfunctional relationships. Painful, miserable, even life-threatening as it may be, that relationship is *familiar*. To the codependent: "This is home. This is another chance to fix it. You deserve this; you always have."

Thus do codependents so commonly end up in exactly the sort of relationships they swore they'd never tolerate. The same old story plays over and over in a million variations.

We asked John Jordan how Gladys and his father resembled each other. He smiled mischievously. "They both cut their toenails over the toilet bowl."

"Think you could dig a little deeper on this one?"

He sobered. "You mean other than the obvious—that they're both cranky and fault-finding? Well, uh, Gladys keeps the house just so. I mean *just* so. Every pillow fluffed, every venetian blind dusted, every doo-dad in its exact place. Dad was like that in spiritual matters. And come to think of it, in other ways, too. Everything had to be exact. I never thought about it before. Get past the obvious physical differences, there are a lot of similarities."

"Gladys, how are your father and John similar?"

"Both wrapped up in themselves, both distant. Neither has any time for me, neither even sees me, really. I'm a fixture . . . a housecleaning robot without ears. To both of them."

The need to recreate the family of origin and, if necessary mend it, is exceedingly, unimaginably powerful in codependents. Even when the marital partner does not really have the repetitive traits (as, for example, John actually did listen—Gladys only thought of him as unhearing), they are perceived in order to complete the picture. It is the terrible trap into which the codependent falls: *If I can be the perfect, perfect mate, I can somehow fix my spouse. Thereby I can realize the failed childhood fantasy that if I were the perfect, perfect child, I could somehow fix my original family.*

Not to tease but to provoke thought, we may bluntly ask the

patient: "Whom did you marry—your mother or your father?"
Many people when choosing a spouse pick a person who in
some way resembles their mother or father. Most commonly,
the adult child will marry a person who emotionally resembles,
or recreates some dynamic with, the parent of the opposite
sex. Gladys Jordan did that. But it can be the parent of the
same sex. A man might marry a woman who somehow recreates a dynamic with the father of his past. Such was the case
with John Jordan.

What you now know about the codependent's need to recreate the past tells you why the Jordans had such difficulty seeing
the very solution they came to us to find. That need to recreate the original family pain blinded them to the obvious solution. The ghosts of their past were there by invitation.

It was their pasts that had to be dealt with—mended, if you
will—before the ghosts could be successfully exorcised. That
is why we took them step by step through realization of what
their pasts actually held, the natural anger about what their
pasts did to them, and grief over what was lost. Then healing
emerged as the fruit of the cleansing.

You can now see why your past holds such a grip on your
todays. Every individual has been shaped by personal history.
The codependent, as always, carries it to extreme.

WARNING

We finally did it! We got dear old Dad dried out. He's in AA,
he's feeling pretty good about himself . . . but what's this? His
family looks like they've been dragged through a war. Mom is
edgy and angry. The kids are hostile, suspicious, jaded. Six
months after Dad enters sobriety, Mom can't take it anymore
and moves out.

It wasn't supposed to end this way.

For convenience in discussion here we're using the example
of the father as dependent. It could quite as easily be the wife.
We're using alcohol as the substance, but it could be any
compulsion—drugs, spending, work, the gamut. The details
are secondary; the causes and effects are what we're looking
at.

In counsel we warn couples carefully that the first year into sobriety is a killer. Three to nine months after Dad or whoever dries out, the family will find themselves beset by crises. The euphoria of achieving the goal—Dad's healing—is buried in acrimonious friction.

But if the family hangs tough, staying in recovery together to weather that stormy first year, the healing will seem miraculous. Wonderful. Here is why.

As Al-Anon and mental health workers first began recognizing and treating codependency, they laid the full cause at Dad's door. Dad's dependence on alcohol generated the family's codependency. Today we see that codependency is a cause as well as an effect, both the chicken and the egg.

Mom and Dad's original choice of each other was no accident, as we have seen. Mom is bringing a certain level of codependency into the marriage right at the outset. At the unconscious level, Mom needs Dad's dependence just as much as Dad needs his booze. To complicate it further, he also needs her codependency. Dad's sobriety ruptures that fragile fabric of interlocked dependence.

The alcohol, Mom's depression—these and other factors are the symptoms which form the top layer of our four-tiered cake model. When that top layer is stripped away, the next level lies exposed. Relationships. No longer can the family blame everything on the symptoms or be distracted by surface concerns. No wonder crises erupt. Now family members must deal with each other anew, up front and personal, at that difficult relationship level.

Once the family reestablishes its relationships, if they persist diligently, healing results. An allusion is the making of a patchwork quilt. All those little odd pieces, some of them left over from old garments, most of them cut from scraps, look like chaos. Then the seamstress begins her work, joining this to that, arranging the pieces and putting them in their places. There emerges a pattern of harmony and beauty, but it takes an awful lot of time and work.

There is a certain cyclical nature to the repetition compulsion. The same mistakes happen again and again. The same things occur over and over. Indeed, the codependent's life inexorably revolves through cycles beyond control, as we shall next see.

PART THREE:

---

*Factors That
Perpetuate
Codependency*

CHAPTER
SIX

The Snowball Effect of Addiction

"I feel like I'm running around in circles."

"What goes around comes around."

"May the circle be unbroken by and by, Lord, by and by."

Cycles. Economic cycles, cycles of history, seasonal cycles, hydrologic cycles, two-cycle engines, cyclotrons, life cycles, motorcycles, unicycles, bicycles, tricycles, Popsicles.

THE LURE OF CYCLES

In a popular book-length treatise, *Time's Arrow—Time's Cycle,* Stephen J. Gould discussed the way classical natural philosophers dealt with the haunting enigma of recurrence and progression. Perhaps cycles of activity and repetition fascinate us in part because they govern so much of our everyday lives. They appeal to our sense of order. And, too, there is a certain comfort in cyclical recurrence; whether something is pleasant or painful, at least you know it's coming.

Unless you are highly codependent. Then cycles are your worst enemies.

By the very nature of codependency, the codependent is trapped in a series of vicious cycles. Some interlock with the destructive cycles other people are playing out. Some wheel along hidden completely within the codependent. They feed the codependency, perpetuating it, intensifying it. They must be recognized and broken before progress can commence.

THE ADDICTION CYCLE

One of the most virulent of these is the addiction cycle. Picture a child at the crest of a cow pasture hill, fashioning a large, icy snowball. He checks the fall line, assures himself no rocks or trees stand in the way, and shoves the snowball over the side. It's a long hill. Clunky and uncertain at first, the snowball slowly picks up weight, speed, momentum. Halfway down, it has already burgeoned into a Godzilla of a monster, mindless and unstoppable. By the time it reaches the bottom and rolls relentlessly across the creek gully, it has become the Snowball of Death. The addiction cycle is that snowball.

At first, counselors assumed codependency was strictly an effect, a syndrome in people who lived closely with alcoholics and other addicts. Now we see that regardless of what launched your codependency, once the condition is in place, the addiction cycle both perpetuates and amplifies it. It now maintains its own internal addictive momentum. No longer can you ease codependency simply by identifying and dealing with the cause. You must do that, but you must also take definite steps to recover from the codependency itself, and you must break the addiction component that feeds it.

THE MECHANICS OF THE ADDICTION CYCLE

Our cycle comes from the old classic model used by counselors and researchers studying alcohol and drug addiction (see page 79). In that model, usually described as a spiraling circle, the subject feels pain of some sort, low self-esteem, guilt, dissatisfaction, pressure, or simply the sheer boredom life can bring. He finds anesthesia in alcohol or drugs, but getting drunk or snorting or shooting up creates consequences—remorse, greater guilt, even more pain. The subject found relief once in his anesthetic, so he returns to it. The consequences increase to include depression, loss of health, perhaps even the loss of job and family. More guilt and shame, more remorse, more anesthetic. The cure has turned into the

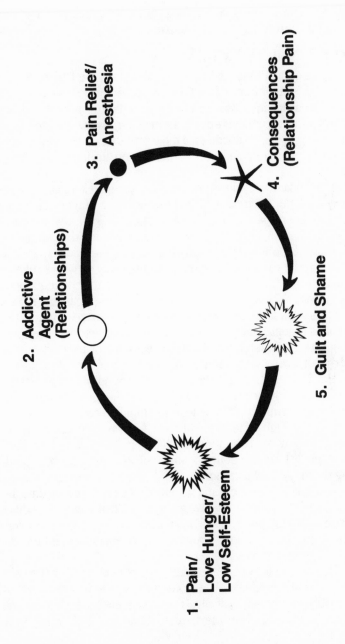

2. **Addictive Agent (Relationships)**

3. **Pain Relief/ Anesthesia**

4. **Consequences (Relationship Pain)**

5. **Guilt and Shame**

1. **Pain/ Love Hunger/ Low Self-Esteem**

cause. The cycle is now rolling on its own, growing without further input from the original pain.

THE SPIRAL EFFECT

Once upon a time, the most popular toy in the United States was the Slinky. Slinky is a flat wire coiled into the shape of a cylindrical spring. As the spring uncoils and recoils, Slinky "walks" down stair steps or an inclined plane. It "steps" in one long, agonized stride off a table top, takes a few quick hops to stabilize itself, and settles quietly on its lees, a cylinder again.

The addiction cycle approximately resembles a Slinky. Seen head-on, it's a circle with several loci, or stages, along it. Some kind of pain marks the first stage or locus, which we'll call 1. This is where the cycle starts. The addictive agent (for example, alcohol, drugs, work) marks the next locus, 2. The agent in the role of an anesthetic temporarily provides relief—locus 3 or stage 3—but there are unpleasant consequences (locus 4), such as guilt and shame, perhaps a hangover. Pain results—back to locus 1. Pain calls for more anesthetic. Around it goes again. In the addict and codependent, the cycle might repeat itself a couple of times a year, or every Saturday night, or even many times a day.

But it doesn't just go around and around in place. As the subject's body becomes conditioned to the anesthetic, larger doses are required. These lead to amplified consequences. It is as if through time the addiction followed the outer rim of the Slinky wire. It continues cycling from locus 1 through 2 through 3 through 4, but it also travels downward, ever spiraling down, as well as around.

Eventually, the cycle spirals out of control. To an extent, the nature of the anesthetic governs the speed at which the addict travels around his cycle. For example, beer feeds the cycle fairly slowly. The most dramatic and time-telescoped effects are caused by the opiates.

Heroin provides perhaps four hours of euphoria. As the user comes down, he feels even worse than he did before, psychologically and physiologically. The doses soon escalate as the body builds chemical tolerance, making the withdrawal ever more pronounced. The downs get downer, but the ups don't get any upper as the user strives to regain that elusive euphoria.

In this classic model the addictive agent—the anesthetic—is no longer merely a stage or locus on a circular pathway. It has taken on a self-perpetuating life of its own. Whether or not it is physically addictive, it has become psychologically addictive for the person in pain.

THE CODEPENDENT'S CYCLE

This addictive cycle is every bit as destructive for the codependent as it is for any addict. Let's take our usual generic example, the time-honored picture of the sober wife of an alcoholic husband. He is locked into his own cycle of addiction. What about her?

Same cycle, same mechanics, slightly different elements.

It starts in the same place, pain. In addition to the normal pain of being human, she feels the discouraging pain of living with that alcoholic man. Her anesthetic—her addictive agent—is not as easily identifiable as her husband's, for it doesn't come in a conveniently labeled bottle. It can be any of a number of things of which she was unaware, and she probably doesn't know she's shooting up.

Her pain killer is perhaps the sense of martyrdom that we all enjoy wallowing in now and then. Martyrdom can be amazingly subjective. If a wife focuses only upon her husband's negative traits, her martyrdom, her sacrifice will not shine as brightly.

Denial might be the wife's panacea. She may well gain a feeling of euphoria and self-assurance when she rescues her husband. She takes a certain noble satisfaction in the sacrifices she must make to hold this home together. The feel-good pill can take many intangible forms.

Next come the sorry consequences, and their results are just as sad as the addict's. By the very rescues and enabling behaviors that fuel her self-assurance and her sensation of being needed, she deepens and intensifies her husband's dependency. When she bails him out, he need not face his own consequences. When she cleans up after him and puts him to bed, his eyes are shielded from the ugliness that is his addiction. He can continue in his dependency freely because he has this guardian angel who faithfully sweeps away the dirty fallout.

But even worse, she must stoically deny her own pain, including a lot of anger she dare not admit exists. To express her true feelings would blunt the anesthetic—lessen the stoicism, reduce the satisfactions that martyrdom provides.

And yet a basic human need is to have feelings validated. If they are unacknowledged, they go invalidated. The more she hangs tough, the more her own needs go unmet. Because she's not taking care of her emotional self, nor is he, her love tank is getting no refill at all. And it was probably low when she entered this union. She has no genuine love to give. The depression, the love deficit, the hunger all intensify her need for another fix. It locks her all the more tightly into the martyr role that gives her that fleeting high of achievement, usefulness, self-assurance.

At the Minirth-Meier Clinic we find this too often in the Christian marriage. The wife (generally speaking; in actual fact it often is the husband) assumes a noble, stoic pose of martyrdom. "No Christian has ever suffered more, but I'll go the hundredth mile with my poor besotted husband." On the surface it sounds good and pious and altruistic when in fact it functions almost as a drug for her as she plays out the role. The fiction is that his addiction is socially despised, hers lauded. His is wrong; hers is right. His comes from weakness of character, hers from strength. That fiction is often perpetuated in the counseling chambers of the church and elsewhere. The facts are that she is perhaps even weaker than he, and certainly quite as deeply addicted.

Consider the case of Howard Weiss, the successful owner of a chain of dry-cleaning establishments. Talk about your clean-cut example of the American Dream in action—here he was. His well-tailored suit told you right away, "This man has arrived!" He stood straight and tall, commanding in his presence. Except for a bit of graying at the temples, Howard looked almost young enough to have stepped right off the college campus.

He sat down in the office and unloaded his deepest secret. "We're Christians, and we maintain a Christian family, but my wife is a full-blown alcoholic. We can't go on like this. I must reach her and pull her out of it. I want to do an intervention."

"Do you understand what's entailed in intervention?"

"Not exactly. I heard about it when a friend described an intervention in his wife's pill problem."

"In intervention, people important to the person, such as the husband, a boss, the children, a close friend, a relative, and a mentor, confront her simultaneously. In preparation, all of you receive training. As a group you all appear on her doorstep to confront her in love. Show her you care. Ask her to get help."

"I see. It worked well for my friend. But shouldn't my wife be in the depths of despondency, so to speak? Is there a point when it's most effective?"

"Usually friends see it as a last resort, when the subject has bottomed out. That's partly because of the friends' reticence and not necessarily the subject's need. It takes courage."

"I see. Yes, I think that must be done."

"Excellent. So tell me some things about your wife. . . ."

The surface picture looked deceptively simple. Here was a concerned husband seeking help for his addicted wife. But this painting on top, for the world to see, covered quite a different picture underneath. A succession of visits rubbed away the surface painting a patch at a time to reveal a view not even Howard Weiss himself knew existed.

The real picture began to emerge when week after week Howard delayed the intervention. "I don't think she's ready yet." "Not this week. Something has come up." "She has the flu—she wouldn't really listen, she's so sick."

Each week, though, he was back in the office, complaining about how much worse things were. "You won't believe what she did this week." "She passed out on the floor and was there six hours." "She's becoming impossible to talk to."

Each time, we would agree. "Fine. That tells us more than ever that we should go ahead and intervene and get your wife the help she needs." And each time, Howard would balk with an appropriate excuse.

What we were discovering was that his addiction to her addiction was so great—his role as stoic and martyr was so powerfully important to him—he could not step aside. He could not bear to see her addiction cycle broken, for then his would shatter as well (we'll confront the dynamics of his denial in the next chapter).

Unpleasant elements revealed themselves in the uncovering picture. Howard's mother and grandmother were alcoholics and he had married one. He intensely hated women in general and his wife in particular. Now here before him was a means of venting his resentment in a socially acceptable way. That hidden part of him, the part not even he recognized, thrived on watching her hurt. He took a certain sadistic satisfaction in following her descent into misery and pain. Her depravity proved to the world how justified his ferocious anger was. On the surface he wanted to help her. But in the reality beneath, he welcomed the punishment she so richly deserved. That aspect emerged vividly as each week he described in careful detail the terrible thing this wife had become.

The picture he saw was a noble God-fearing man who stood faithfully by that irresponsible drunk. In the revealed painting he was an addict as powerfully hooked on his own cycle as she was on hers. The more he rescued, the nobler he felt. The worse she appeared, the better he looked and the more his unspoken hatred appeared to be justified. The cycles spiraled and twisted in and out of each other.

The same basic addiction cycle can describe just about any obsessive compulsion. Any number of factors can label the entry point. In the instance of Cathy Leland, one of our recent patients, the entry point was a sense of uselessness, of being of little value. The basic problem, as usual, was that her love tank was near empty, neglected by a Valium-addicted mother and a preoccupied father.

Her addiction was labeled work. The longer and harder Cathy worked, the more she accomplished. True, her accomplishments were not all on the grand scale of keeping the world safe for democracy. But as the list of nagging little duties and things-that-must-be-done in her appointment book got checked off each day, she felt good. What terrible consequences could possibly accrue from being industrious? It was satisfying, fulfilling, praiseworthy.

Cathy's marriage was entering its eleventh month and already the groom felt neglected, for good reason. She got home at nine P.M. and went to work at seven A.M. She used to swim at the Y twice a week. No more. All during college Cathy had set aside half an hour daily for Bible study, prayer, and communion with God. Now her Bible needed dusting and she wasn't spending five minutes a week with Him. At home she felt intensely guilty; at the office she felt needed.

Going to work equaled shooting up. But because the addiction agent, work, is not only healthy but socially desirable, Cathy's addiction cycle didn't really look like one. She was ambitious, yes; productive, certainly. But sick? She hadn't considered the thought. And yet, her addiction was just as destructive as alcohol or drugs to her marriage and her happiness.

If food is the anesthetic, either obesity or bulimia becomes the consequence. The resulting shame, guilt, and self-loathing calls for more anesthetic. The cycle goes on.

THE EXPANDED CYCLE

Using Howard Weiss to illustrate the process, we can now build an expanded version of the addiction/compulsion cycle. Howard's pain was twofold. There was the lost child's pain he had long ago buried, and there was the current pain caused by his wife's addiction. His anesthetic was, ultimately, watching her suffer, so that his hidden, deep-seated hatred might be justified.

The consequences were obvious—his wife hurt worse and worse, and that made him feel guiltier and guiltier down inside. Guilt and shame were multiplied by the fact that the worse she got, the better he felt.

As an extra locus or wayside along the path, we can insert denial between the pain locus (lack of self-esteem) and the addictive agent (the anesthetic) on the cyclical pathway. To move from the pain back into the addictive agent, particularly when the consequences are clear to impartial observation, the addict and the codependent must deny misusing the agent, must deny the gravity of the consequences, and perhaps deny that the agent or compulsion is addictive. We've all heard of the drunk who won't admit he drinks too much, the smoker who denies the health hazard. The problem spans the spectrum of addictive agents.

Howard necessarily had to deny within himself wanting to hurt his wife. The very thought was repugnant to any civilized person. He had developed a lifelong habit of denying the original family pain. The only thing he did not deny was the depth of his wife's addiction, because his justification and relief from pain depended upon her continuing illness.

The consequences extend far beyond a hangover or a neglected spouse. They may be physical, as when smoking causes lung cancer or alcohol encourages cirrhosis of the liver. They can certainly be spiritual, when God is denied, neglected, or misused. Social consequences accrue.

A northwest rehabilitation hospital has prepared a series of television and radio commercials dramatizing the social dysfunctions of addiction. In one ad a man morosely contemplates his fender, smashed in an accident while he blacked out, as his neighbor tells him about the hospital. In others, wives confront their remorseful husbands about what happened last night, and beg that they call the 800 number now. The commercials work well because these situations are so common and familiar.

The emotional consequences are of course devastating to the addict. But some researchers estimate that the emotional fallout of one person's addiction burns a minimum of four other people.

We also may insert a way station on the route between the consequences and the next cycle of pain/denial/anesthesia, and that is shame. A number of counselors now believe that at the core, most addictions are shame-based. The rational mind perceives the consequences just mentioned. But beyond them lie the guilt and shame of an appetite out of control. "I'm pedaling as fast as I can in reverse, and this cycle is still carrying me where I don't want to go. I've lost it. If I were stronger, if I weren't so worthless, I'd keep a lid on these appetites—maintain a balance. I'm at fault, and obviously I'm too selfish and lazy to pull myself together."

Howard Weiss's shame came from several directions. There

was his wife's socially unacceptable illness, and it was growing. Even if it served his unconscious belief that women deserve scorn, it was shameful to behold. Public opinion fanned those particular flames of shame. Her addiction and his were past control. And below his conscious level, where the real picture was unfolding, shameful, shameful things were happening. How can a *real* man do that?!

Eventually the shame and guilt merge with the original pain until they become virtually indistinguishable. We make it a separate item in this illustration because it is a cause of pain generated by the consequences, apart from the original pain. The shame and guilt must be appropriately assuaged—not glossed over, not dwelt upon, not brushed aside—if recovery is to proceed to completion.

In the early days of television, station managers filled a lot of empty hours, especially on weekends, with old cowboy movies. Old, *old* cowboy movies. Those B-grade flicks John Wayne started out in . . . *The Three Mesquiteers* (actually there were many of these popular cowboy flicks over the years) . . . Ken Maynard. . . . In every one of them, stagecoaches rattled across the open desert. And because of the stroboscopic effects of shooting film at twenty-four frames per second, the stagecoach wheels appeared to turn backwards. Ever notice that?

A codependent's deep problems appear much like those stagecoach wheels. The apparent spin is backwards of the way the codependent is really rolling, thanks to the effects of denial. And two wheels rolling simultaneously is more realistic an illustration than is one wheel.

In counseling we may represent a codependent's deeper problems with two cycles. The first cycle is generated by the original family pain—the abuses leading to lost childhood. As that pain spirals along on its own, building just like the snowball on the hill, it may become so heavy it triggers a second addictive cycle, as a snowball might break in two. They both roll inexorably downward, gathering more weight between them than would one alone. The codependent is now enslaved to two compulsions or addictions.

About a decade ago, Stanton Peele and Archie Brodsky

wrote a landmark work, *Love and Addiction*. He compared the American notion of romantic love with a heroin habit. The comparison would not have amused Barbara Cartland. He pointed out, among many other things, how the full flower of addiction resembles the throes of infatuation, and that withdrawal from heroin parallels a lovers' breakup.

Indeed, we've found that a particularly intense personal relationship follows the familiar pathways of the addiction cycle. The cycle would look like this: The pain might be the self-doubt or feeling of inadequacy—the half person, if you will. That leads to the addictive agent, an overinvolvement with a Significant Other Person (SOP). The consequence is a relationship that is unstable and suffocating for both persons. If you are suffocating an SOP, that SOP's natural instinctive reaction is to throw you off. It's almost as if you two were holding each other under water. The relationship becomes a volatile series of blowups as each, enmeshed, frantically struggles for breathing space.

All those painful effects—the instability, the discomfort of the relationship—feed back into the low self-esteem and self-doubt that triggered the overinvolvement to start with. The only way out appears to be deeper enmeshment, getting so close to the SOP that those blowups won't happen. Soon the cycle hums, fully in place, with both parties pedaling as fast as they can.

BREAKING THE CYCLE

The addiction cycle is so malignant, the only way to break it is to interdict it in several places at once. We have found that a major reason people fail to break an addiction cycle is that they intervene at only one or two points. An example is the alcoholic who gives up his booze. Again and again. Because he has not dealt with the other elements of his addiction—the pain, the consequences, the guilt—he is almost certainly condemned to fall back into the downward spiral. The ten-stage recovery process we use here at the clinic is very broad in scope because we know we must intervene at every point.

For the Jordans, recovery did not simply mean listening.

That addressed only the symptom of their problem, the most superficial aspect. We helped them resolve the core issues— their original family pain, the consequences of their long history of "selective deafness," the shame implied in an unhappy marriage.

The twelve-step program of Alcoholics Anonymous addresses the addiction cycle at several points. Steps 4 and 5, for example, the moral inventory, provide a specific route by which guilt and shame may be addressed. Steps 8 and 9 give practical ways to make amends with persons who were hurt.

Consequences such as lost jobs, lost love, damaged property or feelings require several steps to healing. The addictive behavior itself must be stopped or slowed enough that new consequences aren't constantly being added to the pile. Next the person makes an honest inventory of all the various results of the addiction. This achieves two ends. It shatters denial, as the damage and costs of the addiction at last come to conscious light. And the list provides specifics for which to grieve, item by item. Deep grieving purges. If it is not done, and the list is not thereby relegated to the past, the losses become part of the cycle again, entering at the pain spot. If the pain gets bad enough, the person may well regress again into his addiction.

Cathy Leland's workaholism threatened her marriage while she was yet a bride. How did we help her? The recent pain, her feeling of uselessness, we could somewhat assuage through counseling. The deep pain of an empty love tank took much time and work to heal. We interrupted her cycle at the addictive-agent point by recommending a much-reduced work regimen. Much of her consequential guilt came from lacking time for God and for her unhappy bridegroom. That she eased by deliberately scheduling time for both. She began feeling a sense of accomplishment in areas other than the workplace— in her marriage, her relationship with God, even watercolor painting, which she took up to help broaden her interests and distract her from her addiction.

She's in a maintenance stage of recovery now. And the one thing she has to watch for these days is that watercolors don't become addictive.

WHAT ABOUT YOU?

"Everyone has an addiction of some sort," some say.

"Then what can be so bad about mine?" say others.

Lots of teenagers' parents wish their kids had Cathy Leland's addiction—at least enough to take the garbage out and do the lawn. If you literally can't live without that six-pack, joint, recreational drug or cocktail, you already know you have a problem. Now consider what else you simply cannot live without—the things you keep going back to time after time. Do any of these covert agents, each possibly addictive, apply to you?

Your credit card. Do you maintain an outstanding balance near your credit limit? Have you had to raise your credit limit? Do you put more than ten items a month (barring business travel expenses) on your card? Examine your last credit statement as if it were someone else's. Has spending gotten out of hand?

Your job. Do your overtime hours (either recompensed or not) equal one-fourth or more of the expected hours—for example, if you work a forty-hour week, do you put in ten hours extra (five hours in a twenty-hour week, etc.)? Did you pick that job because there was no hourly maximum and you could put in any number? Do you bring at least an hour's worth of must-do homework home three nights in five or more often?

Look back over the last five occasions when you had to make a choice between doing something work-related or something other-related in the same time slot. Did the work-related option win out three or more times? Pretend you're within five years of retirement; would you consider postponing it? Yes answers suggest your work habits are out of control.

Do you engage in secret activities that would appall friends you respect? An irrepressible need to enjoy skin magazines, erotic videos, sexual material featuring children, slasher movies and magazines, the services of prostitutes, or activities that can lead to arrest if discovered are some but not all of the possibilities. Sexual addictions get lots of laughs at the comedy clubs. They aren't funny.

Do you make nonessential, idle contact with your SOP—the

most important person in your life—at least twice daily (in other words, contact not dictated by work, normal family business, seeming emergencies, scheduling adjustments, etc.)? Have you two had more than one argument in the last seven days? More than three? If you have no contact with your SOP for a week or more do you feel symptoms of anxiety? How about a three-day separation? Has your SOP ever insisted on less frequent contact, more "space" or breathing room, freedom to date others or pursue other interests without you? If your SOP were to die this night, what would your responses be over the forty-eight hours following? The line between normal, healthy bonding and an addictive overinvolvement is hard to see, harder to define. Shine a cold, hard spotlight on your relationship with your SOP. Be as honest as possible. How deeply enmeshed are you?

Examine your life carefully for the lurking presence of addictive agents such as these: rage; repeated plastic surgery; gambling; devotion to an organization or cause; television; computer games and programs; pastimes not in your case associated with gambling, such as card or board games; sports activities such as golf, running, jogging, exercise, and workout regimens.

Many people suffer addiction to more than one agent. Even if you know you have a problem, that may not be all the problem. Other less obvious elements may also be dragging you down the spiral of pain and despair. After surveying your possible addictive agents, assume for the moment that you're trapped in an addiction cycle. What consequences can you think of that accompany your supposed addiction? What sources of pain do you recall? Draw one or more cycles uniquely your own and fill in the loci, or stages, around the circle.

WARNING

If you have a drug dependency, it is of paramount importance that you be under medical supervision during the withdrawal process. Certain chemicals, such as some tranquilizers and even alcohol, can be fatal if you try to go out cold turkey without medical care. If you are chemically dependent and trying to break out of an addiction cycle, you *must* obtain a good medical assessment at a hospital or treatment center or from your doctor.

So far in this book, as we examined the causes and effects of codependency we've been urging you to probe your own feelings and memories. This may be uncharted ground for you, or you may be an old hand at introspection. In either case, we have been urging you to trot out the past for examination. We've been skating around the edge of the pond, testing the ice, getting the feel of it, weighing causes against your particular situation.

From here on, though, the going will be much tougher. You will be asked to deal with feelings and urges you don't want to deal with. In short, as we delve into the mechanics of codependency and then its resolutions, we're going to be playing hardball. If at some point you feel things are too painful, that problems you know you can't handle are beginning to reveal themselves, we urge you by all means to seek professional counsel. *Don't* take chances with problems too big to solve on your own. *Do* see it through.

The misery of codependency need not spoil your happiness. It need not be passed involuntarily to your children and your family around you. The time to end the misery is now. You can pursue and seize happiness. You can reject misery and choose love instead. But there will be a heavy price to pay in pain before the deep wounds are exposed and healed. Your relationships must be revealed and tested, and that will be very hard.

The first and continuing step is introspection. The next is to understand the mechanics of what is happening within you. Then comes the march to true healing. The light at the end of the tunnel will definitely be sunlight and not an approaching train.

CHAPTER
SEVEN

Denial

Gloria Reiner's husband, Gary, was special. He told her so. Because he was such an extremely sensitive person, he said, he required the close company of women as well as men.

And so she closed her smoky gray eyes and believed him.

With her conscious mind.

When resentment and jealousy seethed up inside her, she steadfastly beat them down. "I'm sorry, dear. You're right—I'm wrong to feel angry and possessive. You are being the man you have to be."

And he would coo, "Jealousy like beauty is in the eye of the beholder. Just remember Titus 1:15: 'To the pure all things are pure.' Keep yourself pure by holding to pure thoughts."

Jealousy is wrong. *Let not the sun set on your anger*.

The Reiners belonged to a very rigid, legalistic church. Everything about Gloria's strict church upbringing and her training as a gracious lady required her to keep her feelings under tight rein. Being a staunch perfectionist, she determined to do it perfectly, as she did everything else. She got pretty good at it too; he gave her plenty of opportunity for practice.

Gloria broke, eventually. It got to be too much for her. An intense depression landed her in our hospital, several hundred miles from her home.

About a week into her stay she called Gary, just to see how he was getting along. A woman from her church answered the phone.

On reflex Gloria's rage welled up. Just as reflexively she shut it down. "No. I need to understand Gary. I must maintain a reasonable attitude. He wouldn't do anything wrong. My anger is totally inappropriate."

She recited the litany over and over.

How were we to convince Gloria her anger was not only natural and appropriate but justified? Whether or not he was actually cheating, he was disregarding his wife's needs and callously putting her through a very painful wringer. We began by entering her into group therapy at the hospital.

Now one of the most important functions of a therapy group is to provide a surrogate family. This "family" takes a part in the healing by partially replacing the dysfunctional original family, which bred the codependency problems to start with. The group becomes a caring and nurturing circle for the lost child that is within each of them. And a very nice thing about a therapy group is that although its members may be a little slow to pick up on their own problems, they can quickly see right through the others'.

It's something like the story of the two fish swimming through the sea. They probed wrecks, explored seaweed forests, swam high and low. Finally one fish asked, "Just what are we looking for?" The other replied, "I heard there's water down here someplace."

A codependent can be under seven fathoms of codependency. All the other observers can see what's happening. The sufferer cannot.

Joe, a compulsive eater and spender, was one of the most vociferous members of her group. He chuckled, "Gloria, dear, you're not only in denial, you're in denial about your denial."

"Wrong!" And she spread still another layer on her denial.

With Joe in the lead the group would confront Gloria, force a crack in her armor, bring her to a state of some small awareness. The next day she would be right back at the beginning. "It's not Gary; it's me. I mustn't feel this way."

What a malignant, intense, horrifyingly powerful dynamic is denial!

DENIAL

Consider the addiction cycle. The observer on the outside looking in can see clearly and say to the addict, "Why are you doing this to yourself when the consequences are so obvious?" The answer is denial. The only way an addict (we'll say "she" for convenience, but it operates just as powerfully with "he") can remain in her addiction is if somehow she can maintain her denial.

Declare things better or less harmful than they really are—thus, by magical thinking, she reduces the consequences to manageable size or even to zero. If but for a short time she breaks with that denial, the addiction cycle is revealed for what it is.

This concept is even more important for the codependent than for the dependent. The dependent is dealing with his addiction or dysfunction; the codependent must deal with both his problem and hers. "His problem isn't as bad as it looks. It's going to get better. I myself don't have a problem."

Codependents growing up in a dysfunctional home very early learn how to use denial effectively. Claudia Black, a pioneer and leader in the field of codependency, gives a memorable example. She was quite young—three, perhaps—when she awoke one morning to see her drunken father sprawled unconscious in the front yard. Terrified she ran to her mother. "Mommy! Daddy is lying out there! Something's wrong!"

Calmly her mother replied, "No, dear, nothing's wrong. Daddy is camping."

Claudia clearly remembers nodding at that very tender age and agreeing, "Daddy is camping." Thus as a tiny girl she learned to see a terrifying piece of reality, deny its reality, turn it upside down and say, "No, things are not as painful and frightening as they seem. It's really okay somehow."

Gloria Reiner said that, too, even after she was hospitalized for acute depression.

INTERVENTION

Intervention is a technique sometimes used to jolt an addict into seeing the reality of his addiction ("his" reads "her" just as accurately). As mentioned previously, the method consists of training persons close to the addict in what to do and not to do, then gathering them on his doorstep all at once to confront him with the facts of his problem. There is no judgment, no condemnation, no comparisons—only the facts. The group sits down before him as a body and quotes dates and places in an effort to break through the massive wall of denial. Anytime an intervention is done, the single greatest obstacle is denial.

Intervention works like this: known and trusted people bombard the subject with facts in order to force in a wedge of awareness, however briefly. We compare it with opening a window, in this case a window of opportunity. Sometimes a tremendously negative consequence such as losing a job, wrecking the car, or causing injury can pop the window briefly, providing a few hours or at most a few days to reach the addict. But the window slams shut quickly—the protective membrane of denial stitches itself firmly back in place again. We have learned to move swiftly if crisis occurs in the addict's life.

You will recall that the anorexic student nurse, Louise, whom we met in a previous chapter, was the subject of another kind of intervention. Her supervisor issued a nonnegotiable ultimatum: "Enter treatment or lose your position." Because her student position was an important avenue to achieve praise and acceptance, it worked. Major corporations are beginning to see that this sort of intervention provides superior advantages over the old practice of simply firing alcoholics.

We find that a serious barrier to timely intervention may well be the dependent's codependent, as you saw in the case of Howard Weiss in the preceding chapter.

Why? Codependents are endlessly inventive with their magical thinking. Like Gloria Reiner, Howard Weiss used denial to keep his pain at bay—the truth was too much for either of them to deal with. Done well, denial offers a kinder future someday.

Because they were codependent on a dependent spouse—

addicted to that spouse's addiction—each used denial to keep the cycle of coaddiction in place. Remember that, very frequently, codependents are not just responding to a dependent spouse; they have brought their own fully established problems of codependency into the union.

In these two cases the cycle was painful to ride, but it was familiar and comforting in an irrational way (again, we're not dealing with reason). As long as they were enmeshed in their cycles, Gloria and Howard could not conceive of a less painful existence beyond them. Although interventions and windows and such might help Gloria's husband and Howard's wife, no such intervention short of group therapy was available for the codependents. ("Do an intervention on Gloria? But she's not the one who needs it.") Although they faced less opportunity to be given a window, their addiction cycles were every bit as powerful and destructive as their mates'.

Another aspect of magical thinking that is the special province of the codependent is the unconscious conviction that somehow the codependent is responsible for whatever happens to anyone. Deep inside, Gloria believed (a) she was in some way responsible for her husband's anomalies, (b) if only she were a better wife/lover/human being it wouldn't be this way, and therefore, (c) she deserved to be punished for her responsibility. Although a codependent almost never voices these thoughts consciously, they very commonly lurk beneath the surface, part of the package, if you will. Gloria used denial to keep that good old well-deserved punishment going.

Denial becomes so easy for magical thinkers. They can heap layers of denial one upon the other to prevent anything from breaking through.

OTHER FORMS OF DENIAL

Don't believe that denial is a factor in dependence and codependency only; it's simply that dependents and codependents carry it to an illogical extreme, as they do so many other things. Denial itself becomes, in a sense, an obsessive compulsion. Medical workers outside codependency bump into it time after time. One of the biggest deterrents to timely cancer treatment is that so many people delay seeing a doctor for fear he will "find something."

A classic case of denial that passed only briefly through a nearby hospital involved a young woman named Dolores. She suffered vaguely defined symptoms of who-knows-what. She just didn't feel up to snuff, so her internist ran her through a battery of tests.

"I have good news for you, Miss Ramos," he announced. "Your problem is easily treatable. With proper attention to diet, plus mild medication, you'll live a full and happy life. You have diabetes."

Replied Dolores, "You're a quack."

Over the next year Dolores ricocheted from doctor to doctor, at least half a dozen internists. The diagnosis came back the same each time. Diabetes. When Dolores Ramos died not too long thereafter, the autopsy dutifully reported "diabetes." It should have said "denial."

SUBMISSION

Another aspect of denial and magical thinking that needs examination is the additional dimension regarding wifely submission found in certain conservative churches. Kay Marshall Strom's excellent book *In the Name of Submission* deals in clear, terse language with one of the ugliest of abuses, wife battering. Without mentioning codependency by name she sets down very clearly its causes and effects, particularly on the children.

The Christian wife is taught that the husband is the head of the house, as Christ heads the church. So far, so good. There is no better formula for successful marriage than that found in Scripture, and a tribe with two chiefs and no Indians won't function long. But when a man (whose father probably, according to the statistics, was also a wife-beater) would promulgate an abusive relationship, he'll find plenty of false evidence in Scripture to support his abuse.

It's not hard. In 1 Corinthians 7:4 he need only accept Paul's teaching that the husband rules over the wife's body—ignoring the rest of that verse, of course, that says the wife rules over the husband's body. In that same chapter, verse 10, Paul declares that a wife should not separate from her husband. Yet, how few women are counseled in the rest of that same verse—*but if she does.* . . . Paul left the door open for extreme cases.

Ms. Strom counsels wisely that the abusive husband is almost never going to change unless the wife takes drastic steps to force a change. Separation with the ultimatum "You must undergo treatment before I will return" is just about the only successful means a wife has of easing the abuse. Are the children warped by a relationship in which the husband mistreats his wife? Every time.

The wife is called upon to be subject to her man (Ephesians 5:22), but hardly anyone notices that in 5:21 Paul has used exactly the same word to call every Christian into similar submission to every other. Neither is the wife-beater likely to take seriously Paul's admonition to husbands in Ephesians 5:25 to love the wife protectively and sacrificially.

Discipline? The abusive husband quotes Hebrews 12:7, which extols God's disciplining of His faithful, and twists it to suggest that the man ought to keep his mature adult wife in line in the same way one might discipline a small child, or God might discipline an errant saint.

After all, everyone knows the wife's chief duty is to please her man (the 1 Corinthians 7:32–35 passage so often used as a proof text states just as firmly that the husband similarly should please his wife). Not only is divorce unthinkable, it is construed as trumpeting to the world that the wife somehow failed to make a happy home. Thus in marriage, but too often especially in Christian marriage, denominational interpretation and tradition bind the woman to an unholy union of fear and pain.

Because of her erroneous concept of submission and her strong abhorrence of divorce or separation, the Christian wife may have little recourse but to take refuge in terrible denial. If she entered the union with her own burden of codependency already on her shoulders (and like Beryl Mason, who so often chose wife-beaters as husbands, she probably did), the denial is compounded by false guilt and magical thinking. An abusive

husband will almost certainly reflect the onus of his actions
back upon his victim.

"You realize, dear," says the husband, "that you make me
do these things. You make me hit you." And the codependent
believes it because codependents are certain they are responsible for others' thoughts and deeds.

"If you were in perfect submission I wouldn't have to discipline you." And the codependent believes it, because the codependent, lacking a good self-image, is too often willing to
accept a big unhealthy dose of blame for just about anything.

"You drive me to drink!" and the codependent agrees.

"It's your fault!" and the codependent buys the whole bolt,
regardless how shoddy it may be.

COUNTERING DENIAL WITH TRUTH

Consider some of these statements we at the clinic find
commonly associated with denial and magical thinking. Do any
of them ring bells for you?

"It's not as bad as it appears."
>   No. It's almost certainly worse. Denial makes a bad
>   situation look good and an intolerable situation look hope-
>   ful.

**"I make him/her do those things" (fly into a rage,
drink, etc.).**
>   It's true that in any relationship both parties contribute
>   to the conflict, but what he/she wants you to think is that
>   you are totally responsible. As long as you glibly volunteer
>   to take all the responsibility, that other person may wal-
>   low in his/her addiction without remorse. You're harming
>   that person terribly by not making him/her accept re-
>   sponsibility for all actions, good and bad.

**"If I were better, or tried harder, things would be all
right."**
>   Instead of an overemphasis on trying to do better,
>   backing off may actually do the relationship good because

you are not assuming total responsibility. There is a point at which trying harder will not work.

"You just watch; it will change for the better soon."
While some people do choose to change, be careful of magical thinking. In all of our experience we rarely see a spontaneous improvement. And even if the other person improves, you still have codependency problems of your own to deal with.

"It's a minor problem—certainly not an addiction!"
While there may be degrees of seriousness with any problem, if it has in any way taken control of your life or that other person's, it's an addiction. Start dealing with it. And if it is threatening you physically, it's all the worse.

"There's nothing wrong with me; it's the other person you should fix."
If the other person has a problem, you are affected. Period.

"It's the way he/she is and that's all there is to it."
If the other person is abusive, cold, indifferent, or cruel; if that person is generating unhappiness in you or your children, you have an obligation to begin a change.

"My life is too messed up to mend. Nothing will help."
Peter denied the Lord three times; David sinned seriously. Yet both were restored to fellowship with the Lord. You can be too.

"We're making progress on our own. We don't need help."
While we can make progress on our own to some degree, we all need outside help from time to time. The best of progress makes a step back for two steps forward. And a step back can derail your progress unless you actively work at resolution.

"Whatever befalls me is God's will for my life."
In that case, why pray? And why did Joshua walk for

seven days around Jericho's walls?[1] Why did Naaman bathe in the Jordan?[2] Why do Americans fight and die for free elections? Why eat healthful foods and avoid smoking? Kismet is not where it's at in psychology, either.

"But you don't understand my situation," you might say. Or "My situation isn't like that." These, too, are attitudes of denial. Most importantly, keep in mind that denial is the most powerful and harmful attitude you will ever fight within yourself and that no real healing can commence until it is set aside.

Denial is, in essence, the antithesis of confession. It breeds in the dark recesses of the heart, that heart "deceitful above all things and desperately wicked," as Jeremiah said in his prophecy.[3]

You may not realize how thick and numerous are your own walls of denial. To break through them you may have to seek the honest opinion of a close friend (family members usually are hampered by the same denials you are and therefore aren't good external observers). Whatever the means, you must see your relationships and condition as they are and not as you wishfully think they ought to be.

You remember "denial's" place on the addiction cycle. When that way station on the cycle is rubbed away, when denial is finally and effectively dealt with, you will probably wish it were back. Denial protected you from the next step, which is painful, perhaps even violent, but it is also cathartic. Healing.

We're dealing next with anger.

CHAPTER
EIGHT

Anger

Brad Darren has luminous blue eyes not unlike Paul Newman's, a Harrison Ford body, a smile as bright and dazzling as the national Christmas tree, the boyish good looks of a Robert Redford—and to top it all off, he owns a charming third-floor condo in a truly elegant community. Joan Trask has mysterious deep brown eyes, a Jane Fonda body, a smile that makes you forget all about third-world crises and the threat of nuclear disaster, an elegant natural beauty—and to top it all off, her three-bedroom home in the prestigious North End is bought and paid for.

The moment Brad and Joan met it was love at first sight. They might have married instantly had not both agreed that prudence and certain financial considerations counseled "Wait." Neither was quite ready to abandon freedom. Both enjoyed fast-track careers that ought to be stabilized before taking such a life-changing step as marriage.

It was to be expected that the perfect relationship between these two perfect people would have some ups and downs. Brad's father fought with his mother all the time and they, too, had been perfect for each other. It's the deep natural order of things. Joan agreed; her cocaine-addicted father squabbled all the time with her prudish, straitlaced mother.

As a make-up gift after a particularly harrowing falling-out, Joan presented Brad with an elaborate exercise bicycle featuring all the latest in digital readout, computerized cardiovascular analysis, and the optional rowing function. He was thrilled, and he loved her all the more. He kept the bike at her spacious home because it was really too big for his little condo.

August 2. Following a violent quarrel, they vowed never to darken each other's door again. Enough is enough. Brad removed his exercycle from Joan's home and toted it back to his place, up the three flights of stairs because it wouldn't fit in the elevator.

August 5. Awash in remorse, Joan arrived at Brad's door seeking forgiveness. He responded favorably. Together they carried the exercycle down the stairs and transported it back across town to her home.

August 13. Incensed by what he saw in Joan's relationship with a business associate, Brad exploded. They argued hotly. He yanked his exercycle and hauled it back to his place.

August 14. Brad cooled off and reconsidered. He called Joan asking for a reconciliation. She forgave him. He came to her home for dinner, bringing his exercycle.

September 1. Angered by the way Brad was so chauvinistically taking over her home and her life, Joan confronted him, demanding breathing space. They argued violently. Joan kicked out the exercycle along with Brad.

September 6. Reconciliation. Brad's exercycle by now had lost two rubber feet, and the handlebars with the rowing option wobbled a lot. It didn't help a bit when Brad and Joan dropped it on the stairs en route back to Joan's.

September 17. Brad shocked his friends by announcing plans to undergo cosmetic surgery on his nose and chin. How could he see flaws in so perfect a face? Never one to mince words, Joan informed him that he was an overly self-critical nincompoop. The battered exercycle—and Brad—headed back to the third-floor condo.

As outlandish as this situation seems, Brad and Joan are not stereotypical fictional characters. They are clients whose names have been changed, and we as their doctors watched the exercycle's tenuous journeys back and forth.

How nice it would be to be able to report that through therapy Brad and Joan achieved a measure of peace together. Sadly, it's not so. Both are certain such blowups are normal for sensitive, high-strung young executives, particularly in light of the fact that their parents before them (all four of them also sensitive and high-strung according to the children) experienced similar love relationships. Neither can see how damaging their undercurrent of intense anger and hostility can be. Neither will admit the blowups are becoming increasingly violent and intense.

HIDDEN ANGER

In a way, though, Brad and Joan are fortunate. Their anger is obvious; they acknowledge it even as they deny its power. In both clinical and private practice, we at the Minirth-Meier Clinic find that in *every* codependent relationship tremendous anger builds up on both sides. And when it is not recognized and acknowledged, that anger erupts one way or another. It *always* causes damage to the patient's emotions and often to his or her health as well.

In a codependent relationship, when one or both partners deny anger it goes underground. So frequently does anger emerge as depression, we can cast an overly simplistic lay definition for depression: *Depression is anger turned inward*. Anger is not the only source of depression, but it's one of those causes to look for first.

Denied anger can also express itself in other ways. Anger may emerge sort of sideways, as it were, through passive-aggressive responses. Some examples might include the superperfectionist housewife who keeps scorching her husband's shirts, although she certainly knows how to iron. Or the husband who is constantly ripping up his knuckles when the wrench slips as he's changing the car's oil. Or an adult son, living at home with a possessive mother, who keeps bumping his head on the low cellar doorway—he's been doing it for eleven years. These are actions or activities that irk or cause pain. The person does not consciously feel anger or admit it. The unconscious action provides an outlet for the spate of anger, the pressure release.

Sexual dysfunction is another common response. An older

woman in counsel admitted, "We haven't been intimate in ten years. I love and respect my husband—I simply cannot respond to him sexually at all. Yes, I suppose it's a problem, and yes, I'm depressed, but you must understand, there's no anger here."

The man or woman in denial of anger might experience anxiety attacks—panic at little or no provocation. Whatever the means, in some way, sooner or later, that tremendous anger must release itself. So violently does the anger burst forth, the person experiencing a panic attack may report, "I thought I was going to die, I was so overwhelmed by fear and strange emotions I didn't know existed."

SOURCES OF ANGER

Everybody gets angry now and then—it's normal. But debilitating depression? Self-damaging actions? Sexual problems? Anxiety attacks? Where could so much irrepressible anger possibly come from? We see several sources of extreme anger in codependent relationships which are generated by factors other than the day-to-day little upsets we all experience.

LOST CHILDHOOD

You will recall that a codependent's love tank is most probably running near empty because the parents had been unable to fill it adequately during the growing-up days. Almost universally, the codependent carries a reservoir of old, unresolved anger, a deep feeling of having been cheated somehow, by this failure in the original family. The loss may not be understood or verbalized, but it's down there. If physical abuse was a part of growing up, the anger is further multiplied.

LACK OF COMPLETENESS

A second source, a concept we've not yet discussed, is the sense of personal identity—or lack of it—in a codependent. When lack of self-esteem links arms with this lack of identity, the person senses something is missing. Question marks haunt what should be a solid personality. The resulting frustration expresses itself as anger.

LACK OF FULFILLMENT BY OTHERS

Recall also that a codependent with a nearly empty love tank gravitates toward others with similarly impoverished tanks. The unspoken, unthought expectation when two such half people enter a marriage is, "You are going to fill my tank; through you I will achieve completeness." Neither person has the capacity to do that. A frustrating double sense of betrayal generates what we could call new anger. The reservoir of anger deepens as the love tank languishes.

A wholesome marital relationship between noncodependent persons may be illustrated with two circles. He and she are not half people. Each is a complete circle, a solid entity. By choice, not necessity, each enters into the sacred shared relationship of marriage. Both persons, as well as the marriage itself, possess discrete boundaries. The wedding of these two people is not the totality of their existence. Each is still complete in self as well as in tandem. Thus, for them love is a choice, a voluntary move toward mutual concert and satisfaction.

The codependent, however, may be illustrated as a dotted circle. The person is there but the boundaries are indistinct. The halfness of the codependent is not a halfness of shape but of boundary. One of the traits of the codependent, you will remember, is a certain fogginess about self, a lack of strong personal identity. The codependent asks, "Who am I?" The noncodependent cannot imagine why the codependent doesn't know.

When these two rather vague circles unite, the two lives become inextricably enmeshed. In a sense they pile on top of each other. The yearning of each is to overlap the other, to complete the self, to gain a firm identity, to somehow make a solid line from the dots and dashes. It doesn't work that way, of course. Even a complete overlap couldn't achieve the kind of wholeness these two seek. As a result, each feels pulled at, drained, smothered, and logically so, for each is trying to draw from the other what is lacking in self. Each develops an undercurrent feeling of being violated. Exploited. The chronic sense of violation, of exploitation, becomes a constant source of unspoken resentment and hostility.

As the persons become overinvolved, they will reach a breaking point. One or both eventually will push away: "I need breathing room!" is the cry, either unconscious or overt. An immense amount of anger wells up from this. It's a defense mechanism, in a sense, as each tries to keep from being suffocated by the enmeshment of the other.

To gain a feeling for this powerful and intense suffocation, imagine yourself as a little kid on the bottom of a whole pile of kids—perhaps some wild playground experience, or perhaps a game of roughhouse football where everyone had to get in on the play. You struggle, you panic, you can't breathe. Have you ever been held underwater involuntarily? You experience the same feelings, intensified by the fact that you really can't breathe.

A man named Roger, a near-drowning victim, was hauled from the surf off Huntington Beach, California. Swimming alone, he had ventured beyond the breakers where a tidal current caught him. Fortunately, boaters found him in time. During recovery he described his feelings when he realized he was too far offshore to make it back. "At first I panicked; I guess that's natural. I should have been praying, but so help me I never thought of it. Instead I got angry. I can't tell you who I was angry at—myself, I suppose. All I know is there was this rage, this howling rage, at myself for going out so far, and at the world for doing this to me, and at whatever—I didn't know. I was still enraged when I lost consciousness."

Codependent spouses respond similarly to the feeling of suffocation which the smothering relationship engenders. Add that anger to the boiling reservoirs already churning in their lives. Complicate the picture with those impoverished love tanks. Toss in some surface symptoms of compulsive behavior and addiction. Then introduce the whole dimension of denial, and you can begin to see why unresolved anger is such a potent destroyer of happiness and choice.

Brad and Joan still have not admitted, either to themselves or to each other, that this reservoir of anger exists in their lives. Their failure to acknowledge anger has erected a formidable barrier to healing.

Can you ever hope to sort and unravel such an insidious

tangle? You can, but only if you can dig down to the anger within and force it to the surface. This can be an incredibly powerful and painful experience. It can also be even more debilitating than the anger itself if, once you've forced your anger to the surface, you do not deal with it in an effective and timely way.

For the moment it is sufficient that you recognize the fact that every codependent carries an intense burden of anger and nearly all of it is hidden, unsuspected. Later on, when you have enough background to handle dangerous emotions safely, you will be asked to dredge up that anger and deal with it effectively. You will be confused and amazed—and terribly hurt—by what you find deep inside yourself. But with that pain will come healing, and a delightful new awareness of just how wonderfully you have been created.

Let us let sleeping dogs lie for the moment. First, let's explore in more detail how codependency affects the various kinds of interpersonal relationships.

PART FOUR:

Codependency in Interpersonal Relationships

CHAPTER NINE

Codependent or Healthy Relationships?

Susanna Wesley bore nineteen babies. Ten reached adulthood. She homeschooled them all in basic education plus Latin, Greek, and theology, often from a sickbed. Her rigid, orderly schedules drove her easygoing spendthrift husband, Samuel Wesley, Sr., away for months on end, leaving her to handle alone the household, his debts, and his backwater parish on the English moors. Her middle boy-child, John, adopted her methodical ways so thoroughly, the amazing revolution he forged is called by that name—Methodism. You may also have heard of the youngest son Charles. And then there was Emilia.

Emilia Wesley, the eldest daughter, was known throughout the parish as the pretty one, the smartest girl in the brood, the one you could depend upon. She carried her tall, lithe body with regal grace. Was she stuck on herself? The village oldwives gossiped and argued about that. On the one hand, she kept her place as a vicar's daughter and never acted aloof. On the other, there she was entering her twenties and she wasn't married yet. To her credit, she kept herself pure, but she wasn't even being courted.

From very early, Emilia picked up the slack when her mother was too weak physically to carry her load. Emilia helped with the children and the housework. Emilia learned

Latin, Greek, and theology along with her brothers, even though there was scant use three hundred years ago for an educated woman. She worked her whole childhood because she had to. There was no choice, no other option.

Because of her father's extravagance, Emilia had no money for decent apparel. Every penny went for bread or disappeared into the bottomless chasms of her father's get-rich schemes. Her lack of proper clothes barred her from the better-paid jobs in which she would have excelled, governess or nurse. Desperate to use her knowledge, she established a successful school for girls in nearby Gainsborough. She was forty-four when a man named Robert Harper sought her hand in marriage.

Although she didn't actually love the fellow, he was attractive. He had money and a good job and she was abysmally sick of working. She wanted to rest once, to be treated well and taken care of after a lifetime of always caring for others. And so she married.

What she didn't know was that Rob Harper was just as tired of working. His secret agenda for marriage was to quit work, take it easy, and be kept by a successful woman. When the baby came he left her, taking her savings and leaving her his debts. Shortly after, the sickly infant died.

REPEATING THE FAMILY PAIN

Emilia Wesley Harper's story repeats itself a million times today. Only the details change. A woman emerging from an alcoholic home vows to leave that misery behind forever. She marries an alcoholic and may well become an alcoholic herself despite knowing from experience what alcoholism is. A man whose home life was disrupted by several divorces finds himself constantly and repeatedly "unlucky in love." Claudia Black wrote a landmark book on the problem with the self-explanatory title *It Will Never Happen to Me!* Numerous other sociologists and social workers have recorded the constant phenomenon: adults from dysfunctional families end up with dysfunctional adult relationships, for they have become co-dependents.

Why? Surely the man or woman who grew up knowing firsthand the misery alcoholism or other compulsive behavior causes would know what to avoid. Can't the sufferer see all those blatant warning signs?

We at the clinic, as well as other counselors, note a sadly intriguing fact: somehow, people who are powerfully codependent literally blind themselves to the red flags other people would flee from. No, they don't see the warning signs, because they unconsciously choose not to. Unerringly they find themselves attracted to exactly the people they swear they'll never end up being or joining.

Let's put the phenomenon in picture form. We mentioned previously that codependency is difficult if not impossible to measure, although some counselors are assigning numerical scores to degrees of codependency. Without getting that technical we can, however, build an informal scale for our own use. Let's pretend that deep inside, each person possesses a thermometer that measures codependency.

No one is totally free of the ghosts of the past, so no one would rank zero on our hypothetical thermometer. No one is so enslaved by the past as to rank a hundred, which is to say completely codependent. The large majority of people are somewhere at the low end. Factors in their original families may have given their personalities some interesting loops and turns, but they function well in a family situation and enjoy healthy personal relationships.

THE HEALTHY FAMILY

What is a healthy family? Ask a hundred adult children and you'll get a hundred different answers. Here are some criteria we condensed from our observations at the clinic:

- Sane, balanced parents. No depression, no mental illness, no extreme frustration with either life in general or some element of it. If depression was part of their past, they've dealt with it adequately.
- Non-addicted parents. In addition to the obvious—alcoholism or drug use—problem areas include such obsessive compulsions as workaholism, rageaholism, compulsive spending, eating disorders.
- Mature parents. Self-sufficient, able to deal with life.

- Parents with a positive, comfortable self-image.
- Parents who can relate appropriately to God. In the best-case scenario, God is central to the family structure.
- Parents committed to maintaining a *happy* marriage.

Usually, people with a low level of codependency come from such families and build healthy families of their own. Now let's consider the other end of the scale—extreme, rabid codependency.

A CODEPENDENT FAMILY

Reverse the conditions above:

- One or both parents are mentally unbalanced, preoccupied, frustrated, unrealistic in their world view. If only one parent suffers thus, the other will be preoccupied with the ill mate.
- Parents addicted to alcohol, drugs, work; consumed by rage or hungers; compulsive about things healthy people are casual about.
- Immature parents; especially parents who lean upon the children for nurturance, ego-bolstering, advice, help.
- Parents with a poorly developed or skewed self-image.
- Parents in an uncomfortable relationship with God; one or both may be atheists (no relationship at all) or agnostics. Or they may be intensely religious but strongly behavior directed (if you act exactly right and look exactly right and think exactly right, God will accept you), extremely rigid in their theology (the only right way to relate to God is this way), and just as adamant that the children follow exactly in the parents' theological footsteps.
- Parents who divorce; separate; fight viciously; feel bitter toward each other or toward marriage in general or parents who remain together in a hostile relationship "for the sake of the kids."

ANALYZING EMILIA

Looking at Emilia Wesley Harper across the centuries, we guess at her position on our codependency scale. Emilia's father abandoned her. She assumed an adult role very early, a state we now call emotional incest. She was a second mommy. Her mother was rigidly strict and behavior oriented. That this strictness was necessary to a point, for the teeming Wesley household would elsewise have been chaotic, did not soften its effect. Her childhood was lost, evaporated in a cloud of onerous responsibility from tender youth. In Emilia you can see so many causes of codependency that we explored in Part Two.

In adulthood, lack of opportunity to use her God-given intelligence and education frustrated her. Constantly being poor also frustrated her, for in her society even the most deserving rarely crossed the lines of economic class to better themselves. It is a matter of record that she deeply resented her father's absences and failure to provide. Through no fault of her own, her codependency thermometer would probably register quite high.

Codependency brings with it a kind of radar. A person scoring, say, 80 on our scale will gravitate unerringly to someone who is perhaps between 75 and 90. Two hundred people mill about in a grand ballroom. One ranks 85; all the others are below 20. An 80-scoring codependent who walks into the room will single out that one other codependent in the crowd. Every time. Beeline.

The man Emilia chose appeared industrious, well-off, and stable—everything the adult male she knew best was not. He would surely not abandon her. She was determined never to repeat her mother's mistake, for she knew firsthand the grief which penury and abandonments caused. The qualities she yearned for most in a mate she saw in Rob Harper. The qualities he actually possessed were very like her father's.

It comes back to love tanks. Again, here are two heart-shaped tanks. This time they are not Mother and Father. The one we'll call Henry. His tank happens to be very low (conversely, his codependency thermometer is up around 80). Henry has no concept of the tank inside him, let alone that it's near empty, but he senses a lack in his life, a hollow spot. Of marriageable age, he is seeking the love of his life, his Henrietta. Quite likely, the love tanks of the women he dates, and of the woman he mates, will be at about the same level as his own. Henrietta, the other tank in our illustration, will score right up there at 75, 80, 90.

This need not be an intentional choice on Henry's part. Indeed, if he comes from an abusive background he quite likely has told himself, "By cracky in my family things will be different! We won't be like Mom and Dad." Then along comes that codependent radar to give him a mate just like dear old Mom or Dad.

When Henry and Henrietta court, they mask or shield the emptiness of their tanks. With that deception, plus the radar, it's not hard for each to see in the other the illusion that "Here is the person who will give me the love I crave." The unwritten, unspoken marriage contract says, "You will fulfill me. Deep on the inside something is missing—I'm sure that something is love—and you, my true love, can provide it."

We usually have found that the emptier a person's love tank, the more highly that person values idealized romance. Stated differently, the extent to which my love tank is empty is the extent to which I will give priority to romantic love, to the old Hollywood "some enchanted evening you may see a stranger across a crowded room" convention. It will fill me. It will last forever. When Henry first links up with Henrietta, the fireworks go off, the good times roll. The exaggerated intensity of those feelings reflects the emptiness of their tanks.

If Henry's tank were near full, he would not feel this driving need to lose himself completely in Henrietta. He would, of course, still enjoy warm, romantic feelings toward her (whose tank almost certainly would also be near full). Those feelings, though, would be safely tempered by reason, logic, values, and, in the Christian, consideration of God's will.

But Henry's tank is not full. As far as his unmet emotional needs go, Henry is a half person. And as he joins with Henrietta, down at some deep level lies the unrealistic hope: "If we put my half person together with your half person, we'll be a whole person. You will fulfill me and I will fulfill you."

It doesn't work that way. Figuratively, marriage turns out to be a multiplication, not an addition. *One half times one half is one fourth. Brokenness plus brokenness does not make completion*. It remains brokenness. Henry and Henrietta find themselves worse off than before they met.

But that's not the biggest problem. Down inside, both have been very carefully hiding their love tanks from each other and from themselves, concealing the fact that the tanks are near empty. Each hoped to be loved as a child is loved, that little lost child inside; to siphon off enough love from the mate to fill the echoing tank. You can't keep that kind of intelligence from a marital partner for long. Each soon finds the other's reservoir sadly lacking. As the deception unmasks itself, as the poverty of unmet emotional needs emerges, the marriage dissolves rapidly in a storm of disappointment, bitterness, and anger.

What if Henrietta's tank is fairly well filled? Probably she will soon find the relationship suffocating—draining in a very real sense. She doesn't need another half person to complete herself because she already is a whole person. Something about the relationship doesn't feel right. Alerted to the red flags and not blinded by codependency, she'll likely back off during courtship.

An illustration we use in group therapy is of a man whose car runs out of gas on the highway. He flags another car, and they try to siphon gas from one vehicle to the other, only to learn that the other tank is also empty. What little gas there was is now distributed so sparsely they're both stuck, unable to drive away.

We find it extremely difficult to counsel couples with this strong, magnetic, codependent attraction. Their feelings toward each other are incredibly intense. The couple, certain it's love, can't see what's wrong with such a consuming, almost worshipful, attitude toward one another. Isn't this the very love that Whitney Houston sings about, and Neil Diamond extols?

Think of the number of films, television shows, and top-40 songs that promote and idealize this sort of love relationship:

- The lover's be-all and end-all exists in the lovee.
- If that tingle, that kick, felt in the initial infatuation fades, the love has faded (Neil Diamond and Barbra Streisand, "You Don't Bring Me Flowers Anymore").
- True love unmistakably wallops you (the "across-a-crowded-room" thing). If it doesn't stun you it's not there.

- Physical attraction is where it's at ("You Must Have Been a Beautiful Baby!").
- Real love is overwhelming, beyond control ("I Can't Stop Loving You").

Compare this with what counselors in the field know about codependent relationships:

- The codependent suffers an unclear or faulty self-image and therefore tends to become absorbed into other people.
  Put differently, the codependent lacks a sense of self and personal boundaries—"I am me." Instead the codependent thinks *I'm not sure who I am*. Codependents become confusingly enmeshed with others who are close and entangle their identities with their loved ones'.
- Because codependents' love tanks have been running on empty, they cannot understand and recognize the fundamental human function, "true love." Codependents will erroneously confuse infatuation, mutual love hunger, physical attraction, or simple affection as love.
- Codependents tend so strongly to compulsivity and addiction that they bring these addictive qualities to their personal relationships as well. They easily become helplessly obsessed with the other person, unable to let go.

To the person embroiled in this kind of love relationship, it must be true love because this is the way it is described by the media and everyone else. That person fails to realize two things: the media doesn't picture the stronger but less romantic true love because it's not nearly as exciting. True love doesn't make good copy or build intense conflict the way a codependent relationship does. The stereotype is simpler and easier to express than deep, complex love ties, particularly in our instant gratification culture.

Picture anthropologists digging up the ruins of our civilization 30,000 years from now. One-hour photo. Fast food. Federal Express overnight delivery, guaranteed. Fax. Drive-through tellers and 24-hour banking machines. Painkillers that work *now*, "When you haven't got time for the pain. . . ."

Would those anthropologists be as staggered by our impatience as are people from foreign cultures who step for the first time into our full-gallop way of life?

An American journalist who lived for a while in Japan recently took an assignment in the USSR. She claimed that if moving from American culture into Japanese is a different world, Soviet life is a whole different universe. In Russia you make waiting a cottage industry as you deal with incredible bureaucratic delays and the long lines required for purchase of daily basics. Waiting. In America, it's a lost art.

Given our cultural propensity for I-want-it-now, is it any wonder that our children eschew years of college or apprentice work in preparation for professional satisfaction, when an easily obtainable drug can give them a high in moments?

Combine the instant gratification syndrome with the forms of codependent love promoted by American media, and you have a painfully twisted version of what love ought to be. A popular book of a few years ago told women how to work on a marriage prospect. If he didn't propose in a year, drop him as a bad bet and move on.

We in our culture tend to forget that many highly successful marriages are still arranged. In Japan, that different world, forty percent of marriages are arranged. Their divorce rate is one-fourth ours. No wonder psychologists sometimes claim a strong skepticism about romance.

Even in strong, healthy marriages, the reason for being together usually has to be reexamined at some time in the marriage. Eventually, a certain disillusionment hits. "This isn't what I thought it would be."

When people come together, and most especially if two codependents unite, the relationship exists initially at two discrete levels. We have already mentioned the problem that codependents hide their own love poverty from potential mates. But there is more.

Envision newlyweds as skating on a pond. The surface ice, the veneer, is their obvious and ostensible reasons for marrying. The "This is the one!" attitude. "I love you madly and we both like to figure skate. We will spend an eternity of bliss, figure skating."

Under the ice, though, lurks the lake, the major water body,

the unwritten, unspoken contracts. Eventually, the surface veneer cracks, for it's not strong enough to support marriage—
marriage is both the heaviest and lightest of man's endeavors.
The skaters drop down to the chilling deeper agendas. If they
are not ready to work on these issues, the union will either
break up or impoverish itself in a sea of acrimonious regrets
and disappointments. These marriages end up in our offices
six months after the wedding, bitter and disillusioned.

"I love her with all my heart and now I don't even know
her."

"He's not the man I married. He's a stranger. He changed."

These feelings are typical of couples like Ralph and Darcy
Welles. They looked like a storybook pair. We could tell immediately that Darcy had the mind of a Rhodes scholar to go with
her movie star attractiveness. Ralph, a forty-year-old widower
marrying for the second time, kept the pace—and the
virility—of a college kid. He had the suave appearance of a man
born to wear a tuxedo. And yet, when he kicked back for a
week's vacation on his Colorado ranch, he became the con-
summate outdoorsman in his faded Stetson and checkered
shirt.

Less than a year after their wedding, they sat in our offices
seeking counsel. After a few sessions we were able to identify
the hidden contracts they had brought into their marriage.
Ralph Welles's hidden agenda in marrying Darcy was, in effect,
that he'd done his bit as staid husband of a proper wife. This
time around he intended to marry a glamorous mistress.
Darcy expected to be a cozy housewife, albeit a dazzlingly
beautiful one. She suddenly became very domestic. He expected maribou feather mules and seductive negligees; she
fancied a flannel nightgown and fuzzy slippers. *Whoa!* cried
Ralph's inner man. *Where did my mistress go?*

Simultaneously with their wedding, the Dallas economy
took a nosedive, dragging along with it a lot of Ralph's money.
Darcy's hidden contract: you're going to take care of me and
domesticate me and shower me with affluence—the romantic
fantasy of a money-soaked marriage. The wealthy, secure man
she thought she had married came home one day and mentioned the prospect of bankruptcy.

If whatever romance the relationship provides is limited to the ice level, that romance is likely to shatter along with the dream, when the conquering hero comes home announcing financial penury. If, however, the romance is foundational, on a level as deep as their hidden agendas, the marriage will survive.

Ralph and Darcy were able to give up their original romantic dreams because their love was foundational. Both, however, had to rework their marriage expectations. In doing so, their thinking went something like this:

Ralph: *What I wanted was a siren, a fantasy at my fingertips. What I got, though, was a fine wife. I've been blessed again with a good woman. I'm satisfied with that.*

Darcy: *I honestly thought I was getting a bankroll; it's what every girl dreams of. But what I have is a man who loves me and will do the best he can for me. Considering how many creeps are out there, I was royally blessed. I'll change my dreams and hang onto what I have.*

Sincere, committed couples who are honest about their hidden agendas are able to compromise, giving up some expectations in return for good reasons to remain together. Had Ralph and Darcy been codependent, though, their counseling would have taken much longer, for they would have had to deal with the causes of their codependency as well as the fallacies in their relationships with themselves and others.

Every couple either deliberately or unconsciously must reexamine their marriage expectations periodically because deeper reasons for all relationships exist along with the surface reasons. The stable person who has received love in childhood can usually take the rethinking those hidden reasons require, as the Welleses did. Codependents, already drained of narcissistic love, and therefore of strength, will not have the wherewithal to untangle the deceit and rebuild on new terms unless they also deal with their codependency. The change must take place inside them, and if they are codependent they have a staunch enemy of change—themselves.

Much as codependents say they want to be healed and ease

the misery, deep inside they fight to keep the misery. Their innermost being resists the change. Something was wrong in childhood and until they fix it, they cannot move ahead. Deep inside they yearn to repeat the past over and over until it finally comes out right.

And you are no different. As you begin the work that will bring you peace, you must be aware of this sly and subtle voice within you that will be fighting you all the way.

Is there such a thing as pure, unsullied romance? There certainly is, and it's nothing like the sorry version of love and romance that codependency offers. Let's look at the contrasts between false love and true love.

CHAPTER
TEN

Codependent or Interdependent Relationships?

"You made me love you. I didn't wanna do it; I didn't wanna do it. You made me feel blue, and all the time I guess you knew it. . . . You made me happy; you made me glad. And there were those times, dear, you made me feel so sad. . . . Gimme gimme gimme what I cry for; you know you got the kind of kisses that I'd die for. You know you made me love you."

"You are my sunshine, my only sunshine. You make me happy when skies are gray. . . . Please don't take my sunshine away."

"All I want is loving you. . . ."

"You're everything to me. . . ."

Popular music. If there were laws against pushing codependent love relationships, pop music would be in prison until the albums rotted. So would a lot of movies and a whole lot of books, both fiction and nonfiction.

What is the difference between a codependent relationship and its antithesis, the interdependent relationship? Where is the line drawn between healthy and obsessive? Ten comparisons can help us analyze the health and strength of either an isolated relationship or relationships in the context of a family or group.

Please keep in mind that just as codependency itself is not

an all-or-nothing thing, but rather a matter of degree, even so are these characteristics. The contrasts between a codependent relationship and a healthy interdependent relationship are not either-or comparisons. As you weigh your own relationships in the light of these criteria, think: "How much do I lean in one direction over the other? Am I more like the first-mentioned, the unhealthy alternative, or more like the second, the healthy alternative that invites peace, happiness, and growth?"

COMPELLED VS. CHOSEN

Torvill and Dean, figure-skating partners extraordinaire, speed across the rink, lacing and relacing their arms, their legs, even their necks. They are as one. Suddenly they separate. Still in perfect synchronization, they glide out in spiraling circles, then come together again, a firmly knit single unit.

Now imagine Torvill and Dean trying to perform while tied together closely at waist level. No spins, no separations, no intricate maneuvers. Nose to nose is the only possible configuration. Even the most graceful movements tug and jerk the skaters mercilessly. Gone are that amazing unity, the singleness of purpose, the fluid changes in a complex choreography. What's so amazing about close synchronization when the performers are physically unable to separate or shift position?

There is a certain flavor to a codependent relationship that might be described as "driven" or "intense." There is a compulsive nature to it. The members are tied to each other almost as with an invisible rope. The slightest move in one causes a reaction in the other. The positions are rigid. Every word and thought is guarded, weighed against the other's imagined response.

"Don't talk about this—it will upset her." "Don't admit you are hurting—he'll only laugh." "If I reveal my feelings the world might think our relationship is less than perfect." "I dare not act for fear he will react wrongly."

CHOSEN

How different is the chosenness of an interdependent relationship! The desire is there but not the intense need. Love, whether for a spouse, a child, a parent, or a friend, is a matter of choice. Should the choreography require, the skaters can move about with beauty and originality. Each can stretch and grow without tilting or damaging the relationship.

"I will act in what is clearly our best interest, and if he responds wrongly you'll talk it out." In direct contrast to "I can't live without you, Baby," stands "Nonsense. Of course I could live without you if I had to. Because I love you deeply, I choose not to." This freedom of choice makes a relationship all the richer and more beautiful.

Love is a choice.

IDENTITY THREATENED VS. IDENTITY PRESERVED

Helen Reddy exults, "I am woman!" A bit general, perhaps, but it's nonetheless a statement of identity. Personal identity. Who am I? How do I perceive myself? Robert Burns wished, "Would some god the giftie gi'e us to see ourselves as others see us."

We believe that what happens in part in a codependent relationship is that as two people become enmeshed, they feed upon a mutual illusion: "As I become closer to you, my own identity becomes clearer." This is another way of saying, "If my dotted-line circle just overlaps your dotted-line circle enough, we'll make a solid-line circle." "My half person needs your half person in order to become complete." Each attempts to draw from the other a vivid personal identity, a clear picture of the self. Yet neither has a solid sense of self available for the other to borrow from.

These two skaters, then, tied at the waist, draw the rope in tighter, tighter, ever tighter, trying each to validate his own identity in part by being associated more closely with the other. Ironically, just the opposite happens.

Each has become ever more invested in the identity of the other. Each anticipates or mimics the other's wants and preferences. Each pretends things are perfect when they're not, because a truly great relationship should look perfect and besides, who wants to admit they're involved with a less-than-great person? That hardly serves an ego that is none too firm to start with. Tension, frustration, anger all build and are quickly buried. The compulsivity that marks the codependent makes the relationship seem larger than life, more important than it is, consuming, compelling.

Should one of them feel so suffocated as to take a step away, the other's very identity is threatened. Too much of the self is being drawn from the other person. When the source moves away, distancing itself, that vicarious identity separates, too.

The identities in a codependent relationship can be likened to the birth of Siamese twins. The surgeon faces an agonizing dilemma: if the twins are separated, one or both may perish. And yet they might not survive together. In emotional codependency the persons feel certain they cannot go on if they are separated. Surely they will perish. And yet their present union is damaging.

IDENTITY PRESERVED

In an interdependent association, what holds the skaters in close configuration is the beauty of the choreography. No rope. No awkward linkage. As both associates grow, aspects of the relationship provide new dimensions to each identity, but because each identity was complete and secure already, the association is not one of absolute necessity. This permits a wonderful freedom for each partner to realize a full measure of potential.

The committed Christian in particular possesses the opportunity to reach for the stars, for our God specializes in one-on-one. For many reasons, not the least of which being that God knows the person intimately even before birth, God Himself validates the Christian's identity. Also, the Christian can draw as heavily as necessary upon the identity of God and Jesus Christ and indeed is encouraged to do so. What a complete and limitless resource is the Supreme Identity!

The Christian's self, completeness, and value all exist within; they do not depend upon outside relationships with others. The person is secure within. When that Christian enters with another into a relationship as spouse, close friend, or family member, each will give and receive, but not out of necessity. When the relationship is broken through death or other involuntary separation, life goes on. Grief, of course. Sadness, certainly. Pain, undoubtedly. But not a loss of self.

ILLUSION OF STRENGTH VS. STRENGTH THROUGH REALITY

"A horse that works six days a week is strong," explained Margaret. "Far stronger than a horse left out to pasture all winter. And the pastured horse is a lot stronger than a horse that spent the winter in a barn. Exercise. Activity. Now I figure that's the way it is inside as well as outside. I'm working hard emotionally, so I'm a lot stronger emotionally, you see, than if Pete weren't like that."

Margaret enjoyed a position every teenage girl envies. Not yet thirty, she owned and managed a large horse operation on the outskirts of Fort Worth. She participated in rodeos and gymkhanas (organized horseback competitions), rode whenever she wished with hired hands to do the cleanup. She also had Pete, her alcoholic husband, a quiet drunk who started with beer when he walked through the door each afternoon and drank himself into a stupor every evening.

Margaret tossed her headful of long dark hair and shrugged philosophically. "Pete could be a lot worse. He could be mean or abusive when he drinks. He could be going down to the beer joints instead of sitting home. And he still has his job. And back when I was first getting started he was so supportive. He really believes in me. He's my strength."

"You actually think having a man like Pete makes you stronger?"

"I'm living proof."

Oftentimes the codependent comes to believe that her strength derives from the other person or from the relationship. In a codependency more extreme than Margaret's, one or both partners might be convinced that their vitality and strength, as well as a large measure of their identity, derive from each other. Deep inside a small voice whispers, *If you pull back from me, or we turn down the volume on our relationship, I will lose strength. Vitality. I may even fade away and cease to exist.*

The reality is tragically the opposite. Even as both partners in a codependent relationship are convincing themselves that "This relationship is my lifeblood. I have to stay connected!" the relationship is draining their energy, sapping their strength. Both are drawing from mutually empty tanks. They're either suppressing a lot of anger or dissipating a lot of energy expressing the anger, because anger is there. Simply staying in denial requires a lot of energy. And that's not to mention the very emotionally taxing stress and anxiety caused by the nuts-and-bolts breakdowns of a dysfunctional relationship—embarrassment, dread, neglect, argument, perhaps financial difficulties or problems with the kids that otherwise would not be.

REAL STRENGTH

One of our associates, Bill, designed and built himself a log house in Colorado. This wasn't just a Daniel Boone log cabin. The living room was two stories deep with a balustraded balcony running between the upstairs bedrooms. Bill fashioned a wonderful curving stairway from a bent and gnarled cottonwood. There were a few minor glitches. For instance, he could stand by his huge natural-rock fireplace and watch the balustrade bob up and down when the kids ran upstairs. And it sagged a little.

A local, Joe Ramirez, stopped by. "Bill," he murmured in his laid-back country drawl, "got a suggestion. Peel a couple logs and make pillars. Prop up that balcony before your cat runs upstairs and its weight brings the whole thing down."

"I should have built an A frame, huh?"

"Nope. Two pillars will do it nicely. Don't want them leaning on each other, touching at the bottom or the top—not an A or a V. Together but apart is strongest. . . . Can hold up the whole world."

Sturdy, upright. Together but apart. Separate entities in a mutual role. Therein lies true strength.

MELODRAMATIC VS. CONSISTENT

Think of melodrama, and there are Brad and Joan, hauling that exercycle back and forth across town, up and down the stairs. Their relationship fluctuates from wild affection to even wilder disaffection. Such exceedingly dramatic breakups and reunions are common in codependent relationships.

Astronomer George Gamow earned world acclaim during those heady early days of nuclear physics, as the power and scope of the universe was just becoming known. After defining the four dimensions of space-time, he illustrated his life as a line moving through the space-time continuum, its position described by the points which were random and nonrandom events. Such world lines, he suggested, intersected with others to generate new points and redirect all the lines.

It's a relevant illustration. Should you attend our clinic, we may well ask you to picture your marital, parental, or close friend relationships similarly as sets of parallel lines. No relationship hums along at the constant distance of, for instance, railroad tracks. After all, we're human. Codependent unions, however, suffer such radical fluctuations that the lines separate widely during the bad times. Then the lines actually intersect during their reunions. Identity gets confused and merged. Enmity results, perhaps even violence. The happy times, the together times, become bad times too.

One couple under our counsel, Robert and Edna, have been together eight years. They are enduring a very emotionally turbulent, sometimes physically violent relationship with intense ups and downs. They've tried temporary separations, trying to get some perspective, trying to set some healthy distance. None of their separations has ever lasted more than twenty-four hours. The result: their relationship continues to flounder along, generating misery by the bushel. They cannot and will not come to terms with their base problems.

CONSISTENCY

Compare such wild melodrama with a healthy relationship. Again, two lines draw themselves through life, touching and being touched by others. In the long course these lines record the undulant natural rhythms of a solid relationship. The partners may at times pursue different facets of life—for one or both a career, child-rearing, school, hobbies and pursuits, ministries in and out of the church. These might be shown as a broadening of space between the lines. Then there are other intimate and beautiful times, such as the birth of a child, that bring those lines into warm proximity. The identities remain discrete; the relationship remains, over all, very close.

POSSESSIVENESS VS. TRUSTING COMMITMENT

Perhaps Brad and Joan wouldn't have to lug that exercycle around quite so much if he weren't so jealous. He sees some hunk in Joan's workplace and, knowing how sexually attractive she is (after all, she's performing that "ole magic called love" on him well enough), he suspects the worst. Who could resist her?

Jealousy. Generally, codependent relationships exhibit a fair degree of jealousy. Though born of insecurity, it stretches far beyond the common uncertainties of life to reach, at times, true clinical paranoia. Brad literally lies in wait, seeking that first little sign, some tiny shred of evidence that she might be involved with someone else. Any such hint triggers a big scene and a fight. Although thoroughly modern Joan struggles mightily against any vestige of male domination or possessiveness, she, too, eyes Brad's associates just as jealously.

TRUSTING COMMITMENT

In contrast, genuine commitment gives latitude for comfortable trust. There may, sadly, be reason for doubt in a relationship, even a healthy one. What we find in codependency is a vulture vigil, the partners ever alert to any indication of disaffection. A trusting partner, while not blind and stupid, is slow to suspect and quick to believe. The trusting partner can accept comfortably the fact that the spouse comes into contact with a wide variety of other persons on this planet, some of them attractive. In fact, a good summary adjective to describe a trusting relationship is simply "comfortable."

NARROW FOCUS VS. BROAD SUPPORT

Florence Nightingale is best known, of course, for her work in the Crimean War as she single-handedly shaped modern nursing and made it a respected profession. What few know is that she was a pioneer in the use of statistical graphics similar to our common pie graph. With her "cockscombs," as she called her vivid statistical pictures, she nudged a somnolent British military into major health reforms.

Draw a pie chart of the life you are living right now, based on the time and effort you spend at various personal roles. Mother of Five, for example, would be a much larger wedge than would be Surfing Enthusiast. One wedge may be marriage; others may be parenthood, job, church, friends, recreation and hobbies, alone times. A healthy person's pie chart will consist of many wedges, and although they are of different sizes, all more or less in balance with one another.

The codependent's chart will appear distorted, particularly if the wedges represent the amount of emotional energy spent on the various roles. In terms of emotional effort, the codependent is so obsessed with one overbearing relationship that every other wedge shrinks. There are just so many hours in a day, just so many ergs of available energy. The codependent squanders huge blocks of time and energy dealing with one person and that one person's problems. With one thing absorbing so much of the codependent's focus, precious little time and energy remain to be focused upon the other wedges.

Now you can see graphically why a child receives nurturance from less-than-one parent if one parent is "clean" and the other enslaved to alcohol, drugs, or a severe compulsion. The nonaddict is preoccupied, feeling guilty, feeling resentful, hurt, attempting to handle crises—in short, absorbed in that problematic other person. No matter how loved, the child has become a very small wedge in the parent's pie.

Commonly in malignant codependent relationships, the first to go are friendships. Church relationships flounder. Even if other slices still exist, they're squeezed down to a small area of total energy expended and attention given.

Medical biology provides an illustration with tumors. The tumor itself may not be malignant. But as it grows, feeding on the host energy, it crowds out the healthy tissue. The tumor itself we could live with, but the crowding and loss of healthy tissue threaten life. Look at the codependent, by partial analogy, as a person inflicted with just such an emotional tumor.

The problem relationship crowds out the healthy relationships and activities that would bring balance and richness to life.

BROAD SUPPORT

The term *broad support* means just that. Picture a lovely Florentine pedestal table. Picture hauling off with an axe and whacking out the pedestal. The table crashes. Now picture a Tudor table with a curved pillar leg in each corner. Whack out a leg. The table's hurting, but it's still up there. A person with only one consuming relationship for support is going to crash if that support is removed (at least, the person feels certain that's so). A person with several solid relationships will suffer, but not fall.

What other elements offer support in your life? Are there persons close to you (not dependent children; remember "emotional incest") for support should your major source of stability fail?

STOCK MARKET SYNDROME VS.
STABLE SELF-ESTEEM

"Stocks closed down today. Analysts blame inflation jitters."

"Stocks rose sharply in the wake of the president's announcement that . . ."

"I am tied to the barometer of your moods. If you are up, I am up. If you are down, I am down. I become unhappy by sensing that you are unhappy. Any rumor or problem, real or imagined, really rattles my cage."

That's the stock market syndrome. Very often we see clients who are bound so tightly into the lives and fortunes of others that if anyone in their circle is having a bad day, they, too, have a rotten day. They never act. They react. Reaction is much more taxing than action, because you must attune yourself so closely to another's whims, read signs so carefully, never drop your guard. The worst part: because the reactor cannot influence the actor significantly, the reactor has no control over his or her own feelings. Add frustration, therefore, to the tension.

STABLE SELF-ESTEEM

When you demonstrate healthy interdependence, you are no less sensitive, no less caring than the codependent. But you are not so tied to any person that your contentment and happiness depend on whether the other person is happy and content. The support and nurturance you offer is therefore stronger, for you don't have to respond to the other person in order to satisfy your own needs. The key to this healthy interdependence is self-esteem: confidence within.

REPETITION COMPULSION VS. OPENNESS TO THE FUTURE

The ghosts in John and Gladys Jordan's past are a good example of the repetition compulsion. Unresolved issues in childhood, particularly matters having to do with abuse or neglect, doom the emerging adult to recreate, to repeat, the past. This compulsive need effectively eliminates freedom of choice. The need intensifies for persons in denial—by denying problems, they deny the chance to work them through. They *must* unconsciously restage the past in a fruitless attempt to deal with what they are consciously denying.

It is infinitely worse for the Christian. The ability to hear and follow God's will is stifled. The compulsion becomes the guiding force.

The apostle Paul grew up a Pharisee, the son of Pharisees. No one was more rigid and legalistic than your average Pharisee. And yet, once he overcame the blindness of his religious tradition, with God's help, he became sensitive and open to the sometimes puzzling ways and places God led him. He could not have served God fully had he remained locked in his past.

OPENNESS TO THE FUTURE

In a healthy interdependent relationship lies great openness to the future. The past has been dealt with. The relationship is free to grow, an organic, dynamic thing. A year beyond the honeymoon a marriage has become something even better.

Ten years later it has grown and changed some more. A friendship deepens. A sibling bond matures.

Increasingly couples bring their marriages in for a tune-up, so to speak, through annual or semi-annual participation in programs such as retreats and marriage encounters. During these pauses, they reflect upon job and marriage and options for the future. The success of programs such as these requires that the union be free to change, untrammeled by compulsion.

NEED TO CONTROL VS. WILLINGNESS
TO SURRENDER

In a dysfunctional home, control is the name of the game. Perhaps a perfectionistic, critical, legalistic, domineering parent created a climate of overcontrol. Or a parent mired in substance abuse caused chaos; nobody could control anything because no one knew what to expect next. Many of our clients hear this and cry "Bingo! I had it both ways at once." Very often, if one parent is unstable and out of control, the other will go overboard in the opposite direction.

If control was an issue in the original family, the emerging adult possesses a tremendous need to control. That need will be voiced one way or another. Sometimes control will be the only painful issue in an otherwise nurturing home. Patients describing their relationships with their SOP often say, "We've been battling it out since the day we met, and I have no idea who's winning or losing."

Many factors feed into the addiction/obsession/compulsion cycle. Control is a major one. The addict strives to control his (or her; it's just as true for women) inner moods chemically. The rageaholic *must* impose absolute control. The anorexic teen often lives under a strongly controlling parent or parents. She has no power to be herself or exercise the normal wing-flapping of teenage years, but she can stop eating. All the king's horses and all the king's men can't make her eat.

WILLINGNESS TO SURRENDER

Willingness to surrender power is not a character flaw; it's a sign of good health. The person with a low reading on the codependency thermometer will use control, but he won't need it.

This surrender can manifest itself in any relationship. In the workplace, the boss spreads the choice jobs around liberally; he doesn't have to keep a finger in every single pie. He delegates responsibility well. At home, Mom gives the kids the freedom to make a mess as well as something that might be unpalatable as they learn to cook. Grandpa lets a less-than-perfect car wash get by because his eager six-year-old carwasher did the very best she could.

Usually in the marriage relationship, the husband is physically stronger. He could use his strength to force his wife and children into submission. He could—but he doesn't. The wife could withhold her husband's marriage rights in order to coerce him into yielding in some matter, or perhaps slam the bedroom door in a fit of anger. She could—but she doesn't.

Christians see Jesus as the ultimate example of surrendering power, for repeatedly He demonstrated His ultimate power over man and nature. Demons, disease, and storms obeyed Him. Ten thousand angels could have come to His aid as He hung in agony from the cross. But He submitted. This all-powerful Person completely humbled Himself that God's purpose be accomplished.

FEAR OF ABANDONMENT VS. TRUST IN GOD/CHRISTIAN FELLOWSHIP

Joe skips out on the family and child support and becomes a motorcycle bum. That's abandonment. Mom gets tired of household drudgery so she dumps it and takes an apartment and a job two hundred miles away. That's abandonment. Marie feels smothered by her relationship with Ralph and decides to date him only once a week instead of nightly. That's not abandonment. But Ralph thinks it is. Ralph is strongly codependent.

A healthy step backwards to create breathing room is tantamount to complete abandonment for a codependent in a consuming relationship. Any spaces in the togetherness equate with rejection, even death. Whispering in the undercurrents of the codependent's mind is the warning, *If you are forsaken, too much will be lost; you will perish.* Robin Norwood phrased it vividly: "Terrified of abandonment, you will do anything to keep a relationship from dissolving."[1]

Although the woman may be able to better articulate it— "I'm so afraid of losing him!"—this fear of abandonment haunts the man quite as much. In our office one day sat Robert Helm. Tall, broad, tuned to perfection by daily workouts on the latest bodybuilding equipment—he'd be an ideal fit to the Gentle Giant stereotype except that he wasn't gentle. He was seeing us because of wife abuse.

Thursday he discussed their conflict-filled marriage. "I understand now that it's not going to work. It didn't even in the beginning. I can see why Edna says she can't tolerate any more of this. Neither can I. Time to bring things to an end."

Friday Edna moved out. "Trying to get some perspective," she said. "I need some time alone."

Saturday morning Robert was on the phone to us, literally engulfed in panic. The man who sounded so tough and strong when speaking of separation couldn't handle it. In his eyes he had been summarily abandoned.

Tragically even Ralph and Edna's approach to therapy is codependent. They should be asking, in essence, "How can we healthfully put this relationship back together?" Instead, they want their therapist to join in their dramatic dance, bolster the relationship as it now exists, patch it up enough to make it tolerable. The unspoken message: *Whatever you do, don't require us to face our problems directly.* They don't want to rebuild, for that would require change, painful at first. They want to stabilize the existing shaky relationship by casting it in some magical cement.

TRUST IN GOD/CHRISTIAN FELLOWSHIP

Opposite the fear of abandonment, of course, is trust. The very best trust rests in God. Him alone can we believe when He promises, "I will never leave you or forsake you." Upon Him alone we can lean completely.

And yet, we must trust human beings also, somehow. But how?

The first level of trust lies in parents and spouse. The next involves peripheral relationships. As a rule, to be stable these levels must rest upon the solid foundation of trust in God.

"Trust?!" wails our clinical patient. "Do you realize what my spouse [parent, significant other person] did to me? How can I rebuild trust after that?"

Our response is, "By approaching it indirectly. Do you trust God? Bask in that. Rebuild peripheral relationships. Teach yourself that you can trust others. Reach out to a support group. Given time, trust will build in your primary relationship."

Unfortunately, for the codependent whose be-all and end-all rests in a single person, that answer won't wash. "You don't understand. I have to know whether I can trust this one person!"

Trust, like a good reputation, is so easy to destroy, so difficult to build, and building it is infinitely harder for the person shackled by problems of codependency.

The greatest venue for codependent problems is in marriage. Whether you are married right now or not, you should know where these problems emerge and how to negate them. Let's cover that next.

CHAPTER
ELEVEN

Making Relationships Work

We mentioned in the last chapter that the opposite of dependence or codependency is not independence. It is interdependence. Perhaps our illustration of a relationship wheel can further clarify.

THE RELATIONSHIP WHEEL

At the top of the wheel is that happy circumstance, the healthy, interdependent marriage. Two people stand close together with enough space between them to comfortably make room for God. Growth and beneficial change have room to work there also. The scale that would weigh dependence against independence is balanced.

As we travel the circle in a clockwise direction we tip the scale toward independence. The farther we go, the more deeply we get into independent attitudes. Counterclockwise motion indicates an exaggerated dependence in the relationship. Neither will serve the marriage well.

In some groups, the motion to the left, the counterclockwise drift, is promoted as being a healthy model for the Christian marriage. The newest trend in business dynamics casts the chief executive officer in a servant position. To him above

all is given the role of serving selflessly both the corpor
and its employees. Let us see what this movement to the left
generates.

The first stop on the counterclockwise route may be labeled
simply "dependence" or "a dependent relationship" wherein
one person begins to lean excessively upon the other. The
dependence might be caused by random or innocent
circumstance—one of the partners becomes gravely ill, perhaps, or is incapacitated. It sometimes happens simply
through laziness or convenience; let George do it. Or authorities may counsel the couple that the wife must be subservient,
dependent upon the husband's whim and will. Less frequently,
the husband may surrender independence to his wife. Should
substance abuse enter the picture, the couple almost invariably slides counterclockwise, as the addictive partner leans
ever more heavily upon the spouse.

Whatever the trigger mechanism, however random or innocent the beginning, both partners stand at great risk of slipping
down into the next stage, "codependency."

REVERSING CODEPENDENT TENDENCIES

In a healthy union the couple will work back up toward the
top of the circle. For example, an associate at the clinic suffered a heart attack and was laid low for several months. Ron
had to depend upon his wife for many functions and activities
he had taken for granted as his prerogative since their wedding
day. Suddenly it was she who handled the finances. She got the
car lubed. She fixed the stopped-up drain, for he could not
physically assume the stand-on-your-head positions it took to
work on the grease trap.

As soon as he was able (and, frankly, in some cases before
he was fully able—he had always lacked patience), Ron resumed a little normal activity. He picked up some of the more
quiescent chores that had been hers, thereby spreading the
work load fifty–fifty, even if the fifties were not the same ones
they used to be. Although his impaired health prevented them
from restoring their relationship identically to what it had been
before, the overall balance was restored. By deliberately moving in the clockwise direction of independence—and not just

physically but in mind and spirit—Ron brought them back again to the top of the wheel.

But what if dependence develops and the couple slides the other way, downhill counterclockwise? The leaner leans harder. The leanee, the "strong" one, in unconscious ways begins to lean as well. Each needs the other for a prop, a fix. They have assumed the A-frame configuration we call codependency. Both are dangerously off balance.

AN INDEPENDENT RELATIONSHIP

In its effort to get away from the dependence of the counterclockwise motion, the women's liberation movement thundered off the other way. Moving clockwise from the top of the circle poses hazards just as great.

- "We've drifted apart somehow."
- "I am me and he is he and we're not we anymore."
- "We don't know each other anymore. We live in separate worlds and they just don't seem to overlap at all."

As the couple moves farther clockwise the estrangement grows. Move far enough and the estrangement becomes antagonism, alienation. Instead of adding to the richness and diversity of marriage, differences become divisive. Usually, most of the differences were there from the beginning. Such a premium, though, has been placed upon independence that the differences become excuses, rationalizations, perhaps eventually weapons with which to attack each other.

Clients who study the wheel will nod. "Yes, I see. That's us, alright. Yes." But they are often startled by what happens at the bottom of the circle, at the extreme lower end from healthy balance. Both unhealthy codependency and unhealthy independence can end up in malignant codependency. Galloping codependency.

Our poor couple, both estranged and tilted, are now at nearly cross purposes. And yet, they're intricately bound. The lines become something of a braid, twisting, enmeshed, but never touching. There is monumental antagonism. There is a powerful sense of entrapment. Most of all there is intense anger at this point. Always.

GOING IN BOTH DIRECTIONS SIMULTANEOUSLY

The wheel illustrates most of all how codependency and independence operate simultaneously. An excellent example is workaholism, and the classic workaholic is Tom Chambers. He sells real estate, not an easy job under the best of circumstances. At the height of his workaholism he would show you any property you wanted to see at any time of day or night. If you preferred talking business over dinner, he whipped out his credit card and took you to dinner. If you had time only to catch him in the morning, he closed the deal over the breakfast table. Weekdays, weekends, he was always available for business. He paid cash for the family's second BMW.

All this time his wife, Judith, the dutiful enabler, took on a disproportionate amount of the everyday family chores that were as much his responsibility as hers, such as time spent with the children. She handled all the nickel-and-dime, time-consuming details required for the maintenance of their cars, their home, and their lifestyle.

Tom and Judith became increasingly dependent upon each other. He couldn't spend that much time and effort on work if she didn't pick up the rest of the slack in his life—everything from stopping at the dry cleaners to making sure no insurance premiums and household bills went unpaid. She even wrote his thank-you notes to his parents for gifts they sent him. And yet she was utterly dependent upon him for the money and social prestige she enjoyed. They were completely enmeshed in each other.

After a time, also, they had become almost completely independent of each other. He had no part in her domestic world anymore. She certainly had no part in his business dealings. As enmeshed as they were in some ways, their daily spheres of living overlapped hardly at all. They became estranged, emotionally unavailable to each other as all these other factors crowded into their lives. Judith especially harbored intense anger for Tom's neglect and emotional distance. Alienation and distance deteriorated into open hostility. That hostility and anger spawned fights and noisy rounds of argument and blame.

Tom and Judith's simultaneous descent down both sides of

the relationship wheel is typical of couples in which one or both members are caught up in addiction or compulsion.

Not always do couples slide clear to the bottom of the wheel. They may drift clockwise, eventually to float away from the wheel into their separate universes. The union ends. Or they may find some sort of equilibrium partway down, living lives of quiet desperation, trying to survive until death.

How tragic.

WHEN INDEPENDENCE PREVAILS

Elizabeth Metrano's Old Country Italian grandfather grew up in a rugged urban section of New Jersey. He parlayed an eighth-grade education into a multimillion-dollar estate and escaped from New York into the wealthy suburbs of New Jersey. Beth has inherited his savvy and ambition. With twenty-nine aunts and uncles and fifty-three cousins, her family reunions are pretty much big happy gang wars, orchestrated annually by Uncle Joe Taglioni, for which he usually books the Union County fairgrounds. She loves noise, bustle, and lots of people around.

Caleb Johansen first rode a horse unaided at age twenty-two months. Born and raised on a Montana ranch, his concept of heaven includes a good horse under your favorite saddle and a horizon straight and clear enough that you can see halfway to forever. When Caleb says "three's a crowd" he means it.

While at Southern Methodist University, Beth and Caleb met and married. Their friends claimed it would never last. *"High Noon* meets *The Godfather?* Forget it!" With Beth's ambition and Caleb's steady common sense, the couple built a rich life. They owned a lovely home in Highland Park and a ten-acre retreat in Grapevine near the reservoir. Beth served in an advisory position on the Highland Park school board. Caleb chaired a large service club. They were very active in church activities. They enjoyed an important ministry with inner-city young people; they would haul a dozen children out to Grapevine for a weekend of fun with boats and horses. And they had become strangers.

Because of their religious convictions they would not consider divorce. And yet, their marriage had disintegrated into sharp words and a daily contest of wills. They needed help, and they had the good sense to seek it early.

"Her idea of a quiet trail ride is *Lawrence of Arabia*—five hundred screaming horsemen strung out across the desert."

"His idea of sleeping in on Saturday morning is lying in bed till seven."

"She runs up a hundred-dollar-a-month phone bill just talking to relatives on the East Coast."

"At least I talk. He doesn't. At all."

"Her activities always come first, no matter what."

"His activities always come first, no matter what. He eats three meals a week at our dining room table," Beth griped. "The rest of the time he's out somewhere else doing something. I'm up and out by seven-thirty, to get to work. Still he's gone before I get up. The only evening he's home, I'm at the executive board meeting. He has never once put a load of laundry in the washer. Or even taken one out of the dryer."

"My sister in Bozeman has three kids and a big-money career as a CPA. She swings it by handling her accounts out of her home; computer, modem, fax—she's connected to the world. And yet she can still be a housewife and mother. It can be done. Beth isn't a mother yet, but she's a wife, and where I grew up the wife handles the household. It's scriptural. Proverbs 31."

Pretend you are in the counselor's chair facing Beth and Caleb. First and foremost a counselor must be a listener, attuned to both the words and the nuances, and you are. You perceive an undercurrent of agitation and impatience here. They both look a little tired. Both are neat and well-groomed, but Caleb presents a very casual, laid-back air while Beth is all crisp and businesslike. His rural drawl contrasts sharply with the vestiges of her New Jersey twang. On the surface it appears their friends were right—these two people are so totally different, the notion of a lasting union is fanciful.

Now do two things. First, analyze Beth and Caleb's situation using what you know of love tanks and the relationship wheel. Then compare and contrast their situation with your own. You may not be married. Chances are excellent you can't ride a horse. But that doesn't matter. Beth and Caleb are each other's Significant Other Person. Weigh your relationship with your own SOP, be it a parent, friend, or spouse. Contrasts are as instructive as similarities. Examine them all.

What counsel would you give the Johansens? Who should change—Beth, Caleb, or both? In what ways? Before continuing, spend a few moments at least considering ways they might restore peace and contentment to their union.

Although it's not exactly a cookbook formula, we at the clinic usually suggest a series of steps for couples with needs similar to the Johansens'. The sequence of steps varies according to whether the problem is one of dependence or independence, for the idea is to move back the other way on the wheel.

COUNTERING THE SLIDE TOWARD INDEPENDENCE

If the couple has been experiencing a clockwise drift into potentially damaging independence, we recommend the following four steps:

First, *the couple must confront the problem,* which means declaring to both self and each other that a problem exists. Even in mild cases there may be subtle denial. "That's just what happens when you've been married as long as we have." "You don't expect as much enthusiasm as when we were first married, do you?" "We've grown. Of course we're not as close." "It's okay. It's normal."

Second, *we recommend doing a time inventory*. Where, how, and under what circumstances does this couple come together? When do they share time and space, or fail to? The inventory is best done on paper, in clear black and white.

Third—and this step is best not only committed to paper but performed in the presence of a third party, such as a counselor, a pastor, or a trusted friend—*the couple must cut a new covenant,* make a new deal, promise a recommitment. The essence of the new deal is to spend more time together and to create more points of convergence to narrow the distances that now separate them. This recommitment might take any form that works and will be different for every couple. In order to execute it, the couple almost always must reduce outside demands on time and energy.

Fourth, we work out some way in which *the couple will maintain accountability*. The third step is useless if it drifts into oblivion like so many other good intentions. Here is where the third party can be an immense help. If the couple make themselves accountable to a trusted third person, the commitment will almost certainly stand. Couples in our counsel frequently make periodic inventories on their own, to heal rifts and see how well they're doing.

COUNTERING THE SLIDE TOWARD CODEPENDENCY

A couple drifting counterclockwise into dependence will need help going the other way. Spending more time together may well exacerbate their problem, weaken their bond.

With them we recommend first (as with any couple) to *acknowledge the problem*. Admitting dependence is difficult and challenging when the dependence is unavoidable, as for example with a chronic or debilitating illness. But it must be done.

Again, the second step consists of an inventory, in this case an analysis *of where boundaries are being violated*. Boundaries are violated when one person takes false, unnecessary, or excessive responsibility for the other. They are violated when one partner clings excessively to the other. In an overly simplistic example, a wife with cerebral palsy needs help getting her shoes on over her twisted toes. Her husband puts her shoes on her. But when he puts on her stockings and laces her shoes—aspects she can handle herself—he is taking on an unnecessary task. The same wife may violate boundaries by calling her husband at work four or five times daily concerning inconsequentials or perhaps nothing at all.

The secret to success lies in resetting boundaries so that dependence is not intensified.

The third and fourth steps should be committed to paper. In the third step, *each party declares the boundaries he or she believes are appropriate*—the amount of personal interaction he or she wants. Understand the party may not get them, but they should be listed.

The fourth step is *a list of what each party is willing to give up*. In essence, this statement says, "I hearby declare which rescuing and enabling actions I am willing to give up. This is how I will back away from you. This is what I want to give you."

Fifth, we ask *each person to commit to new ways of caring for self*—for self-responsibility. Note we're not just speaking to the more dependent person, but to both. This statement says, "These are the ways I will take responsibility for myself so that you do not intrude across my line."

Finally, and this may be most important of all, we ask both persons to carefully *look at their relationships with healthy third parties*, and at healthy activities the two persons do *not* share. A man who feels trapped in a marriage—who needs breathing room—might join a support group or common interest group. He might increase his role in church activity, develop friend-ships with other males who share his interests. In this he is not abandoning his marriage commitment; and if the marriage has slipped down toward dependence/codependency, these will be healthy moves toward a comfortable and fruitful balance.

The "dependent" partner in such a marriage is encouraged equally to develop outside interests. This step is just as impor-tant for the leaning party and probably more so.

The relationship wheel is not limited to marriages. Parent-adult child relationships, friend-friend bonds, perhaps even bonds in the workplace, church, or school will profit from a close examination.

An exercise of this sort is especially fruitful when a couple is approximately at points A or B on the wheel—just beginning the slide into dependence/independence. There the situation can be reversed without a major overhaul.

And what about you? If you have recognized clear symptoms of codependency in yourself after reading this far into the book, a simple tune-up will not be enough. If chapters 3 and 4 rang bells you didn't even know were in the belfry, patching up the surface symptoms is absolutely the *worst* thing you can do.

Insight is the first requirement of recovery. To quote Dr.

Minirth, you can't shoot ducks till the sun comes up. Insight into the mechanics of your relationships and insight into the reality of compulsions, obsessions, and addictions will provide immense benefits as you tackle your problems.

Tom and Judith Chambers are just beginning the long slow climb back up the wheel toward a healthy relationship. They are both so drained and weary they have hardly any energy left to improve their relationship. The story has no end yet.

And finally, regarding the Johansens—we assessed the state of their marriage as being either at the antagonism point of the relationship wheel or perilously close to it. Because both were so grimly determined to make the marriage work, they were willing to accept some serious sacrifices.

We asked each to list all the activities that required more than fifteen minutes of the day. When we asked them to prioritize the lists, though, they hit a snag. Nothing on the lists was fluff. Every item was not only worthy but God-centered. On their own they decided to consider priorities one year at a time. Beth resigned from the school board for a year, and Caleb gave up his chairmanship with the service club. They limited weekend outings with kids to two a month and reserved one weekend per month for themselves—an extended date, preferably out of town somewhere. Time together became one of the most effective healing balms to the marriage.

In other sessions they arrived at agreements about work schedules and routine chores. Most important, they took inventory of each other's strengths and weaknesses and invented ways to capitalize on them, both at home and in the church. Their differences again became rich sources of strength.

All these decisions and agreements were essentially Band-Aids, but Band-Aids were enough, because the shallow wounds in the Johansen union were being tended before they festered and deepened. For another couple, these surface changes might well be inadequate.

The romance is back in the Johansen union, fortified by time together and healthy differences. Beth and Caleb are already planning next year's priority list. They're thinking of starting a horsemanship camp for troubled teens. He'll handle the horse end; she, the promotion and business. And four weekends a summer, the camp will provide a horsemanship retreat for couples.

Participation in the couples retreat will be strictly limited to keep the experience quiet and prevent bustle. But the teen camps will probably look a lot like *Lawrence of Arabia*.

CHAPTER
TWELVE

*The Roles
People Play*

Sean McCurdy could talk the skin off a grape. In a people who boasted the Blarney stone, Sean stood forth as an Irishman among Irishmen. Named John at his birth in Perth Amboy, New Jersey, he legally changed over to the Gaelic form of the name the day he turned twenty-one. He had honed and polished his golden gift of gab his whole life. In his early years the wiry redhead sold more magazines and candy and personalized stationery than anyone else in his school. The band obtained uniforms, the library bought books, the debating team traveled to the state competition—all financed in part by his glib tongue. In high school he sold advertising space in his school paper, almost single-handedly turning it from a single-fold news sheet into an eight-page weekly tabloid, replete with the fancy inserts and photocopy that only money can provide.

Now here he sat in our office for vocational counseling, the Texas sun streaming through the window, his career as a salesman on the rocks, and his twenty-seventh birthday only a few days past. What was going wrong?

As he wagged his head, his bush of unruly copper hair glowed. "I'm so frustrated I can't stand it. I'm the best salesman you're ever going to meet and I can't stay with a job more than a few months. Six months max. It just . . ." He waved his hand. "It just falls apart. I can't see how most of the things that happened were my fault. And yet, they keep happening to me."

"What do you sell?"

"Whatever's in the warehouse. No computers. I'm not what you call computer literate and there's too much to learn—the customer's bound to know more about the product than I do. Anything else. I've sold shoes, used cars, new cars, food processors. Everything. Even baby furniture. You know, I really enjoyed that job, selling baby furniture."

"What happened that you quit?"

"Didn't quit. Fired. Nursery section of a major department store. Minimum plus commission. We handled two national lines of cribs, playpens and such, and carried our own store brand. Selling the national brands was where the money was, of course; they cost up to a fourth more. And yet, even while you're pitching the expensive stuff, you don't dare badmouth the house brand. You see the challenge? I sold seventy percent name brand merchandise and the sales gross in that department jumped a hundred and six percent the four months I was there."

"But they fired you."

"My immediate supervisor fired me. He promised a bonus check in addition to commissions for anyone exceeding the monthly quota. The first month I got a slow start because I was still learning the lines. Second month I exceeded quota and got a dinky little check, but it was okay. The third month was *really* hot. But no check. I gave him three weeks to come through and then filed a formal complaint. Bam! Gone."

"What was his reason?"

"Said he couldn't work with somebody with an attitude."

"Any reason why the check was held back?"

"Said he forgot about it. What else is he going to say? 'You sell too much and I'm backing out on my promise'?"

"The job before that?"

"Two months with a downtown car agency. I was just getting the product line down pat."

"Why'd you quit?"

"The sales manager was always on my back. Never a nice

word. Just comments like 'Why did that couple leave without buying?' 'That old coot—you should've shown him a black model, not the yellow one. Old guys like those shiny black cars.' "

"Fired?"

"Quit after a big fight. Sure a salesman's out to make money, but the real secret—the *real* secret—is you gotta care about people. Genuinely care. Your customer deserves the best, and it's your privilege to help him own it. That manager didn't give a hoot about his customers or his sales staff. I couldn't work under those conditions."

I couldn't work under those conditions. The department store manager couldn't work with somebody with an attitude. As Sean McCurdy recited the details of his checkered employment record—thirteen jobs in the last four years—a vivid picture emerged.

The surface pattern was easy to discern because it was so repetitive and uniform. A bright and charismatic salesman, Sean had no trouble obtaining a position. After a few weeks or a few months, his boss would do something terribly unjust. Following the inevitable fight, Sean would either quit or get fired, ricocheting from job to job.

The picture behind the pattern, though, became the key to helping Sean. His father had abandoned his mother and him when he was four. In the nighttime of his mind dwelt an immense and hidden anger toward his father and by extension toward male authority figures. He had never acknowledged or dealt with that anger.

Each time he got a boss, then, he would set very high expectations. This boss was going to be a loving, perfect, and absolutely just father figure. Remember the intense need a codependent feels about fixing the past—to repeat the past and this time around get it right? Of course the boss/father/authority figure, being human, would blow it sooner or later, usually sooner. The unrealistic image of perfection shattered, Sean's anger would come bursting out. The past was not mended; his love tank was still on empty; the need for a caring, perfect father was not met. He was painfully frustrated and he hadn't the slightest idea why.

There was no malice in these surrogate relationships. Sean didn't hate the persons. He was playing out a role, blindly and without understanding.

Sean had to realize, not just with his head but also with his heart, that when he entered an employment situation it became much more than just a job to him. Deep inside he was recreating a powerful family dynamic, a father/son relationship.

Sean is by no means alone. Nearly everyone does it to some extent; as always, the codependent carries it to the unconscious extreme. Gladys Jordan, whom we met at the beginning of the book, recreated her father/child relationship in her marital union. So did John, and those ghosts soured their marriage. Sean went farther. He was constantly restaging a father/son relationship that he dreamt of but never had. Not only did those re-creations spoil his work relationships, they were unconsciously set up to fix the past—something they could never ever do.

THE COMPLEXITY OF INTERPERSONAL RELATIONSHIPS

Our personal lives are basically an intricate web of interpersonal relationships. Codependency can distort that web dramatically. It can create roles that should not be part of our lives, and it can warp those roles essential to us.

Almost as a playwright or author might do, codependents build elaborate relationships far beyond the obvious, subtly turning employers (in Sean's case), spouses (in the Jordans'), or others into father figures; changing doctors or pastors into surrogate parents; substituting one role for another in the back rooms of their minds.

Consider the many intricately woven interpersonal roles each of us fills just on the observable level: parent/child (and the same person is probably both simultaneously, playing different roles with different relatives), husband/wife, boss/subordinate, teacher/student, coach/athlete, doctor/patient, clergy/layman, sister/sister, sister/brother, brother/brother, to name a few—and all that fails to take into account birth order: eldest, youngest, older brother/younger brother, older sister/younger sister in all the combinations. The person who grew up in a dysfunctional family, the person whose love tank is low, unconsciously shifts these complex roles around, seeking to recreate with the persons available at hand the original family dynamic, the original family pain, the original family situation. This time around the problem will be mended, the pain eased, the situation corrected.

Incidentally, probably nobody bears the brunt of such role shifts more than pastors (females in counseling roles, for example, are equally vulnerable). Being an authority figure, being a man of God (which in the minds of some may translate into being God), makes a pastor a walking target for codependent persons who want to set him up as a good or bad parent, spouse, or whatever. We often serve pastors in the clinic and we are constantly amazed by some of the war stories they bring from the front lines.

The pastor may find in his office a man or woman who is expecting him to become the stand-in spouse (perhaps even in a sexual context) or parent that person hungers for. The parishioner's grasping needs place incredible demands on the pastor, who feels suffocated, drained. Unless the pastor's boundaries are comfortably and firmly in place—in other words, we could depict him diagrammatically as a sharp, solid circle—he may feel engulfed and rightly so.

An hour later another parishioner is sitting in the chair blindly unloading anger. The pastor is hearing exactly what he's doing wrong, how he isn't perfect, why attendance is down or the collection declining. Not only is that person venting unseen personal angers and frustrations upon the undeserving pastor, he's probably certain he's doing the pastor a favor.

In a church of a hundred souls, let's say eighty are healthy, loving Christians. The remaining twenty may have some serious emotional problems. If they aren't dealing with those problems in some way, they may well set the pastor up as a hero or villain, perhaps both. Not only must the pastor have excellent personal boundaries in order to deal with the broad spectrum of problems both obvious and hidden, he must understand the mechanics of codependency. Unfortunately, few pastors are trained to recognize and deal with codependency problems.

Also—and this is one of those sweeping generalizations that may mean little or nothing—the helping professions tend to attract people with unresolved codependency issues of their own. Assuming that the pastor has been genuinely called of God to the ministry, he may still be subject to the emotional dynamics of his own codependency—the need to help, the need to fix things up, the need to be everything to everyone. When this pastor's codependent radar blips the radar of a codependent parishioner with unmet emotional needs, particularly if the pastor cannot set internal boundaries, trouble will surely follow.

Early on, psychotherapists recognized how powerful these dynamics could be. The client had a blank wall to look at. The analyst was out of sight behind his head, avoiding eye contact. Psychologists today usually enter into a more personal relationship with the client but that relationship is guarded; appointments are limited to regular hours in controlled settings, for example. In contrast, the pastor doesn't enjoy that safety. Parishioners' needs arise at all hours in all situations, multiplying the possibility of problems.

THE EFFECTS OF CODEPENDENCY ON FAMILY ROLES

The above-mentioned interpersonal relationships are only the bare outline of the picture. Psychologists have come to recognize certain roles, or stereotypes, that persons assume within the family.[1] All families develop them to a mild extent— the hero, the scapegoat, the lost child, the mascot, the enabler. For persons in a dysfunctional family situation, though, the roles become a coping mechanism, a way to get through life with a minimum of upset. They become rigid, mindless patterns of behavior easily visible to those outside the family, unrecognized by those within.

The roles were first recognized in families of alcoholics. They have since been identified in just about every other dysfunctional family dynamic as well. And because codependents unconsciously change and shift these roles, they emerge in adult relationships also. Roles that functioned satisfactorily as coping mechanisms in the original family simply do not work in adulthood, when all the interpersonal relationships change. If they aren't altered, they destroy happiness and peace with God.

What are these roles? The children assume them very early. There is, for one, the hero.

HERO

The hero is the fixer-upper, the glue man. The hero keeps the dysfunctional family functioning and takes up the slack where the parents don't have it together. The hero may get the laundry done, fix meals, mind the smaller kids, perhaps even nurture a disabled or dysfunctional parent (as when the hero child tends to the needs of an alcoholic mother or father). The hero may or may not receive praise and support within the family—but from the outside, the hero is acknowledged as the trustworthy, conscientious, mature, capable kid. The hero is usually but not always the oldest child. Emilia Wesley was a hero.

Either male or female, the hero often earns straight A's in school and/or excels in sports. The hero has substituted a teacher/student dynamic in part for the parent/child relationship. The hero can't fix up Mom and Dad and make them happy, but pleasing Teacher shoots a little juice to the love tank. Teacher sees the near-perfect paper and lavishes praise. Honor and prestige accrue. The accolade in the Gospels, "Well done, good and faithful servant" is a powerful incentive.[2]

SCAPEGOAT

The scapegoat is the black sheep. Regardless what sweet words of denial the scapegoat hears from his parents' lips, he knows down inside that this household just isn't cutting it. He probably cannot articulate his loss, but his love tank is staying on empty. Obviously someone is to blame, and children, you will recall, are quick to assign any anomaly in the universe to their own fault. The scapegoat deserves to be punished for this mess. Besides, when he takes the blame he also gets attention. Ask any celebrity: bad press is better than no press at all.

James Dean played the quintessential scapegoat. In the classic fifties film *East of Eden,* he is the restless, nonconformist son. The good he tries to do is misconstrued; the bad is contrasted against his goody-goody brother's "correct" behavior. Again in *Rebel Without a Cause,* the free spirit with the unorthodox behavior is painted as a juvenile delinquent by the selfish, insensitive, straitlaced adults. In both films, the character is basically a misunderstood but highly sympathetic round peg in a square hole. That interpretation is not too far from the mark.

MASCOT

The mascot is the black sheep with a white reputation, the family clown. He earns his attention by grabbing it. Problems? Dissolve them with a laugh. Pain? Joke it away. Distract, bring a smile, present a happy face. The mascot is out to make you— and himself—forget for a few moments that life hurts dreadfully. Frequently the grinning little guy who makes the tension bearable with his zany humor is sadder inside than any other family member.

How universally recognized is the suffering merrymaker! In opera there is Pagliacci. Ballet has its Petrouchka. One of the most tortured of early television performers was Morton Downey. Now Morton Downey, Jr., boasts openly of his own codependency. Alcohol/substance abuse and divorce run rampant among comedians and afflict a high proportion of other performers. Our Beryl Mason is no anomaly among the well-known.

LOST CHILD

The lost child makes the perfect hero in a classic western or romance novel, the loner who keeps his own counsel. While the hero is excelling and the mascot is goofing around, and the scapegoat is getting into scrapes, the lost child simply isn't noticed. Not there. The lost child might be alone in her room or playing out in the garage. She doesn't say much, doesn't stick out in the bunch, probably enjoys escapist reading. The lost child is nice. Constantly, unbearably, doggedly nice.

Okay, so maybe the scapegoat isn't much fun to have for a family member, but aren't the others healthy? What can be wrong with a kid who makes all A's or a nice little girl, or even a clown, for that matter? The problem is not with the patterns of behavior themselves but with the identities. If those displaying these pattern types were to be drawn as circles, the circles would be at best dotted lines. They lack a strong sense of identity, of personal-ness. They don't really know what they need from life. And down inside, these delightful and desirable children (and adults) are extremely miserable. As they get older the misery will not ease.

The roles of hero, mascot, scapegoat, and lost child may shift from person to person as family circumstances change. An only child may move from one to another. Louise, the anorexic referred to our hospital by her nursing supervisor, played two roles. She was a hero when she excelled in school and kept the home scene from crumbling. But when she went away to nursing school she became the scapegoat, criticized by her mother for abandoning her first responsibility to the family.

SHIFTING DYSFUNCTIONAL FAMILY ROLES

Several other roles appear in a dysfunctional family, but they differ from the above in several ways. The above roles occur in every family to a limited extent and are magnified by codependency. These are generated by codependency itself. Usually each family member assumes different roles at different times as dictated by the situation.

ENABLER

If it weren't for the enablers, a family's dysfunction could not long exist. The tragedy is that the enablers can't grasp that fact. Every member in a dysfunctional family plays the enabler role to some extent. This role was first identified in families where a "normal" spouse was married to an alcoholic. Let's say for convenience only that Dad is the alcoholic and Mom is not. She's keeping the family together—heroic, martyr Mom.

(Remember this works exactly the same if Mom is addictive and Dad the "clean" one, or if both are addictive to some degree. And the addiction need not be alcohol—drugs, work, rage, extreme religious rigidity—any addiction may be plugged into the "alcoholism" of our generalized case here.)

How does harried, put-upon Mom enable Dad to drink, when Dad's drinking appears to be the source of all her problems, and she yearns aloud for him to quit? Many ways, ways of which she is not aware.

She keeps his drinking a secret and enlists the children's cooperation in deceiving the world. Thus he need not face public approbation for his behavior. "We don't take family problems to outsiders." "Little pitchers have big ears, but you keep your mouths shut!" "It's not as bad as it looks." "Don't worry." "When Mrs. X asks you those nosy questions, you tell her your mother says it's none of her business."

She lies to the boss for him when he calls in sick. She bails him out of scrapes and sometimes out of jail itself. She cleans up the messes, both physical and situational, that he's constantly making.

The children, regardless of the other family roles they assume, become enablers also. Assuming in their innocence that everything happening in the family is somehow linked to their behavior, they accept just as much guilt and responsibility as Mom. They learn to keep their mouths shut. They play intensely the roles described above. That is *all* enabling. By adjusting everything to the alcoholic, they all make it easier for him to be one. The kids have no choice. This family is all they have.

Counselors believe that Mom has little choice either. Mom almost certainly brought her own codependency into the marriage. She was set up for all this before ever she met dear old Dad.

All these codependents, mother and children alike, have become so absorbed and enmeshed in the life and problems of another person that they lose their sense of self-determination. Just as much as the dysfunctional family member (the alcoholic father in the above case), they are victims of the family illness. They practice enabling because they feel helpless, yet they could exercise great power in the situation by ceasing enabling.

THE ENABLER'S ADDITIONAL SUITE OF ROLES

Perhaps you have prepared or eaten rainbow gelatin dessert. To make it, you pour an inch or so of grape-flavored gelatin in each clear dessert glass and let it set. Next add an inch of cherry. Give it time to gel, then add orange and finally lemon. The end product is an eye-catching treat in colorful bands.

The roles codependents play are similarly layered. The foundation layer is the universal roles such as mother/daughter or sister/sister. The roles of hero, etc., form a second layer upon the first and are healthy unless carried to extreme as a coping mechanism. The orange layer, the enabler, derives from the codependency itself, and the lemon layer is built upon the enabling. A healthy family would have purple and red layers only.

The roles of this final layer are the enabler's instinctive adaptations to the stressful situation, and they change as the situation changes. They are the placater, martyr, rescuer, persecutor, and victim.

PLACATER

Even a very small child can adopt the placater role. The placater is going to make it all better somehow. He might distract and heal by being a clown. He is often the hero. The placater knows what words to say to reassure siblings, soothe Mom, get around Dad. A born negotiator, the placater recognizes in advance the waves that might rock the family boat and tries to still them and may even use an occasional white lie to keep the family friction to a minimum.

MARTYR

The martyr will pay any personal price to alleviate the family situation. The martyr sacrifices time, energy, and happiness to keep the family together, to try to get the dependent to quit drinking or shooting up. She will stick it out for a hundred years and go to any extent to make things work out right. By "right" the martyr means "the way the martyr wants them to." She will burn out or go nuts or both. The only thing the martyr will *not* be able to do is make a difference in the dependent's habits.

RESCUER

The rescuer is going to salvage the situation, whatever it is. The rescuer will get a second job to pay the bills. He will bail out the dependent, hire the attorney, pay the estranged teen-aged child's rent, do the jobs that would otherwise go undone.

At first glance the rescuer and martyr seem to be one and the same. They overlap in some ways, but in other ways they are separate. The martyr's actions go far beyond rescuing. The martyr's frame of mind is *Sacrifice! Give more! Deny self and ignore the cost.* The rescuer rescues. His frame of mind is *Hurry! Fix up this immediate mess! Cover it up. Minimize the damage. Get this behind us quickly.*

PERSECUTOR

Persecutor says, "It's all your fault!" The persecutor lays blame liberally everywhere but on the self. He tells all the family members exactly what they are doing wrong and why they have not achieved perfection. The persecutor is not a pleasant person to be in the same county with.

VICTIM

Oh, poor victim—she didn't ask for any of this. The victim could be happy if only all this weren't happening. She is the soul most to be pitied, because she is so very nice down inside that none of this is deserved. This role is not to be confused with actual victimization. True victims usually do not perceive themselves as victims in this intensely self-pitying sense.

Because these four roles, the lemon layer of gelatin, all belong to the enabler, one person may play them all, first this role and then that one, as the situation suggests. In fact, the roles shift so amorphously, we find enablers extremely difficult to counsel well.

Irene, the wife of an alcoholic named Walt, came to our clinic not for her own problems but for Walt's. These statements from her lips were collected from our first several interviews with her. Like all enablers, Irene played each of these roles as the occasion called for them.

"If Betty hadn't called me and told me where Walt was, he'd be downtown in the drunk tank right now. I literally had to pick him up off the street last night in front of Wanamaker's." *(Rescuer.)*

"Do you realize where the kids would be if I didn't keep this family together? Foster homes. My sister certainly won't take them. Mom doesn't understand. She doesn't even want them around, Billy especially. It's all up to me." *(Martyr.)*

"It's Walt's fault, all of it. He promises and promises and then he takes that first drink and he's gone. And like a fool, I keep believing him. He's supposed to love me. How can he do this to me?" *(Both persecutor and victim.)*

"I don't deserve this. You can't begin to imagine what a rotten childhood I had. If anyone should get a break from misery, it's me. I've paid my dues, believe me! Why is it always me?" *(Victim.)*

". . . So I had to go down to the school in person and talk to his teacher to save him from getting a suspension. He's just like his father—he goes out looking for trouble. He'd probably be in juvenile hall if I didn't keep him walking in a straight line." *(Back to being a rescuer again.)*

"I can't take much more of this. You just don't know the pressure I'm under all the time." *(Pity the poor victim.)*

Biochemists are now reconstructing not just the chemical components of complex proteins but also their physical shapes. A single molecule of a complex protein is a long chain warped into an incredible wad of kinks and loops, fused here and there at odd intervals. That's the way the roles in a dysfunctional relationship work, too, all kinked and tied at incongruous points.

Martyr, rescuer, persecutor, victim, enabler, placater, hero, lost child, scapegoat, mascot—these roles help codependents survive their family and the members learn them well. But the roles are warped. Anomalous. When they are applied outside dysfunctional situations, as for instance in employment, church, and friendships, they don't work. The rules have changed; the relationships differ; healthy people are involved now. And yet, the family members who came to depend upon the old rules don't know how else to play the game. The co-dependents are stuck with a twisted system of interpersonal relationships that cannot help them cope with the real world.

PROFESSIONAL RESCUERS

Gary Ellis had the world's greatest job—paramedic—and he loved it! The call they were responding to was a two-car accident on Mercer Road. Gary hit the lights and siren as he confirmed the accident's location with the radio dispatcher. His lowly assistant, Emergency Medical Technician Melinda Bennet, did the driving; Gary got to play with the toys. As the man in charge of this medical aid van, Gary felt like the king of the road. Full lights and siren really made the traffic scatter!

At the accident scene they helped a young woman with possible neck and spine injuries, applying the routine cervical collar and rigid backboard, using the fancy Velcro-coated equipment that has made sandbagging obsolete. Gary kept up on the latest technology and made certain his boss, the manager of this ambulance company, was aware of useful new inventions.

Gary wasn't the biggest guy in the world—five-nine, one hundred and fifty pounds—but he knew how to use leverage. By the time the fire truck arrived, he and little five-foot-four Melinda had dismantled the second car and were extricating the middle-aged driver.

In his three years as a paramedic and one year as an EMT, Gary had cleaned up some truly bad wrecks. He could tell stories that would curl your hair. He knew when to go by the book and when to get innovative—always within protocol guidelines. Gary had steeled himself to blood and death; he reveled in that ultimate feel-good experience that occasionally came along—delivering a baby. Of the hundred and sixty paramedics in this Midwest county, he was as good as there was.

Surprisingly, within two years he would quit the profession

altogether. So would twenty-eight other paramedics in that county.

Trying to combat the extraordinary burnout rate among EMTs and paramedics, public health officials circulated a questionnaire asking, in effect (but more tactfully than this): What do you want? Shorter hours? More money? Greater recognition? What will it take to keep you guys in the profession long enough to make your costly training pay off?

The answer, unfortunately, is usually not the surface perks the questionnaire reflected, desirable as they are. The causes of burnout run much deeper.

There are two kinds of people who enter the caring services such as medicine, law enforcement, clergy, counseling, and social work: those who are called by God and conscience to the work; and those who are driven by the hidden whip of codependency. If workers of the former group burn out, it will be because of the problems the questionnaire addressed, such as exhausting schedules, inadequate pay, too many frustrations per reward. Given a satisfactory work climate, the former group will remain productive for years.

The latter, the workers driven by codependency, will go down in flames and may well take others with them. We believe the reasons have to do with one of the most powerful forces in codependency, the rescue dynamic. Gary is a rescuer.

Rescuing and enabling take place in nearly any dysfunctional situation, not just the classic model. And the children growing up in this milieu will be drawn like magnets to the rescuing professions. We believe there are several reasons for this.

For one thing, rescuing distracts. The rescuer, encouraged to noble sacrifice at every hand, can struggle and work, care always about others, never be selfish. The rescuer is praised for rescuing. That's the good news. The bad news is that by being noble and selfless the rescuer need not consider himself or herself. "By keeping my focus firmly on others, I need not look, let alone focus, upon myself and my needs." Unmet needs, denial, pain—in short, the personal things that are unpleasant to deal with—get buried. Unfortunately, they do not fade. They fester.

For another thing, rescuing satisfies that hideously powerful repetition compulsion. This circumstance works just as did Sean the salesman's compulsion to recreate the father/son relationship with his bosses. The rescuer recreates another chance, and another, and still another, to somehow rescue the family of origin and make everything come out all right this time around. The overt rescue might be successful every time, but that covert rescue always ends up the same. Failure.

Finally, when the rescuer performs a rescue, he or she vicariously rescues himself or herself from the past. The paramedic isn't just patching up the victim, he's patching up that little lost child within. The clinical psychologist isn't just fixing up this nice client's life, she's fixing up her own as well, by transference. "Self-nurturance" is another way to say it. Doesn't sound rational? That's right. It's *not* rational, but it's the way the water circulates in the hidden rivers of our minds.

Looking at it from the love tank point of view, the rescuer deep down believes, "If I fill your tank, mine will somehow be filled." It doesn't happen that way and the rescuer's tank drains further. With love tanks, dry-out equals burnout.

Down beyond the conscious level, the rescuer is not just hoping that the self will be nurtured, the wrongs of the past righted, the personal hurts magically healed without being examined. The rescuer is counting on it. Of course, it doesn't happen. The only things the rescuer fixes are whatever the rescuer is fixing on the surface. The self, the lost child, goes unfixed. The buried wounds fester. The pain and anger grow.

Burnout.

"This job isn't doing what I wanted it to."

"But you're doing good, you're saving lives—or whatever your occupational goal is. Doesn't that satisfy you?"

"No. And now I feel guilty because it ought to but it doesn't." Just what the burned-out rescuer needs—the self-inflicted pain of failure and guilt piled on top of the hidden pain already driving him to distraction.

And yet—and this is most important—unless the person deals with the underlying codependency problems, unless the wounds are opened and cleaned and healed, he or she is doomed to a recurring sense of failure. The burnout will persist. It will taint all the jobs that follow. Surface resolutions such as "I will do so-and-so to pace myself" will provide only ephemeral relief. Before the codependent realizes it, the old patterns are back, cycling ever more viciously: rescue to help the inside; the inside goes unhelped; rescue harder. More. Longer. No. The only answer is to uncover and solve the root problems.

Not at all incidentally, the divorce rate in the caring services, such as medicine, law enforcement, psychology, is extremely high. Marriage and family satisfaction depends just as much upon healing as does career satisfaction.

There is another complication. If the codependent is also a workaholic (and many are), health will suffer as the rescuer neglects physical needs as well as the deeper needs. Worn-down servants do not function well in any arena.

At the clinic we see many Christian workers who have just come in from the field, domestic fields as well as foreign missions. You can almost see the pain and weariness on their faces. But should we tell them, "Look. If you hope to serve others you must first take care of yourself," big neon lights flash on. *Selfish! Selfish! Selfish! A good Christian worker puts self aside. Selfishness is a sin.*

The perfectly proper Christian ethic of service to others becomes distorted when pressed upon by codependency. "Help others" becomes "Do not help self; help only others." "Deny self" becomes "Deny even the sensible, ordinary needs of self." Jesus tore Himself away from needy crowds to convene with His Father in solitary prayer. While He walked among mankind, He knew that to fill others' tanks He had to restore His own. We all do.

Frequently, people who are driven to rescuing by codependency become adamant in their refusal to take care of themselves. "Deny self; serve others" is carried to the extreme of a compulsion. And compulsion is exactly what it is. The culture-supported need to rescue sacrificially, with all its pluses and minuses, may grow into a true obsession.

Gary Ellis is a workaholic of a different sort. His hours are regulated by scheduling authorities beyond himself, and the ambulance company does not permit overtime. He puts in his forty hours weekly and goes home. But he is so enmeshed in his rescuing role as a paramedic that his job has become an obsession. He reads all the technical magazines, browses the catalogs, putters with his personal jump box. He has no interests outside of emergency medical care.

Gary Ellis is hooked on emergency medical service. When he burns out, and it's coming soon, he will become hooked on something else. Whatever that something else is, it will give him no more lasting satisfaction than what he's doing now. His life will spiral along, the same story retold with different scenery, and with each episode his bitterness and disillusionment will cut a little deeper, for bitterness is the hidden root in burnout. If he is a Christian, the bitterness will unavoidably taint his relationship with God and other Christians. His spiritual walk will be adversely affected. Burnout spreads like wildfire.

THE ROLES YOU PLAY

Now that you know the multifarious roles you and the people closest to you play, spend a few minutes identifying the players. Who was the hero when you were growing up? Did one child take on two roles? When was the switch made? Analyze your own family and those of your close friends.

If you inadvertently play exaggerated roles, codependent roles, in your personal relationships, you are crippling those relationships because the roles are inappropriate. This is particularly true in the relationship between you and God. Let's look at that next.

GOD AND SUNGLASSES

How does a codependent relationship with God differ from a healthy one? Think of it in the terms you've been exploring so far.

John and Gladys Jordan and Sean McCurdy all suffered from dysfunctional relationships with their fathers. They stand in grave danger of transferring those feelings about fathers to the father figure God. God is the perfect Father. There is no dysfunctional relationship in Him; He is all-sufficient. But without meaning to, John, Gladys, and Sean may see God in terms far too human.

Gladys, you will remember, grew up with a father who could not or would not listen to her. She unconsciously attributed that trait to her husband, John, as well, despite his good listening ability. If, similarly, she unconsciously attributes that same human imperfection to God, her power of prayer will be severely muted. She will be unable to enjoy and appreciate the loving nature of God. She may well agree with those who say an intimate relationship with God is unattainable, and in her case she will be right. The intimacy will evade her grasp not because of God's nature but because of that codependent blinder she's wearing.

If John sees God as authoritarian and legalistic, he may forget that no human being can earn his own salvation by somehow winning God's approval. John stands in danger of missing the whole point of the gospel—salvation by grace. *Mercy* and *grace* will be alien terms for him. Moreover, although he may agree with his wife that an intimate relationship with God is unattainable, their reasons for believing this will be completely different. His vision of God and hers will be nowise similar. Gladys sees an unresponsive, distant God, and John sees a police officer in the sky who records his every flaw.

Sean is looking for the perfect father. In God Sean has found him. But will Sean realize that? If bad things happen—if Sean suffers grievous loss or believes his prayers have gone unanswered—he might view God as unworthy of full faith, just as he regards his temporal employers who mess up. In short, Sean (as do so many of us) may measure God with the wrong yardstick and find Him wanting. Do you see how the tilt in the bottom half of the four-tier cake is distorting the top half, particularly in this case the second layer, personal relationships, which includes relationship with God?

Study closely a brilliant-cut diamond (the larger the diamond, the clearer and more obvious the allusion). Note that each facet is cut at a different angle to every other facet. The facets along one edge seem almost to lie in sharp opposition to those of the other edge. Tilt the gem and first one facet flashes fire, then another. There are fifty-eight facets. Fewer would not serve; the stone would appear dull and listless, unable to flash its brilliance. Just as critical to the brilliance of this jewel is the acuteness of the angle at the bottom of the stone—how sharp the point.

This is the God of Scripture, a God of many facets. Some are nearly identical, facing almost the same plane. Other facets appear to oppose each other when examined as if isolated from the whole. "Ours is a God of love" appears the opposite of "Vengeance is mine, says the Lord." Perhaps one flashes fire, riveting our attention for a moment. Then our attitude changes slightly and another seizes our eye. Because God is infinitely more complex than the diamond, no man can adequately perceive Him—no person can take in and admire all the facets.

A person with a full love tank and a thermometer registering low on the codependency scale will see the diamond as bright as it can be seen by mortal eye. The codependent, though, will be blinded to many of the facets, perhaps most of them. Because the codependent sees only a few facets, the glorious vision of God has been reduced to a dull and listless portion, lacking fire.

As therapists and psychologists we do not presume to tell anyone how the Bible ought to be interpreted. Scripture is God's love letter to each of us individually. How it speaks and what it says is a very private matter between that person and God. What we emphasize—what we work toward—is that each person may have the chance to fairly and objectively hear God's words, unfiltered by codependent bonds and preconceptions.

It is always intriguing from a psychological point of view how two readers can study the same passage of Scripture and, depending upon each person's emotional predisposition, walk away with radically different senses of what it means. Such unconscious winnowing is normal. The deep recesses of each person's mind sifts incoming information. But the sifting process in the mind of a person from a dysfunctional family—a person whose love tank is impoverished, a person in whom great hidden anger seethes—has been skewed and truncated.

The codependency *must* be dealt with before that person with unmet emotional needs can hope to grasp the reality of God and the gospel. Until the deep problems are resolved, anything God says to that person is subject to gross misinterpretation.

In short, it is not just to improve lifestyle, encourage real happiness, and solve problems that you should seek to root out codependency. The Christian's foremost privilege and responsibility is to hear and respond to God. The codependent can neither hear clearly nor respond adequately. It's that simple.

How does the filter of codependency work? Look on it as being something like a polarizing lens. Light polarization is employed to many uses in both industry and everyday life, and one of the commonest uses is in sunglasses. Plain old tinted sunglasses cut glare by partially blocking off some of the light coming through the lens. All the light, regardless of the angle it enters, gets the same degree of blocking and filtration. A polarizing lens, however, almost completely blocks light waves entering at a certain angle and lets other light waves through untrammeled. Polarizing lenses, in short, block out light selectively.

So do codependent traits. Codependents view God as through a polarized lens. The light is blocked in all but one narrow dimension. Codependents, with their unmet needs and deep, unresolved anger about their experiences with non-nurturing earthly mothers and fathers, look right at the sun/Son as through a polarizing lens and see only a narrow portion of the reality.

All those problems codependency generates in relationships between people also crop up in the believer/God relationship. Consider for example, the ghosts of the past—that is, the repetition compulsion—that plagued John and Gladys Jordan. Gladys feels compelled to recreate the original family situation, in part to rectify it, in part to live with the pain that seems so familiar. God is the only Person in the universe with a zero codependency thermometer. But that old repetition compulsion comes through so strongly, Gladys assigns her father's imperfection to God. Of course she does not call it "imperfection"; everybody knows God is perfect. But upon analysis that's what it turns out to be. Those ghosts can whisper so loudly, the voice of God in the Bible goes unheard. Seeing God in limited, humanistic terms suggests that codependent tendencies are spilling over into her God relationship.

And then there's that deep, unresolved anger. How does the codependent feel toward an abusive parent? Fear and hatred on one hand for the parent(s) who is supposed to be providing nurturance and is not. On the other, the intense, driving, natural love of child for parent. The child (and later the adult child) works desperately to fix the dysfunctional situation, to change the ending, to win the needed approval and nurturance of that parent. That dramatic love/hate ambivalence buries itself deep. It may erupt in the spiritual dimension.

A woman we worked with recently illustrates this well. Rebecca came to us absolutely convinced she was experiencing demon possession. We know better than to rule out such a possibility, but from all we could see and sense, there were no signs whatever of demonic activity. What we finally dug down to was that very ambivalence of love/hate.

Rebecca's daddy was a rigid, perfectionistic dentist, a military man. Every two years the family moved, from base to base, state to state, country to country. Rebecca never completed two full years in the same school. Her role was to smile and agree that whatever Daddy wanted, that's what the family should do. Neither she nor her mother was allowed to express anger, frustration, or hurt at having to put down roots and rip them out again.

Now, years later, part of her—the part that showed—loved God the Father. Indeed, Rebecca is a beautiful and committed Christian. But she was also getting in touch with the hidden part, the unresolved anger and resentment. She had transferred that ugly side of her relationship with her dad to her relationship with God, just as she had transferred the love-thy-parent aspect. Because it was so incomprehensible to her that she might be angry with God, she assumed there must be some outside force within her.

By leading her through the stages we will discuss in the recovery section, we helped her deal with her hidden resentment. She exposed and cleansed the anger. The "demons" hushed.

In summary, two things may happen in a codependent's relationship with God. First, because of that polarizing filter, the person sees and hears only a narrow portion of God, not enough to get the necessary scope of both His judgment and His mercy. Moreover the person cannot adequately perceive what *agape* (unconditional) love should be. Second, the person unconsciously tries to develop a relationship with Him on that limited or skewed basis.

We most frequently see cases wherein the persons try to win God's approval with certain behaviors or rigid self-imposed thought patterns. Anorexia is one such behavior. A rigid, stilted view of "correct" living is another. Sadly, because those persons never won the earthly parents' complete nurturance and approval, they never feel completely accepted by the Father. The best is never quite good enough. Frustration supplants godly love and contentment.

In the clinic we frequently serve Christians who are extremely knowledgeable regarding Scripture. Counseling sessions become marathon theology discussions with rapid-fire exchange of proof-texts and verses. A case in point is Edith, a woman treated in the hospital by clinic personnel. Edith, now a teacher in a church school, was raised by an abusive father, then married a spiritually abusive man. Those first few weeks of her treatment were a debating contest. We would suggest, "You ought to get better in touch with the grace of God." Like a teletype, she'd respond instantly with Bible passages that emphasize God's judgment. Back and forth, back and forth.

So often with well-versed Christians whose love tanks are running near empty, finding God becomes not a quest but a hopeless struggle. Deep down inside, beyond reach of gentle reason, such persons feel bad about themselves emotionally. When feelings of inadequacy and unworthiness run so deep; when these persons emotionally see God the Father as unloving, unforgiving, or unattainable; they can read the message of hope in the New Testament until their eyes cross, and still they come out with a fundamental sense of condemnation. Over and over we see them put themselves into a relationship with God in which they feel they must win His approval through legalism, perfectionism, self-sacrifice, self-abuse—whatever mechanism they feel will best prove to God their worthiness, even as they doubt that worthiness in their own hearts.

Jesus used this concept of a strong family under a loving, nurturing father when He said, "What man is there among you who, if his son asks for bread, will give him a stone? Or if he asks for a fish, will he give him a serpent? If you then, being evil, know how to give good gifts to your children, how much more will your Father who is in heaven give good things to those who ask Him!"[3] The earthly family becomes the shadow of the heavenly family with God the all-wise, all-nurturing head.

The basis of codependency—unsatisfied narcissistic hunger—is thus not something new under the sun. Four thousand years ago the Word of God warned parents of their responsibility, and the warnings continue throughout Scripture. A solid, nurturing, stable family became the God-given pipeline to happiness, long life, and a clear understanding of love and of the heavenly Father.

Here then is still another powerful reason to deal with codependency in your life. Your children and your children's children (by which we mean any children under your influence, whether biologically yours or not) need full love tanks if they are to find happiness, enjoy true love, and know God well. You cannot satisfy their emotional needs so long as you suffer lack. Scripture affirms that you are the key to their future.

No man can see the full extent of God. But when the whole of Scripture is absorbed and examined, there emerges the multidimensional picture of a wonderful Master and Lover beyond human understanding. Even as He demands, He understands. He loves faultlessly, guides perfectly, reigns absolutely. Every man sees the truth as through a glass darkly, even the apostle Paul. But the codependent, tragically, sees as through a twisted glass *very* darkly, the vision warped into a dwarfed view falling short of truth.

"See here!" says Jesus in a paraphrase of John 15:15. "More than servants, you are my friends." When your best friend is God, surely you want to know Him the best you can.

PART FIVE:

The Ten Stages of Recovery

CHAPTER
THIRTEEN

Exploring Your Relationships

So here it is, a three-storied glass and brick building on stilts—the Minirth-Meier Clinic. Coming from the shade of its underground parking, you step into an elevator and hum purposefully up to the reception area. Amid bustle and tasteful furnishings and an occasional potted palm, friendly smiles greet you. Still, you feel ill at ease.

This business of accepting counseling—of being on the receiving end of advice—is not natural to you. Even as your head says you need help, your heart whines that you should be able to handle your problems without hanging all your dirty laundry out for strangers to view. The mere fact that someone probably saw you come into this building identifies you (in your mind) as an emotional weakling who can't get a grip on life.

But you persist. You thumb through a magazine and pretend you're in a dentist's office, not a psychiatric clinic. You persist because your life is a shambles. Things are going wrong—and the shambles and the wrongs are taking too much of a toll on your emotions. They will invariably rub off on the people around you, the people closest to you.

If you were to enter our counsel, what would you expect in the way of treatment of codependency? Here at the Minirth-Meier Clinic we employ a ten-stage model for recovery from codependency. Through it we lead clients to deal with lost childhood, with what are called adult child issues, and in so doing, recover from codependency. These ten steps or stages are not meant in any way to compete with or replace the twelve-step recovery programs of Alcoholics Anonymous, Al-Anon, and similar groups. These stages do, however, touch upon those twelve steps and recast the principles behind them.

In this final section we will explore the stages, one by one, as steps to relief and healing. You have already learned about some of them. You have learned much about codependency that is essential in understanding yourself. Now we bring it all together into a useful form.

And again we caution you—codependency is not a constant state but a continuum. Most people are slightly affected and the adjustments this book offers will lead them to healing and a happier, more productive lifestyle. Others may be so deeply affected that a self-help book cannot provide all the help needed. If your codependency patterns are controlling your life powerfully, your thoughts and feelings may at some point become too heavy to bear. If so, by all means do not delay to seek out competent professional care.

Also, let us repeat the warning that codependency, just like the dependencies that first led us to recognize it, is chronic and progressive. When codependency manifests itself as abuse, depression, eating disorders and such, it can actually be fatal.

Those important disclaimers made, it is time to lead you forward as a client would be led.

THE HEALING ROLLER COASTER RIDE

It's a classic, one-of-a-kind, that's been thrilling people for over half a century. It's the grandpa of all roller coasters, the Jackrabbit at Hershey Park. And you've just climbed into its end car. The car catches into the chain drive with a jerk and you begin the long, slow grind up the trestled hill. You wonder, as the expectation builds, whether this silly little bar across your lap is going to be worth beans if you *really* need it.

For half an eternity you poise on the brink. You're never quite prepared for that first screaming swoop straight down. Your head reverses directions before your stomach reaches the bottom and you're clattering up the next hill—and down—and up. . . . The humps and hills get lower, the right-angle turns become negotiable. The first wild plunge far behind now, you coast casually into the unloading shed, and lurch to an anticlimactic stop.

That's just about the way recovery will go. Because we've used the term "deeper into pain" before, let's put it to work now. Picture the process of healing as that first indescribable loop in a classic roller coaster ride (see illustration page 180). The direction Up indicates less emotional pain, the direction Down leads to more. The bottom of the loop is the nadir of your emotions, the deepest of the pain.

There are differences between our recovery roller coaster and an actual one. In ours, a person entering the ride comes not from the top (free of pain) but from a point part way down. Pain is already a factor. The first five stages of recovery take you what seems like the wrong way, deeper and deeper into pain.

In a classic roller coaster, the only outside power applied to the ride is that chain drive at the very beginning. Once the chain pulls the car to the top of the first hill, the highest point, gravity and inertia power the car for the remainder of the ride. The higher and steeper that first hill, the more kinetic energy is available for the rest of the ride (this is why the subsequent hills get lower and lower; the car is rapidly losing energy to friction just staying on the track as well as the energy spent in subsequent hill climbs).

In our recovery model, the first steep drop will provide the impetus and the wherewithal for the uphill healing. There will be other hills in your future, but none will be as high, and you'll be equipped with the means to roll up over them.

STAGE ONE: EXPLORATION AND DISCOVERY

Archeological digs are fascinating places. Long gone are the days when diggers pawed through the sand until they found

THE TEN STAGES OF THE RECOVERY CURVE

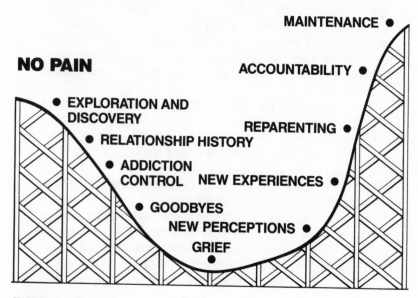

NO PAIN

MAINTENANCE ●

ACCOUNTABILITY ●

● EXPLORATION AND DISCOVERY

REPARENTING ●

● RELATIONSHIP HISTORY

● ADDICTION CONTROL   NEW EXPERIENCES ●

● GOODBYES

NEW PERCEPTIONS ●

GRIEF
●

DEEP PAIN

some valuable artifact worthy of display in a museum back home. Today a dig is divided up both horizontally and vertically in a grid of labeled sections. Diggers use trowels, delicate paintbrushes, and dental picks rather than shovels. Screen sifters separate out tiny shards and bits of refuse. Every find, whatever its significance, is identified by section and layer. Years later, analysts can know precisely where and how each piece was found. Broken pots, worn-out sandals, bits of metal—the cast-offs from ten thousand yesterdays lie neatly arranged in row after row, filling endless tables in stuffy Quonset huts.

In this first stage you are to conduct an archeological dig of your own life. You've already been doing that to an important extent as you've been reading. Now is the time to lay out these gems of self-discovery and to seek more. You are not just clawing out the big, spectacular events for display. You're looking also for the small things that seem insignificant now but may well play a key role in understanding the past. We're going to fill a Quonset hut with the details of your past, and also your present, the compulsions and addictions in your life today.

In counsel we help patients acknowledge two things. One involves the elements which are addictive, compulsive, and obsessive in their present lifestyle. The other involves the issues of lost childhood.

Now nobody likes to admit to an addiction or obsessive compulsion. Such dysfunctions happen to other people, not me. So look instead for elements in your present life that are taking an inordinate amount of your time and energy. What can you not live without, either figuratively or literally? TV? Your job? That SOP? What means so much to you that you will spend time and money on it to the exclusion of other things? Most important: what in your life will you hide or sneak around to do, lest someone find out to what extent you're doing it? Sexual excesses? What are the legal and moral criteria of your most secret actions?

Do not pass judgment on what you find or assign "right" or "wrong" to anything at this point in the process. Simply sift them out. Know them.

The other target of our exploration and discovery is lost childhood issues. If necessary, reread chapter 3 to remind yourself what you are seeking. The loss of a parent through death or divorce, the emotional unavailability of a parent—whatever.

We're performing two functions simultaneously here. We're examining what is going on in your present life, and also what happened earlier in your life. Were you in actual counsel, by the second or third counseling session you would be asked to describe your childhood. We would ask about your relationships with peers and neighbors, your parents and siblings, your pets. What did you dread as a child, and what did you look forward to? Can you recall specific instances of discipline, affection, loss, gain . . . ? What's happened to you? Review the questions and material regarding lost childhood in chapter 4. Lay the pieces out on the table as you find them.

As the last part of stage one, we encourage you to tell your story. Tell to whom? An extremely close and trusted friend; a spouse, perhaps (though not usually; if you are enmeshed in a codependent relationship, it will almost certainly be with that person). A self-help support group would be excellent.

Regardless whom else you entrust with your confidences, the person who can listen best is God. The more you bring Him into the process, particularly from this point on, the easier and swifter will your recovery progress. Self-help books and programs both secular and religious all acknowledge the healing power of faith in God.

First, ask Him to lift the codependent blinders from your eyes. Everyone practices denial and minimization to some extent, but the codependent's very emotional life depends upon them. These distortions blunt your ability to see yourself, and only God can really open your eyes. Now tell a human friend or counselor your tale, but tell it also to God (in fact, He's a good person before whom to rehearse it, if you feel rehearsal is necessary). The seemingly simple act of telling one's story can, in itself, exercise a profound healing influence. Here's why.

Again the classic codependency model of the family under an alcoholic father is the best model for understanding. The common thread running through all the pieces on these family members' tables is shame. The family has a secret, a shameful, embarrassing secret. The family is different from everyone else in some terrible way. The family stands alone against the power of world opinion. Regardless how the family appears on the outside (and the members all strive to look as good as possible), the inside is nothing like those happy families on television, or the comfortable fit every other family in the neighborhood seems to enjoy. This family is dreadfully wrenched out of sync. And every member, truly or falsely, feels responsible for the dysfunction. Shame.

In part because of the shame, the child who grew up in a

dysfunctional family has almost surely never told anyone. If the adult child discussed it at all, certain parts were left out. After all, never before has that child had permission to openly talk about it. Indeed, the parent(s) even now might well be shocked and dismayed to hear the story voiced.

But when that child garners the courage to verbalize the whole story of childhood to a friendly and understanding ear, good things happen. The sheer telling cracks the wall of denial. It breaks through some of the shame. The child emerges, perhaps just a peep, out of the isolation and aloneness characterizing the childhood experiences. Thus does telling the story become a powerful healing tool even though it is but one small part of the full recovery process.

Consider the incident of Jesus and the woman at the well in John 4. Around noon, a Samaritan woman approached the well in Sychar to draw water. Jesus asked her for a drink. She questioned His motives, for Samaritans and Jews did not mingle. He offered her living water. Again she questioned. When Jesus asked her to bring her husband, she claimed to have none. Jesus then replied in effect, "That's true. You've had five husbands, and you're not married to your present man." Astonished, she shifted her questions to the spiritual level, where Jesus had been all along. She came to trust Him as Messiah and eventually testified throughout her village to His messiahship, bringing to Him many believers.

Regarding this incident we may ask patients, "What took place in Jesus' revelation of her life history? How might that lend itself to healing?"

To summarize patients' responses, variously: Jesus did not say or imply, "I ignore what you've done in the past and so should you," or "Your past doesn't matter," or "I don't know about your past." Rather He said, in essence, "I know all about your past. I know your story, and I accept you anyway." That is an intensely supportive insight for codependents.

Various books and counselors may suggest prayers you might use to address God or express yourself before Him. We recommend you do so, by all means, at each stage along the way. Some people struggling with recovery find it helpful to write to God, not that they expect the letter to be delivered.

Rather, they keep something of a journal or diary ("Dear Diary, Today I went . . .") addressed to God ("Dear God, Today I want to tell you . . ."). Such a series of letters or entries serves several purposes. By putting it down on paper you can literally see what you're thinking. It is certainly a form of prayer. And it makes God more immediate, particularly if you and He have not been all that close of late. And some time in the future you can look back and see how very far you've come.

STAGE TWO: RELATIONSHIP
HISTORY/INVENTORY

All those priceless pieces dug from yesterday's middens cannot lie in the Quonset hut forever. They must be sorted and inventoried. It's a mindless, mechanical task, but it's immensely important. Each piece receives an accession number. Each is categorized, arranged, wrapped, and boxed. Some, once packaged, will never see the light of day again. A few, quite frankly, might simply be taken out and reburied. Most will be gently and reverently scrutinized by experts. A very few will emerge as important keys to our understanding of a culture long hidden.

In this second stage our patients, and you, are asked to complete a careful, in-depth relationship history or inventory. Specifically, you are to identify all the persons, past and present, who either left a memorable mark for some reason or who exercised an obvious influence in your life.

CONSIDER FAR-FLUNG FAMILY MEMBERS

Although we've been assuming so far that "family" means the nuclear family of parents plus children (with perhaps an occasional addition, such as a resident aunt or grandparent), the reality of "family" is much more complex. One way or another, each of us maintains relations and is nurturing or nurtured (not nurturing or not nurtured) with all the far-flung members of our greater families.

With the exception of the very few institutionalized abandoned or orphaned infants, nearly all of us are born into a nuclear family. That primary family relationship remains ongoing; one way or another, we carry our family with us our whole lives. That is, we maintain some sort of relationship with our parents and siblings throughout life, whether they be living or dead. In technical terms, this is the family of origin.

By marrying, most adults make a family of procreation. This grouping includes a spouse and perhaps one or more children. In addition there is the work family comprised of employer(s) and fellow employees, the church family, usually a civic family including friends, relatives, and others in the community. And then there is the extended family, which may consist of just a few in-laws, aunts, uncles, and grandparents, or like Beth Metrano Johansen's half a cityful of kin. To further complicate things, persons other than yourself may possess membership in two or more of your different families. For example, your sister-in-law might also be a cousin.

If you have deep codependent patterns, in some way or other those patterns will affect every family you are in. It will shape or distort your membership in each of those groupings. Frequently someone will enter counseling saying, "I only want to work on this one relationship. If things were just better with my [wife] [husband] [child]; if he/she would change, everything would be fine." Unfortunately it never works that way. Change in any one member of a family group ramifies into all the other members, whether that change is in you or in someone else. The family—whichever grouping pertains—must be dealt with as a unit. When we aid a patient with a self-assessment, it becomes glaringly obvious that where codependency rears its ugly head, ripples extend into every aspect of that person's life.

An analogy is found among the old riverboat pilots of Mark Twain's heyday. Piloting was a highly prestigious job and a demanding one. Not only need the pilot know the course of the river intimately, he had to know what was going on beneath the water. Where were the shoals, the rocks, the sandbars, the currents that could either ensure success or wreak instant disaster? Similarly, deep codependent patterns are like the hidden perils the pilot faced. The formations below the water determine the direction and the success of our journey through life.

Think how many people you have been emotionally involved with. Codependency patterns have influenced each of those relationships. As part of the healing process you will be called upon to untangle the relationships, call to mind the persons both living and dead, and make peace individually with each one in an appropriate way.

Our clinic frequently serves adults who were adopted or who lived in foster care. We counsel that they must come to terms with both their adoptive parents and their biological parents, whether they know them or not. Any foster families of which they've been a part, mentors, coaches, or teachers who exercised strong influence in their lives—the list goes on. It is fascinating how many families these clients have been part of.

Multiple marriages, however brief, are each a very significant family, which represent a grouping into which powerful feelings are bound.

"That was a terrible marriage," a client may complain. "I don't even want to think about it. Besides, it only lasted six weeks. It's behind me now. You can't call that significant."

Yes, you can. Right there we blow the whistle. "Back up. We'd better talk about this."

A major task is to help people realize how many families they have, past and present, how many families they lived in, and to what extent codependency can spill over into each and every one of those groupings.

Consider Marian Walsh, an intelligent and attractive woman, who had been a victim of incest by her father. She came to us because she was about to get fired from another job. She's a competent professional woman, a credit to any company. And yet, time and again she got the boot. On the one hand she always tried her hardest to keep the job and perform well. And yet, on the other, she always seemed to do something to sabotage it. Often it was something she neither recognized nor anticipated. When she came to us she already harbored the sneaking suspicion the problem ran a lot deeper than just job competence, for she also encountered troubles in her church families. In four years she had joined, and then for various reasons unjoined, three major churches. She claimed persecution because of her divorce, but her denomination is actually very tolerant of divorce.

Part of what we helped her see was that she still carried tremendous resentment and unresolved anger toward her father. These powerful, negative feelings affected her family of origin, her job family, her church family, her family of procreation. Her churches were headed by males. In every job, she worked under male superiors somewhere in the managerial chain, usually as her immediate supervisor. And every time she walked into a work family she developed the same mixed feelings she would get stepping into her family of origin. She was at once trying to please Dad and live up to his expectations, and simultaneously outraged at Dad, desperate to somehow pay him back. Bosses became father figures, and with every job came all that heavy baggage.

Marian's is not a pleasant story neatly tied in a bow. We worked with her awhile, then referred her to a center nearer her home that specializes in the treatment of codependency, for Marian simply could not handle the devastation wrought in her past. As she came to grips with the pain and fury, she began to crater—a devastating collapse from the top down. She still cannot comfortably face the truth. It will be years before she can begin to build solid ties with work and church families. Marriage? Not yet. Not for Marian.

YOUR RELATIONSHIP INVENTORY

Bring your relationships into clear and deliberate focus. Caution: there will be none of this "Tee hee. Oh, this one's too silly to mention." Again you are not to pass judgment, assigning right or wrong or arbitrarily dismissing a memory as being irrelevant or perhaps even embarrassing. You must be conscientious and thorough, as is the clerk who accessions the finds from the dig, for this inventory will become a key piece in your personal recovery puzzle.

Some patients can paint their inventories in broad strokes. Ask them to talk about all the significant people in their lives and they tick them off one after the other. The relative importance of various relationships becomes clear quickly.

Others, though, need a little more attention to detail. In counsel, if we pick up a particular problem early in the therapeutic process, we may probe deeper, ask for greater detail in some certain part of the inventory.

For example, Jerri Aynes grew up with a physically abusive father. By the age of twenty-nine she weighed a hundred and ninety-five pounds and had become emotionally involved with seven abusive men in a row. In her first session with us she sported a black eye. Even before coming to us she had obviously made some progress. Rather than insisting she walked into a door, as she would have a year ago, she now admitted her boyfriend had slugged her.

For two sessions we listened to her story. On the third we gave her a written assignment: "Write down the first names of all the important men in your life. List them chronologically. For each one, note how you were hurt, how you supported that person, and what attracted you to him."

"For *all* of them?"

"Every one."

It took Jerri two weeks of pondering before she was satisfied her list was complete. Then we sat down with the list and in a marathon session talked about every name.

"Now Larry here, my sophomore year of high school; he was a pill. He was overweight, too, and I felt comfortable around him. We did homework assignments together, pigged out on ice cream sundaes together. He was the only one who didn't try to hurt me. But he had to move away. His father's in the army. We lost track, you know?"

"He was never abusive."

"Never raised a hand. Didn't even argue much."

"When you went for ice cream, who paid?"

"He did. Always insisted on the biggest they had, too."

"Who profited more from the homework sessions, you or him?"

"Him. That's why I put it in the 'how were you supportive?' column. He wasn't real sharp in school and I was an A student."

"Did you date on other than homework sessions?"

Jerri had to think about that a few moments, dredging the far recesses of her memory. "No, not really."

"What did he offer you emotionally? What did he do for you that was just for you?"

She stiffened, frowning. "Oh come on. Stop and think. I was the fat girl. I didn't get the dates or the praise, I got the jokes. Larry was willing to be seen with me and I was willing to settle for that. You don't know what it's like to be the fat girl."

"We were talking about kinds of active and passive abuse last week, do you remember? Lost childhood issues? We looked at them in the light of the parent/child relationship. Now consider them in regard to boyfriend/girlfriend."

"I don't get it."

"Larry used you for his advantage, taking what he wanted and giving nothing in return. Even when he treated you, it wasn't a treat conducive to your health or well-being. He fed you fat food, in fat quantities—almost deliberately, it seems, as if he wanted to be sure you stayed fat along with him. He was unsupportive and unavailable emotionally. Does that ring any bells?"

"Passive abuse, right?"

Right.

As so often happens, this act of walking through the inventory produced startling revelations for Jerri. Recurring patterns literally jumped off the page, not just for the therapist but for the patient as well.

Dave Johnson's father was alcoholic. The only way his mother could cope was with tranquilizers. Since the age of seven Dave had been the little man of the family, picking up the slack where Dad and Mom couldn't cut it. Now, six years after leaving home he was dependable, a college graduate and a good worker, a fine-looking young man with a tousled mop of dark blond hair.

And he was on his fourth serious girlfriend. The other three had decided not to marry him after all. Now Sue, the latest, had just declined his proposal. What was wrong with him? Why couldn't he attract a girl enough to marry her, settle down, and build the nice little family he dreamt of?

At first, Dave saw no similarity at all in the two latest women of his life, Sue and Annie. He sat across the desk from his counselor and studied the list.

"Sue, here, is very cultural. Refined. She took seven years of ballet." He smiled. "Oh, you should watch her move! Annie, though, is not cultured. She's an athlete, but without the grace. In fact, she's the kind of athlete you'd expect in a weight-lifting commercial. She'd laugh her head off at ballet."

"External appearances?"

"No similarity in coloring, build, manner of movement."

"Personalities?"

"Sue is reserved. Quiet. She's not the least expressive. Annie is very outgoing, but only to a point. She lets you a few inches below the surface and there she builds a wall. She's very protective of her private thoughts."

"Would you say, then, that both women have great difficulty achieving intimacy?"

Dave nodded. "Good assessment, yes. In fact, I'd venture that's their only common denominator."

"How about the others? Emotionally demonstrative?"

The light bulb flared on. Every woman Dave gravitated toward, although they dwelt at polar extremes in many ways, shared the common trait of being incapable of emotional intimacy. Here was that repetition compulsion back again. Dave's father and mother, strung out on booze and pills respectively, had both been unavailable to him emotionally. He grew up in an emotional vacuum that he was now unconsciously recreating in every relationship. Note, too, that the women he found attractive all had their own codependent problems with intimacy. That codependent radar was in full working order, blipping away in both directions.

You as a reader probably have no therapist to provide knowledgeable interaction. However, such an inventory of relationships may lead you to a great deal of self-awareness. Prepare your list and examine it carefully, deliberately trying to pick out patterns. If you can share the process with a trusted friend, pastoral counselor, or similar confidante, the list might bear further fruit. Most particularly, share it in private conversation with God. He remembers those people better than you do. He can provide insight. The goal is to seek and find recurring themes in your relationships.

This is why finding patterns is invaluable. The repetition compulsion generated by significant unfinished emotional business, as illustrated by the case of Dave Johnson, will echo through all the intimate relationships of your life. That echo of repeating patterns can lead us back to the voices of past ghosts, that at last we might still them.

CHAPTER FOURTEEN

Breaking the Addiction Cycle

STAGE THREE: ADDICTION CONTROL

The fellow knew he was an alcoholic. He openly admitted to abusing alcohol. But was treatment worth the sacrifice? "Okay," he told us, "I'll make you a deal. I'll come in for six months. If you can help me find out why I drink, then I'll stop."

We turned him down. "Sorry. We can't work with you on that premise. If you continue to drink, you'll erode and wash out any progress we would make."

Any major addiction, compulsion, or obsession is a massive distraction. A hypnotic message plays twenty-four hours a day, for addictions are a form of deep self-hypnosis, a spell, if you will, cast by the lost childhood experience. To the anorexic: "You're still not thin enough." To the substance abuser: "You're nothing. You need another drink or fix." To the workaholic: "Prove yourself! Get this next thing finished." We must first pull the person out of that hypnotic spell and thus break its cycling, gripping distraction.

Hypnosis? Yes. The old Marx brothers' way to create a hypnotic trance is to swing a pocket watch back and forth in front of the subject's eyes. Apparently the technique works well on Daffy Duck, Sylvester Cat, and Bugs Bunny, too; they go into hypnosis that way in lots of old cartoons. Repetition, the swinging pendulum, becomes hypnotic, and the addiction cycle we are now familiar with is extremely hypnotic for that reason.

This is why a client caught up in some kind of ongoing addiction must, as part of the recovery process, go into at least a temporary abstinence from the addictive agent or behavior. When patients come in with alcoholism as part of their codependent behavior complex, we are happy to work with them, but we insist they dry out. If they need hospitalization and detox, so be it. Only while the addict is abstaining, we have learned, can we work together and make good progress. If the person continues in the addiction, we end up wasting each other's time.

Again we caution you. If you are in the grips of addiction to alcohol or drugs—any chemical dependency—that addiction must be interrupted. And for your safety it should be done under medical supervision.

The need to dry out, as it were, is essential clear across the board of addictions. Eating disorders must be brought into a state of arrest. A sexual addiction or extramarital affair must be halted. And yes, we do get offers of "deals" such as: "If you can heal my marriage and shape up my terrible spouse, I'll give up my outside lover."

When an obvious compulsion problem such as substance abuse is the issue, the lines are clear, firmly drawn. The lines become fuzzy when the problem is an outrageously codependent relationship. And yet, a strongly codependent relationship is just as taxing and damaging as substance abuse.

You remember Brad and Joan, the couple with the poor, put-upon exercycle. Brad, bless him, was able to give up dating Joan for about three months last year. During those three months he made splendid progress both in individual and in group therapy. He was beginning to gain a full appreciation of what was making himself tick, and he was well on the road to recovery. Then Joan called. Like a drunk falling off the wagon, he went on a bender. Suddenly they were back together, fighting again, abusive toward each other. During the six weeks following, the therapy came to a standstill, and Brad's happi-

THE TEN STAGES OF
THE RECOVERY PROCESS

1. EXPLORATION AND DISCOVERY
You will explore your past and present to discover the truth about you.

2. RELATIONSHIP HISTORY/INVENTORY
You'll examine and perhaps reset your personal boundaries.

3. ADDICTION CONTROL
You'll get a handle on your addictions and compulsions and take the first steps toward mastering them.

4. LEAVING HOME AND SAYING GOODBYE
You'll say the goodbyes appropriate to healing. You may think you did that years ago. Probably you didn't.

5. GRIEVING YOUR LOSS
Grieving is both the bottom of the curve, the very pits of your emotions and feelings, and also the start upward. It's almost like your dentist hanging up his drill. You know he's not done yet, but the worst is over.

6. NEW SELF-PERCEPTIONS
You will gain fresh perceptions about yourself and make new decisions. What an eye-opener this stage is!

7. NEW EXPERIENCES
You will build a foundation of new experiences to bolster the decisions you've just made.

8. REPARENTING
You will rebuild your past in a sense, and also the present and future, as you become involved in what we call reparenting.

9. RELATIONSHIP ACCOUNTABILITY
You will establish accountability for your new and refreshed personal relationships.

10. MAINTENANCE
You will embark on a maintenance program that will keep you on the track for the remainder of your life.

ness and emotional attitude deteriorated markedly. Even his physical appearance nosedived.

The healing of codependency is not just limited to marriages in progress. The single who looks to wed one day can heal the marriage before the fact, in every sense of the word. Almost never does a couple come into premarital therapy. They wait until the marriage has become uncontrollably acrimonious and bitter, making counsel a move of last resort. And yet, in many cases, marriages could have been sweetened immeasurably simply by nipping problems in the bud.

If you have not yet married, but are assuming that eventually you might, treat the material on marriage here just as carefully and seriously as any other help. To heal a marriage, you see, you must begin by healing yourself. And that can happen before or after the wedding. So when we talk about marriage relationships, apply the information to yourself just as vigorously as you would apply help in any other venue.

Because Brad and Joan were as yet unmarried, we could comfortably counsel separation to the benefit of them both. When the man and woman are husband and wife, and especially when they are Christians who eschew divorce for reasons of faith, the picture turns murky in a hurry.

Understandably, our counsel must be carefully tailored to each individual situation; rote steps or standardized actions won't serve here. We address couples in any of a variety of ways.

"We're most happy to work with you, but we perceive you both are locked into a very unhealthy codependent intertwining. You love not by choice but by need. Unless you can give yourself *some sort of a time out from this,* slow this down and build healthy boundaries, your mutual addiction is going to rampage roughshod over any psychotherapeutic progress. And unless you make healing progress, your union is going to remain unsatisfying, frustrating, and spiritually unproductive."

What do we have in mind when we counsel "time out"? The theory is to break the addiction cycle, whatever that takes. The practice can take many forms. The object is to suggest specific boundaries by which the couple may lovingly put some space between themselves. Without those spaces they cannot begin their own individual recoveries.

SETTING BOUNDARIES

In an extreme case (as for example if Brad and Joan were married) where the man and wife are literally or figuratively constantly at each other's throats, we may suggest actual temporary separation. In dangerous cases of physical abuse, that's normally the necessary first step. Never is this suggested as a trial separation preparatory to divorce. Rather it's a means of prying apart those two dotted-line circles long enough to help them each become a complete circle, or more nearly so.

The codependency may be vicious, short of being physically abusive. Accusations, finger-pointing, mutual blame are so intense that we must work on some structured way in which the two people can leave each other alone. At the same time we urge both parties to independently become very active in the ten-stage process of finding and straightening the bottom layer of the cake. To accomplish that we may set strict guidelines to be followed during therapy, often as a condition of therapy. Here again, decisions and actions must be tailor-made for each couple. From there we seek out some of the codependent links that must be interrupted.

These are some of the classes of boundaries we might recommend for embattled couples in a committed marriage. As healing advances, the couple might move from one sort of boundary into another.

Brief Residential Separation. A couple in our counsel now are at once extremely grasping and also extremely verbally abusive toward each other. We suggested an in-house separation wherein they might leave each other alone long enough to commence healing. Invariably, one spouse would end up literally pursuing the other through the house, loudly demanding that the issues be discussed and resolved. Only when one of them moved out temporarily did we begin to make any progress whatever. They are now able to live in the same house again without constant acrimony, but it took intense work.

Temporary Cessation of Sexual Involvement. The sexual union is a powerful force. It bonds a marriage together as nothing else can. But when spouses use it as a lever to gain concessions, or make it a control issue, the force can become destructive. Sometimes the only way to open a window of opportunity for healing is to counsel temporary abstinence. Sexual involvement can be a major distraction.

Time Limits on Exposure to Each Other. "We're okay for an hour or so, but then we start getting to each other."

"I can stay at my in-laws' for three days and we get along. But that fourth day, it always falls apart."

"I didn't realize how incommunicative he was until we had to ride in the car three days. We never had a solid three-day dose of each other before."

We frequently counsel warring couples to develop outside interests as a means of temporarily limiting contact with each other. This is especially helpful in those codependent unions in which the spouses are tightly enmeshed in each other. Couples in a too-close-for-comfort situation might be asked to whip out their appointment books and schedule their days (including time together) in such a way that contact is controlled. They might also reschedule their workdays to avoid contact when both are weary or trail-worn.

Set Specific Physical and Verbal Abuse Boundaries. "If such-and-so happens, regardless of the circumstance, the victimized spouse leaves immediately." We have recommended that boundary on occasion when a spouse or other family member is endangered or intimidated. We recommend it also when the victimized spouse is prone to retaliate in kind.

Were Brad and Joan married, this might be a good boundary for them to set in order to stop their shouting matches and physical battles. Remember, the addiction cycle must be broken before healing can proceed.

Suspend Victimization. When a spouse blames, accuses, and/or punishes the mate, that is victimization. It's not a matter of who is right or wrong. It's a matter of breaking the codependent behavior patterns. One of our clients, extremely self-righteous, constantly explained to his wife how her faults were spoiling their marriage. It was very difficult for him to exercise the necessary abstention by simply keeping his mouth shut.

Suspend Any Outside Romantic Interest or Affair

Immediately. Period. The end. No "ifs," "ands," or "buts."

Suspend Individual Compulsions. This is a primary step in individual healing. But because spouses in a committed marriage are so closely united, the actions of one profoundly influence the union, and we therefore consider it here as well.

Should you and your spouse enter into counsel, we might spend several sessions listening to you as a couple. If major codependency problems surface, we may break off combined counseling in order to work with each of you independently. Later (sometimes soon, sometimes six months from now), we will all come back together into a couples counseling situation, this time with the enriched insight that promises good fruit.

In the case of Brad and Joan separation was crucial. With John and Gladys Jordan, separation would be the worst approach, because their problem was a severe inability to communicate. Identifying and overcoming those loud ghosts paved the way to healing. But they then had to learn how to hear each other. That takes practice and practice requires proximity—the opportunity to communicate.

Read the Dear Abby and Ann Landers columns, and you'll find a smorgasbord of codependency problems. A common letter, usually from a young woman, will say something like this:

Dear Ann,

A couple months ago during an argument my boyfriend hit me. Right away he felt very sorry and apologized. He promised it would never happen again, but last week it did. Ann, this man is a wonderful person and I love him, but everyone says I should quit seeing him. What should I do?

Signed, Bruised in Biloxi

Or this:

Dear Abby,

My husband is having an affair with his secretary. He says he'll go to a marriage counselor if I do, but I'm too heartsick. It's not me who is unfaithful, and I know he's still seeing her. So don't tell me to get counseling like you tell everyone else. What can I do?

Signed, Betrayed in Birmingham

What would be your advice to these two ladies? Write it in the form of a letter—brief and pithy if possible, long and detailed if necessary.

AVOIDING THE NEW YEAR'S RESOLUTION SYNDROME

11:55 P.M., December 31. I firmly resolve to limit my calorie intake to 1800 or less and give up sugar cookies. I also resolve to exercise daily and hit the gym at least twice a week.

9:05 A.M., January 2. I take out a lifetime membership at the local fitness center.

1:45 P.M., January 11. I eat four sugar cookies at an office potluck.

April. I'm back to eating as much as I used to eat or more; I eat sugar cookies almost every day and I haven't been to the fitness center in weeks.

That's the New Year's resolution syndrome. Ah, such good intentions, but everyone knows where they pave the way to. Setting boundaries, halting addictions, and curbing compulsions are all lovely on paper. Played out in real life, they are beyond your ability to maintain. At this point, God's power is essential. Addictions and boundaries simply do not yield to pure will, not even so sturdy a will as yours. You must have God's enablement in this.

For the alcohol abuser, the wife-beater, or the workaholic, the addiction requiring arrest is fairly clear. When everything a couple says to each other ends in shouting and anger, the need for boundaries is obvious. But what about someone like Sean McCurdy, the salesman who could hold a job for only a short time? His addiction, so to speak, was not so clear-cut.

The telling of his story and his relationship inventory revealed that he was unconsciously seeing his bosses as surrogate fathers. Knowing the problem, however, is far short of devising a solution. For Sean, as for anyone else, abstinence is a day to day, minute by minute thing. A broad, sweeping "I shall do such-and-so no more," must be implemented in the much narrower confines of the moment.

Sean did three things, specifically. First, he prayed daily for insight and the strength to act upon it. Prayer was not an easy thing for him. He had never been what he called "the religious type." The first few weeks he had to prop a 3×5 card against his alarm clock to remind himself. Second, each time he made contact with his boss, however casual that contact might be, he mentally reminded himself, "This man is not perfect and I have no right to expect him to be. I must be more tolerant of human error." Note that he did not intend to change the boss. He worked to change himself. And last, Sean inventoried his relationship with his boss and workmates frequently, staying alert for the troubles that had cropped up before. His problem temporarily halted, he could move on to the next stages of healing.

What problems should you put on hold? Go back to stages one and two, Exploration and Discovery and the Relationship Inventory, and consider carefully what you came up with. What compulsive behavior(s) can you call your own? And, as the action needed in stage three (Addiction Control), what are you going to do about it *now?*

The groundwork thus laid, you are now ready for stage four, Leaving Home and Saying Goodbye. It may sound like a snap, something you did years ago. Actually, it's an elaborate stage that must be performed thoroughly and completely.

CHAPTER FIFTEEN

Leaving Home and Saying Goodbye

She was a gorgeous girl, petite and graceful. At five-foot-two, she couldn't weigh more than eighty-five pounds. Her blond hair shone, even on such a dull and overcast afternoon. The cabbie who had brought her to this cemetery leaned against his yellow taxi and watched her walk purposefully out among the markers, a small parcel in her hand. What was she up to?

She stopped at a recent grave.

MARIAN HOLT

BELOVED WIFE OF JAMES

MOTHER OF PATRICE

LAID TO REST THIS 6th DAY OF

A mound of flowers obscured the rest of the engraving.

"Hello, Momma." She took a deep breath. "I don't exactly know what I'm doing here, but I'm determined to do it. There are some things I never told you before you died, and I should have. So I'm telling you now." The tiny shoulders shrugged and she smiled faintly. "Better late than never, right, Momma?"

A damp breeze picked up, riffling the loose petals of the silk poppies.

"For one thing, I never told you how much I appreciate your love. That was the biggest thing in your existence—making sure Daddy and I were cared for. You gave us your whole life. I'm very grateful for your sacrifice.

"But, uh . . . it wasn't all rosy, Momma. Like being clean, for instance. When you gave me two and three baths a day when I was little, I about screamed. Then I got used to it. By high school, when you were making me shower morning *and* evening, I was numb to it. I wish now you hadn't bleached my hair since I was eight. 'Mousy, dirty brown' you called it. I'm thinking about dyeing it the color of the roots and letting it grow back in its natural shade, Momma. I'm sure you'd have a fit—if you could—and you know? Here I am twenty-six years old, and this is the first time I've ever thought about doing something you might not like.

"I threw away the nailbrush. You never knew, because I never told you, how bitterly I resented scrubbing my finger-nails before every meal. I resented the whole cleanliness and tidiness thing, especially when I watched all my friends play in dirt or in the sandbox or outside when it was raining, and I couldn't.

"And the enemas you gave me when I didn't go on schedule. I was fourteen years old, Momma, and you still made me show you my B.M. every morning. I realize you meant it in love, but I was so miserable." Her voice rose. "I was so messed up, miserable! And you had such a lock on my thoughts, I didn't even know how unhappy I was. I only knew about the tummy aches and the headaches and you constantly harping at me not to get dirty. Momma, I . . ."

The wind did its riffling in silence for a while until she could pull herself back together.

"I love you, Momma, but I hate what you did to me. Anyway, I'm here to tell you those things and also to tell you I'm starting to get my life together, finally, after all these years. I have the anorexia pretty much under control. At least now I can make myself eat. I'm clean; no more coke. And because I'm in group therapy the boss said he won't fire me after all, at least for a while. So it's coming together.

"And I'm here to say goodbye too. You wouldn't let me do that before, when you found out about the cancer. You wouldn't let any of us talk about it. Did you really believe you might beat it, or was it like when I was in high school and I'd get these mad crushes on boys, and get my heart broken, and have to keep it all to myself because you called it nonsense? It seems that any feelings at all were nonsense to you. I feel sorry for you, Momma, for the emptiness in your life. The sterility. That's what it was. I can do that now, at last; feel things, I mean.

"So, uh . . . goodbye, Momma. I love you. I really do. And one other thing. It's a, well, a symbol, you know? The anorexia—you said that was nonsense, too, but I almost died with it, a few weeks after you left us. And this package symbolizes that I've said goodbye to that, too."

She sobbed to herself a few moments, whispered one last goodbye, and laid her little parcel on the marker. She walked back to the waiting taxi and sat in the backseat, sobbing uncontrollably as the cabbie drove away.

In the parcel was a candy bar.

STAGE FOUR: LEAVING HOME AND SAYING GOODBYE

A key step in recovery from codependency sounds so simple—leaving home. Why, nothing to it, right? Everyone does that. Except that it isn't one isolated event; it takes place in stages, and not everyone accomplishes it. Also, there are two separate ways in which we must leave home: we have to make certain we have genuinely left the family of origin, saying goodbye to Mom and Dad. And we must literally say goodbye to false security symbols. Neither step is easy.

In our culture the children's dependence usually ends in late teens or early twenties. By then they're through school, on their own, and have probably begun a family. It's not quite that simple, though. There are many levels of independence and they don't all happen simultaneously. Children achieve residential independence by leaving the actual parental home. They may, however, still be totally dependent financially, as for example when an eighteen-year-old goes away to college.

Social independence is completed when children develop a circle of friends that are their own. The friends may know the parents or share the parents' friendship, but the children count them friends for their own sakes. Vocationally independent children pursue their own careers. Spiritually independent children have literally separated themselves in spirit. This includes establishing their own sets of beliefs and mores, which may not reflect the parents'. None of these steps to complete independence need be made simultaneously.

Then, somewhere in their mid-twenties or early thirties, the children take the final step, making the separation complete and clean, by leaving home emotionally. Apparently children need a few years out there on their own in order to build a solid foundation of confidence before tackling this final separation. Achieving emotional independence is wrenching. It's the last hurrah of childhood, the final vestige of times past. Making the jump takes strength and guts.

There are splendid rewards for persevering with that final break. It is ultimately rewarding to emerge from the shadow of the original family into full status as an independent adult. It enables one to lead a healthy, nonaddictive, productive life of one's own.

There is a long-term benefit, too—an eternally long-term advantage. Pioneering psychologist Carl Jung, in discussing the second half of life, claimed that most people cannot begin to deeply know God until they are in their mid-thirties. Although we do not agree with many of Jung's premises, we recognize the spiritual and emotional benefits that accrue from leaving home. Jung asserts they must first leave home and disconnect emotionally and spiritually from their mother and father. Then they are free to move into a much deeper, richer, spiritual walk with God.

HEALTHY VS. CODEPENDENT

We are, after all, born into families so that we might eventually leave them. In a sense, baby begins leaving home at birth. Independence grows daily. Learning to walk unaided, exploring, embarking upon the terrible twos, entering first grade, getting that driver's license, leaving home physically, and on and on leads eventually to graduation into the heavenly family.

The problem is, codependents never seem to make that final break. They get hung up at some stage short of completion of the independence process. This is another reason we at the clinic so often see codependents during a mid-life crisis. It would certainly seem they've left home; they live apart, they have the college degree, perhaps a family of their own, a career. . . . Somewhere in mid-life the whole thing begins to unravel. The final break was never made, the final step not taken. Quite often it boils down to goodbyes that have been left unsaid.

There are two kinds of goodbyes and this stage requires both. There is the fond farewell: "Goodbye, I'm off on my journey now. I'll see you when I see you." And then there's the acerbic "Goodbye, you creep. Get out of my life!" When you say goodbye to false security symbols, it will be in that latter sense of "I am turning my back on you forever." Saying goodbye to parents has none of that finality. This is not a severing of all ties but rather a declaration of independence. It is the goodbye said prior to going on a trip. "I am still your child, but I'm off on my own now. From now on if I come to see you at your home I will be not an emotional resident but a visitor." This sort of goodbye pertains whether the parent is living or deceased.

How do you know if you've emotionally left home? It's not always easy to tell. What is appropriate or necessary behavior for one person might be clinging and dependent for another. For example, Lisa calls her frail old mother every morning around nine. It's a reasonable safety precaution. Should Mom fail to answer the phone, Lisa would drive right over there to make certain Mom wasn't sick or fallen down. In contrast there's Brad—yes, our Brad with the exercycle. He calls his Mom every day, too, but she's as healthy as he is. He has a powerful need to touch base with her, to affirm his day and his thoughts. Lisa is not relating codependently to Mommy. Brad is. He has not left home.

THE CRITERIA FOR BEING HOME

For adults with codependent problems we may do a brief inventory of the connections they hold with their family of origin. What medical professionals call a "gimme"—an almost sure sign—is ongoing financial subsidy. So very often, adults who have not left home emotionally still maintain some financial dependence. For instance at a group therapy session on a Saturday morning, we quizzed adult children ranging from mid-twenties to mid-thirties, all of them with codependency problems. As we went around the room, every one of them admitted receiving some financial aid from their parents. Residentially they had left the nest. But Momma and Papa Bird were still providing the worms.

Adult codependents may have trouble leaving the nest at all. They bravely declare their independence and move out, often to marry. But something goes wrong. Crisis descends. They move back in. On an early episode of the Bill Cosby show, wife Claire briefly considered having one more baby. Her mother counseled against it. "You'll be too old." "You mean when they leave home?" "No, when they move back in with their kids." The concept was played to comic effect but the thought was there. Sometimes baby birds seek the security of the old home nest.

Another indicator of whether you have left home emotionally is codependent behavior itself. Dependent behaviors usually stop when that emotional goodbye is made, the very reason the act of leaving home *must* be completed. Consider the contrasts in Lisa and Brad. If Mom's circumstances change, Lisa will no longer have to call her daily. Lisa doesn't need that fix. Brad does. He is so wrapped up in his Mom that he can never let it rest. If she doesn't call him by five or so, he's on the phone to her.

Here again, altering the obsessive or compulsive behavior paves the way to change and healing. We counsel Brad to limit calls and letters to his Mom, not so much to end symptomatic behavior as to break that addiction cycle.

An excellent example is Sophia, a woman in her late forties. Sophia came to us when she was already in the throes of a particularly messy divorce. She was still, at that age, highly dependent upon her parents, who were in their eighties. She maintained daily phone contact and wrote frequently because deep inside she felt, *I can't make it through the day without reporting to Mom and Dad how I'm doing. I have to get my fix from them*. She was hooked on their affirmation. So we met with both sides of the generation split, her and her parents, and secured an agreement. Both parties promised to limit phone contact and we set an upper limit to permissible postage costs. Sophia is still working on making that final emotional break, but now she doesn't have the addiction cycle dragging her backwards.

"Ah," said Kim Park, as she sat in counsel in our offices. "That's not a problem with me. My father ended contact with me over six years ago, and by choice I have not attempted contact with him. The goodbyes were said long ago."

No, not exactly. Kim's situation is, in an important sense, the same as failure to leave home physically. Rebelliously breaking all ties with the nest is a good indicator that the appropriate emotional goodbyes have not been said. Kim is still in an emotional bondage to her family of origin. The goal of health is always balance in relationships, avoiding estrangement as much as enmeshment.

THE ACT OF GOODBYE

How do you make that final emotional break if it hasn't been done already? The easiest and least exotic method is to sit down and talk to your parents. Discuss your life and literally say goodbye. In many cases, though, this can't be done. Perhaps one or both parents died or divorced and left your life before that important break was made. It still must be made, though. Perhaps, as in Kim's case, the parents refuse to speak to the child or refuse to participate in what is an experience as wrenching for them as for the child. Perhaps physical distance separates them. If Dad went to Kuala Lumpur and Mom works in Buenos Aires and the child lives in Kalamazoo, contact is difficult if not impossible.

One technique often used by therapists to make contact with uncontactable persons may be useful to you. Sit down in a chair and place an empty chair in front of you, facing you. Mom is sitting in that chair. So talk to her. Tell her what it was like to grow up in her home. Talk about the pain, the joy, the pride and frustrations. Now you may successfully begin the process of saying goodbye. Next put Dad in the chair. Do the same thing with him.

Patrice Holt, the petite blond in the cemetery at the beginning of this chapter, demonstrates another method. She visited the gravesite and literally made her formal goodbye. Quite frequently this technique brings highly charged emotions pouring forth, a marvelous catharsis of soul and spirit.

Still another method is the time-honored written letter. Frequently persons who cannot say what they feel can put it into a letter to the parent or parents. Obviously, if the parent is deceased, the writer is never going to mail it; rain and dark of night may not stay the noble carriers from their appointed rounds, but the black veil does. When the parent is living, we suggest modifying the letter-writing procedure somewhat.

When a patient in our counsel chooses to communicate with a letter, we request that the person actually write two letters. The first, in regular letter format (date, Dear Mom, body, closing, signature), is *not* under any circumstances to be mailed. In this draft we urge the patient to be as expressive as possible. Let it all hang out, as the saying goes—love, tenderness, anger, bitterness, admiration, frustration, all of it. Almost always, the very act of casting this draft unleashes memories and emotions important to the client's recovery.

The second draft, which may or may not be mailed to the parent as the client prefers, is usually much gentler, more tactful, less expressive. If unresolved bitterness is surfacing at this time, though, this draft might also be filled with invective. Its purpose, however, is to be a document that could comfortably be mailed, whether it ever will or not. If you are an adoptee, you may wish to use this form of expression to say goodbye to all your parents, biological and adoptive, alive or dead.

So what, you ask, ever happened to the good old Judeo-Christian ethic of honoring thy parents? Here's this letter which, if you're codependent, may be hot enough to be delivered in a bucket of sand. Isn't that dishonoring?

No. We never ever ask clients to dishonor their parents. Not only does God forbid that, it's demeaning to parent and child alike. No dishonor, no insult, no belittling. Description of hurts; yes. Praise where praise is due; yes. Expression of how you feel; yes. Troweling it on in an exaggerated victim/martyr role; no!

The greatest honor you can give your parents is to become all the person God intended you to be. If unfinished business, emotional baggage, hinders your growth as a Christian, it is important that you shed that baggage. That means you must lovingly but firmly deal with that business. We can't think of a better way to honor parents than to develop your natural gifts.

The notion of emotionally leaving home is nothing new. The "leave your parents and cleave to your wife" principle goes clear back to Genesis 2:24. As you say that fond farewell to Mom and Dad, you enjoy better intimate relationships with other persons in your life—spouse, kids, co-workers—in addition to that deeper relationship with God already mentioned.

There is a sad paradox in this leaving home concept. Co-dependents, the persons most in need of putting the original family behind them, have the greatest difficulty making the break. Goodbyes and transitions are never easy for a healthy child. The first day of school, graduation, marriage may all bring a tear or two. Such events are poignant but do-able. Healthy families release each other. Appropriate goodbyes are difficult, bordering on impossible, for persons emerging from a painful, dysfunctional, abusive childhood.

"That's crazy!" these people say. "It doesn't make any sense. Things were so painful back then. Why am I still so bound up in it when superficially it looks so easy to just get out? And yet I see it's true."

The answer in part you already know—the repetition compulsion, that overpowering sense that something back there is still unfinished. If the codependent leaves home, he/she can't fix it. Another answer is that codependents tend to get hung up on some element of the complex leaving-home process and just sit there forever.

Codependents also suffer the bondage of guilt or shame much more so than do healthier adult children. Because they harbor so much anger and resentment, they feel compelled to stay with that family of origin, to remain tied to the source of that anger, to restage it. Even if the anger remains buried—in fact, especially if the anger remains buried—it still forms a powerful bond of high energy emotion.

Harold Walker, a stock broker who is in his late forties, is an example of such buried anger. In his counsel with us he swears up and down that this anger business is baloney; he doesn't feel bitter toward his alcoholic mother. He also denies any anger directed at his wife or family. But during the past twenty years, he has put his family through bankruptcy multiple times. He has had homes and cars repossessed. His wife finally and reluctantly decided to divorce him when he began robbing from the children's trust funds. Even though he denies any anger, it is obvious from the outside that he's taking out tremendous anger on his wife and kids. Until he can get past this, he and they are doomed to misery and continuing financial crisis.

There is one other step to stage four—saying goodbye to false security symbols. Another word for them might be *false idols*. And this time *goodbye* really means goodbye forever. It must be permanent. A false security symbol is anything functioning in your life as something revered, something to which you are inappropriately devoted. Saying goodbye does not necessarily mean you completely expunge that thing from your life. It means saying a firm goodbye to the idolatrous aspect.

Patrice Holt did it both mentally and symbolically when she laid the candy bar on her mother's grave. As an anorexic, she was obsessed with the thought of food. She compulsively controlled it. But she could not simply put it out of her life. Not only is that physically impossible, she nearly died doing that very thing. It was food's stranglehold on her life and health that was her problem.

In Dallas, wealth and influence are prominent issues. In the past, some of our clients had to say goodbye to the inordinate hold wealth and power had on their lives. They had to put away the primacy of money. As part of their recovery they had to be able to honestly say, "I can take it or leave it." Then came the collapse of the oil boom. Suddenly it wasn't academic anymore. Some of them had to say goodbye to some major dollars.

False security symbols. Idols.

The notion is at least two millennia old. Jesus called upon the young man in Matthew 19:16–22 to make money secondary in his life. The lad couldn't do it.

It's an easy enough thing to tell persons what must be done.

It's quite another to help them in practical ways to accomplish it.

This doesn't sound very exotic or wonderful, but in counsel we talk about it. More importantly we get our patients to talk about it. We encourage discussion of two things: admission that these false idols have an unhealthy grip on them, and a commitment to do something about it. You may well find it productive to discuss the matter with yourself, either mentally or aloud. The best route, of course, is to find a trusted friend or counselor with whom to talk it out. And whomever else you find to share your determination to say your goodbyes, by all means do so with God.

Everybody has parents; you don't glibly shed them. When you say the appropriate and deliberate goodbye to your parents (and stepparents and foster parents and surrogate parents, if such exist), you must fill the blank parent-space somehow. The correct filler is God, the ultimate parent.

You see, saying goodbye to parents is more than just saying goodbye to parents, for parents are a shadow of God. When you were very small, you viewed them as if they *were* God. Now you are saying that no human being is adequate to kiss the hurt and make it better. You are saying goodbye to the myth that human resources are adequate. That is painful and wrenching. You have arrived at the place where no other human being can be God in your life.

Saying goodbye to those false security symbols is also wrenching, because they are—well, they're dependable. For example, Brad and Joan were always fighting. It wasn't pleasant, but in a very negative way it offered the comfort of familiarity and predictability. The familiar is very hard to give up.

The commitment we request as part of the therapeutic process might take the form of a formal or informal contract. Any method that makes the person accountable is a good method. Are you willing to scale back, to set a boundary, to create distance between yourself and the thing, whatever it is? Find someone to whom you can be accountable, enter the pact, and stick with it.

If things went well with stages one through four—Exploration and Discovery, Relationship Inventory, Addiction

Control, Leaving Home and Saying Goodbye, you have been descending deeper and deeper into painful memories.

This is therapy? you're wondering. You are on the roller coaster now, almost literally, plummeting down the pain-of-recovery curve. No one starts at the tiptop, pain free. Everyone has a certain amount of pain; that's probably what led you to this point in the first place. Screaming, you expose your life and relationships even as you abstain from the anesthesia of the addictions you've been called to give up.

Stage four, saying goodbye and giving up false security symbols, can be frightening as well as extremely painful. By stage five, though, you are at the bottom of the curve. Everything in stages one through four is designed to lead you into greater awareness of pain. The people of Alcoholics Anonymous refer to the bottom of this recovery curve in just those terms— "hitting bottom" or "bottoming out." In stages six through ten we will move back up the curve and get healing underway.

It's important to know you are going to feel worse preparatory to feeling better. Above all, you don't want to give up at the bottom. You've already undergone most of the painful part. No time to quit now!

CHAPTER SIXTEEN

Grieving Your Loss

The child who has to memorize a verse of Scripture for Sunday school every week picks up right away on John 11:35: "Jesus wept." That's it; the whole verse. Piece of cake.

But what an astonishing verse it is! When Jesus' good friend Lazarus fell ill, his sisters Mary and Martha called for Jesus to hurry to Bethany, that He might restore Lazarus to health. Instead He hung back until Lazarus died. He knew what He was going to do. He knew what His father was going to do. Even before He reached the village He knew He was going to be eating dinner with a risen Lazarus that night. And yet, when He entered the house amid all the sorrow, He wept. Indeed, the depth of His grief impressed people accustomed to seeing the crocodile tears of paid mourners.

Grief. It is the part of death played by the living. But there is much more to grief than mourning death. Other losses require the grieving process, including losses buried so deeply and so long ago that they're no longer recognized as such.

STAGE FIVE: GRIEVING YOUR LOSS

The grief process, pioneered by Elizabeth Kubler-Ross and now common knowledge among psychologists, is a largely spontaneous chain of events and feelings. The stages through which every grieving person passes are (1) *shock and denial,* (2) *anger,* (3) *depression,* (4) *bargaining and magic* and, finally, (5) *resolution and acceptance.* To that progression we have added another step. In our frame of reference, *sadness becomes number 5, moving resolution and acceptance to 6.*

Under the normal exercise of grief you don't need a therapist to get through the stages. The codependent, however, tends to become hung up on a step along the way, and then remains stuck there. To advance to a satisfactory conclusion, that person needs guidance from a source such as this book or a counselor. He or she needs to back up through the stages and repeat them as needed until the blockage shakes loose and grief proceeds.

THE GOODNESS OF GRIEF

Grief is essential for the adult child who is codependent, who needs powerfully and emotionally to grieve for all the things brought to awareness in stages one through four. It is very important that the person grieve the details of loss in lost childhood. He or she must also grieve the losses incurred because of addictions, compulsions, and obsessions, past and present.

Silly as it sounds, persons must grieve for certain aspects of healing, as well. Your addictive behaviors and feelings once occupied a significant part of your life. Now they are banished. Grief is appropriate for something that once meant so much to you. In particular, after saying goodbye to the original family pain, you must next grieve the loss of the pain you lived with for so long. Good riddance, perhaps—but what an empty hole it leaves.

As a specific example, let's look again at John and Gladys Jordan. They learned to still the ghosts of the past. Their marriage was infinitely better for it. Still they had to grieve, for giving up the codependent behavior at first felt like a loss. After all, residual anger and the lack of communication had been a big part of their lives for a long time. Ugly as it was, it was comfortable. Familiar. They needed also to grieve over half a lifetime of lost love and affection. Here was a long, savage, bitter loss, a consequence of the codependent behavior, that need not have been.

It is also necessary to grieve secondary losses. The alcoholic who enters a treatment center is asked to build a list of losses consequent to the drinking. Perhaps that person lost a job or promotion, marriage and family, a driver's license. The practice applies to any compulsive behavior. The workaholic must grieve for the time lost to his family, for it can never be replaced. The overeater has the grief of obesity to deal with. Sean McCurdy grieved for all those opportunities to advance his career, which he bungled because of his misplaced obsession. And so on.

ANALYZING LOSSES

If you discovered losses because of your lifestyle, those losses have to be grieved. But how do you know what you lost? Will you grossly overestimate grievances and losses, perhaps finding fault where there is none? "My mother wasn't June Cleaver, so I lost out on all those cookies." Probably not. Codependents almost always go too far the other way. Being such experts at denial and minimization, they underestimate the pain and loss rather than form an overly idealistic picture of what their family life should have been. Even the sexually and physically abused tend to downplay the pain. Remember as you analyze your losses that by nature you're almost certainly minimizing them.

This analysis of loss is not an objective assessment. It is highly subjective, and rightly so, for different people weigh different losses differently. When Mamie Dykes lost fifty dollars at bingo, she didn't care. When she lost a fake cameo brooch worth seven dollars, she grieved deeply, because her daughter now deceased had given it to her. The rule is, if it's a significant loss to you (regardless of the value the world would place upon it), it's a loss.

In summary *there are four areas in which you should grieve,* and appropriately. *One is grief for the original family pain* if there was a high level of abuse or dysfunction in your family of origin. *The second is grief over saying goodbye to Mom and Dad,* which for most codependents and adult children has been delayed or deferred. Having to say goodbye now, so late in life, is particularly grievous.

The third area is grief over the addictions, codependencies, and other coping mechanisms you are abandoning. They were important to you for years, like ugly friends who played dirty tricks on you. But they were friends, none the less; it is right to mourn their loss. *The fourth area is the losses accrued over the years as by-products of your codependency.* Think of the misery, the waste, the errors made, the tears, the pain and friction. Much of that did not have to be: your codependency made it so. And that is very sad.

All these griefs and realizations are converging upon you at once. The angers and resentments, the remorse and the regrets, all have to be expunged. In the hospital we see dramatic cases as patients break open and wash away with tears the pus of old wounds.

There was, for instance, an ex-pastor, a tall, scrawny man with thin gray hair and a perpetual frown. His name was Walter Morgan. He had grown up under a strict, emotionally distant, highly perfectionistic father whom he admired immensely. Walter became very perfectionistic himself. Driven by his codependency, he *had* to be the perfect pastor. He *had* to meet everyone's needs. He most of all *had* to be perfect before God, to win Dad's, or God's affection.

Of course it all eventually came crashing down—the task Walter set himself is impossible. When during treatment he finally got in touch with what was actually happening in his life, and what his life had truly been until now, that quiet, mild-mannered man sat and sobbed. You could hear the mourning three rooms away. It came tumbling out, it crowded its way through the doors of his heart and into sunshine for the first time ever. The wounds of a lifetime he cleansed in a torrent of salty tears.

THE GRIEVING PROCESS

How did Walter Morgan reach that point? His catharsis adhered to a progression you, too, will follow. Although we'll take it in sequence here, you may find that, like many others, you will zip right through some steps easily and may backtrack a bit to handle others. That's normal.

1. *Shock and Denial.* Psychologists believe that many codependents and adult children (some psychologists say all of them) walk around in a chronic state of emotional shock not unlike the first step in the grieving process. These people are hung up right at the beginning, before they've gone far at all. They show all the symptoms of a chronic posthypnotic trance.

You read about living cells in high school: a semipermeable membrane surrounds a nucleus, perhaps a nucleolus, and a lot of itty-bitty organelles that may or may not be contamination from a dirty slide. Various chemicals, such as oxygen, carbon dioxide, nutrients, and wastes enter and leave through the membrane to keep the cell vibrantly alive.

Now let's picture a normal family as being like a cell. It is held together by a healthy, though invisible, membrane. Nutrients and wastes—friends and pets—move in and out through the membrane, but what belongs inside remains safe and intact. There is space in there for the nucleus and nucleolus and all the little organelles to move around. In time the membrane ruptures and what were the organelles leave to become cells themselves.

Not so in a dysfunctional family. If for example the mother is the member who is substance addicted, she sends out shock waves every time her substance abuse disrupts normalcy. When she fails to connect emotionally; when she neglects normal tasks and cleanliness; when she flies into inappropriate rage or dissolves in foolish tears; when she waxes wildly hot and cold in paroxysms of unpredictable change—wave after wave after wave pounds upon the other elements of the cell.

Several things happen as these shock waves radiate through the family cell. Relationships become distorted as people get pushed into corners or actively try to avoid the source of the waves. And around each member, shells or walls (in psychology they are called defense mechanisms) form. Within the cell this protective coating is essential, for it provides a buffer against the pounding waves. In normal families, the persons are not this heavily guarded. Their walls are not so thick that they can't form healthy relationships with others.

Walter Morgan's parents had no such problems as alcohol or chemical dependence. But when his perfectionistic father roared (itself a form of abuse), the reverberations through the family cell built Walter's walls up all the same. As he assessed his relationships in stage two, he came to realize his mother had used him for support from early childhood—emotional incest. More reverberations. Walter emerged from his family cell so encased in protective coatings he was called "undemonstrative" by all who met him. Many people are quiet by nature. Walter was quiet much beyond nature.

In the wall-bound family, not only is leaving home difficult, but the emerging members are burdened with all that extra emotional weight. Once, the protective shell was necessary; now, outside the family, it hampers and just plain damages its wearer. Addictions, obsessions, and compulsions form part of it, but it is mostly emotional frozenness. There is no sense of animation. The intellect functions, but the emotions appear to have been either turned off or drained out.

Walter sounded almost like Mr. Spock of the old *Star Trek* series when you talked to him. He was polite to a fault, precise, logical. Were you to ask him, he would convincingly disavow any trace of anger or emotional damage.

Though not as popular as they used to be, there are still a few stage acts featuring a hypnotist who works with members from the audience. Besides the watch swinging back and forth in front of the subject's face, one of the stereotypical actions was this: "When I snap my fingers you will wake up, but you won't remember anything that happened here."

Adult children and codependents are just like that, and a posthypnotic trance is exactly what it is. The codependent fails to remember the full extent of the pain; that selective memory is a major source of denial.

This trance quality is particularly vivid in cases of sexual abuse. Assume the model of a father abusing his daughter. The father will say, "This is the way fathers love daughters. It's normal. Tell no one or Daddy could get in trouble." Coming from Daddy, these are powerful hypnotic messages, fed during an altered state of consciousness—for when a child is being traumatized that child is highly vulnerable. Many women can remember that after the moment of abuse or intercourse Daddy said very forcefully, "Do not tell anyone. This is okay." The fact that this was a violently conflicting message didn't register. The message itself did.

To advance the grief process, persons must get beyond this numbing shock. They must work past this first stage of grieving. For one thing, it is very hard to feel anything emotionally when in a state of shock. For another, shock and denial go hand in hand, and both will hold persons back from further grieving. And the grieving is essential. Nearly every response in stages one through four is designed in part to break through denial.

An example comes from the field of medicine. When something sudden and vicious happens, the body goes into shock to save its own life. Certain blood vessels close down and others open. The heart and lungs make rapid adjustments. Adrenaline flows freely. In many other ways as well, the body compensates for this violent threat to its well-being. Even the skin goes into defensive action. The new emergency procedures minimize blood loss and make certain the brain continues to get the oxygen it needs to remain alive and functional.

But should the body stay in this mode of emergency action, called by medical personnel "traumatic shock," the shock itself becomes life-threatening. If the traumatic shock is not alleviated (by positioning the victim to improve blood flow to the brain, regulating body temperature, giving oxygen, introducing fluids intravenously, and administering certain drugs), the patient may die, not of the primary injuries but of the body's emergency response to them.

Similarly, the child in a dysfunctional family went into a para-traumatic shock in order to survive. The move was life-saving at the time. But once the child emerges into the real world, those defense methods become highly detrimental. Staying in shock in adulthood costs that child true intimacy, often marriage, always balance. Emotionally, the shock can deny the child a meaningful relationship with God.

Shock and denial go hand in hand, even in everyday speech: "Why, I'm shocked! I don't believe it!" Not only is the shock deleterious, so is the denial, as we have learned.

In dealing with Jill and Jerry Braley and their son Bill, the multimillionaire family you met in chapter 2, we had to crack through shells as tough as Walter Morgan's. Walter vaguely suspected he had a problem, primarily because he had studied God's concept of love in Scripture and found himself wanting. But the Braleys couldn't imagine themselves encased in an emotional shell. Jill had trouble with anger, but she released it. And old Jerry was so genial and outgoing. Poor Bill had his problems, but he tried so hard most of the time to be a good businessman, husband, and father. Surely they weren't in a state of shock.

With the Braleys, we had to talk away the cracks in their defenses.

"Jerry, how did you compensate for your shame about the place you lived as a child?"

"I told you. I'd ask my ride to drop me off two blocks from home. A lot of people I grew up with still think I lived on Mulholland Street."

"That's the outside. How did you deal with it inside?"

"Don't know that I ever did."

"When you were handing your savings over to your mom, what did you think?"

Jerry took his time, brushing away the dust of many years. "I guess I felt a certain pride. Superman, you know? Came through again in the nick of time. And sadness. It was expected of a family to help each other out, and I never questioned it. They needed what I made."

"Jill? When your father screamed at you, and you weren't certain just why, how did you feel?"

"I got used to it."

"Exactly! But picture yourself as a little child. You don't know yet what's right and wrong, and you're getting mixed messages. This is right one time but another time it sets your father off. You're frightened when he does that because you can't control it with your behavior, at least not consistently. What emotions does that evoke?"

"Fear and confusion in some children, I suppose."

"Why not you?"

"I got used to it. I adjusted to it."

"And how did you adjust?"

"Well, I suppose I . . ." You could almost see the wall loom up before her eyes. She was finally beginning to see.

Jill built that familiar shell around herself, while Jerry essentially told himself black was white and made himself believe it, as a protective mechanism.

Many people in counsel say, "Most children would respond as you describe, but I was different." And that is true. They were. But they did not start out differently. They had to compensate, change their reactions, fight down the natural response and replace it with another. That's exactly what building a shell is.

You, too, may have been a different child, a child who did not respond as most would be expected to. That very fact suggests that you built a protective shell. Imagine yourself as a little child. Pretend you're still innocent of the world and don't know how you're supposed to respond to things. Your reactions are primal and very elementary. Now picture some of the incidents you described when you were telling your story. How would that unaffected little child have responded? Are you beginning to see your shell? Everyone builds a shell to some extent. That's a healthy response to the unavoidable buffeting of life. The codependent, though, because of those abusive experiences, builds too thick a wall.

2. *Anger*. Following almost spontaneously behind shock and denial comes anger. To test this statement in everyday life, run up to someone and stomp on his foot (just don't tell him we sent you). His first reaction is shock: "What . . . ?" The next is, "That didn't really happen, did it?" Then comes anger. "What do you think this is, doing that to me!" All those may flash through his mind in the few moments before he hauls back his fist and belts you. However prolonged or momentary, those steps in the process happen.

Some people take to anger like a two-year-old to mud. For others, anger is nearly impossible to identify and express. Perfectionistic, people-pleasing codependents, born servants such as Walter Morgan, have spent a lifetime masking personal feelings in order to make others comfortable and happy. With a lifestyle pattern like that, such persons find it extremely difficult to give themselves permission to voice anger. Their deep posthypnotic suggestion often is, "Whatever your family of origin was like, you have no permission to get angry."

Ever have to prime a pump? We mean the old-fashioned iron pump-the-handle-up-and-down pump every farm used to have. Usually you pumped up and down rapidly a few times "dry." Then came the water cold and sparkling, pouring first at a trickle and then at a torrent out the spout. But some pumps were less cooperative. For them you kept a big tin juice can full of water nearby. You dumped that into the top to prime the pump. If you didn't thus prime it, you would whang up and down until you were blue in the face without getting water. Of course, you never forgot to refill the can for next time.

On the treatment floor of the hospital our pump-primer is a room with tumbling mats, punching bags, boxing gloves, whiffle bats, pillows, and other esoterica. Therapists can take patients there and encourage them to flail away, to get some sense of what it's like to vent anger. For people who are deeply emotionally repressed, getting the anger to flow is like trying to prime the pump. Sometimes the therapist has to explain what anger is. Anger, so natural for most folks, is an alien emotion for these people. Sometimes vigorous activity, such as using a punching bag or jumping up and down or whacking away at Nerf balls with a whiffle bat, will get them back in touch with that most basic of emotions.

Jerry's wife, Jill, needed no help at all releasing her anger. That was her specialty. Walter Jordan used the room to help his anger surface. Jerry Braley found a unique vent for his. It was finals week at the university when Jerry happened to drive past UCLA. Several fraternities had parked older-model cars along the curbside. A buck or two bought you the privilege of beating on the cars with a sledge hammer. It was a delightful diversion for all the final exam takers, and a dandy little money-maker for the frats. For easy going, people-loving, good-ole-boy Jerry, it was the safety valve he needed. He took off his sport coat, plunked a hundred dollar bill in the cash box, and laid into a '72 Toyota.

We do not necessarily recommend demolishing automobiles. We do suggest that if you are a person who never gets angry, you are actually a person who suppresses anger. It's there somewhere, like steam in a pressure cooker, and you must somehow hit the valve. Our clients have devised all sorts of means you might try. Some of our patients have tried physical expressions of anger. Others have simply sat there and worried themselves into a state of anger.

One lady in our care had a terrible time getting in touch with her anger. She was leaving our clinic when she chanced to see a small boy deliberately stomp on a beetle. The callous act enraged her. As she began to berate the boy (mostly to his back, for he fled instantly), the dam broke. She stumbled back inside sobbing and screaming and spent the next two hours gloriously draining her long-pent-up rage.

Whatever appropriate means it takes for you to pop the cork and get your buried anger to the surface so you can resolve it, go for it.

"Forget that!" you fume. "You're not turning *me* into one of those angry people."

No, we're not. Quite the reverse. We're trying to liberate the hidden, seething anger already there. You must acknowledge it, release it, deal with it, and expunge it. Anger is a natural, healthy, God-given emotional mechanism for dealing with pain and loss. Paul told the Ephesians, "Be angry, and do not sin: do not let the sun go down on your wrath."[1] He was saying, "Come to an awareness of anger, before it becomes sin." Only by getting in touch with your anger can you put it behind you. We're not creating anger, we're flushing it out. We're lancing an emotional pus wound, getting the emotional toxin out.

There is good evidence that deeply held and repressed anger can suppress the immune system of the body. It is a spiritual toxin for sure. Studies in the past found that large numbers of cancer patients had areas of deep hurt and resentment apart from health concerns. This is not to suggest that this buried emotion caused cancer, but that it may have in some partial way paved the road.

3. *Depression*. Another reason you must deal with anger and put it behind you is depression, which in many ways resembles a secondary shock syndrome. It is anger turned inward. When anger goes underground, the resultant deep depression or numbness can last a lifetime. Healing is nearly impossible under those conditions.

Look at the way pain can express itself. It can be handled promptly and cleanly by grieving through it. It can be projected as anger turned outward. Or it can be introjected—turned inward. If it is buried thusly, it will express itself one way or another, as depression, addictions, or other self-destructive mechanisms.

Depression does not only result from anger turned inward. It also follows anger in the grief process. You'll also find false guilt to be prominent here, which is usually anger that has been turned inward against the self.

"Peachy," you grumble. "The last thing I need is deeper depression. It's bad enough already."

Ah, but wait! We're pleased to tell you there is a wonderful difference. The depression involved in the grief process is temporary. It resolves itself. As you're grieving, depression may be more intense than before you entered the process, but it's a way station—it's not the destination.

After that initial outburst, Walter Morgan's anger erupted off and on for several days, and for a week he languished in a deep depression. But he emerged spontaneously from his depression, as do the vast majority of persons going through the grieving process.

John Jordan described his home as "gloom and doom" as he and Gladys were working through their own grieving. Incidentally, the two of them pretty well kept pace with each other in the process. That doesn't always happen. If you and a spouse are working together on codependency problems, you may go at drastically different rates. Don't spend a lot of time worrying about it. You'll end up in the same place, whatever the speed.

If you should get hung up at the depression point, you can shake loose by recycling through the preceding grief steps.

You may even have to go back through the recovery stages from the beginning. One or two of those recycles will get you going again.

4. *Bargaining and Magic.* And now comes the bargaining-and-magic stage. Bargaining and magical thinking take many forms, some of them barely recognizable. Others might be blatant. Elizabeth Kubler-Ross found that cancer patients may bargain with, or downright bribe, radiologists to get more time in the therapy, to receive a bigger zap. It doesn't make sense logically. If you get X amount of radiation, 2X isn't going to be twice as good; it might be very harmful. But logic flies over the veranda rail when magical thinking is involved. Trying somehow to get an extra edge is the name of the game, and it happens both consciously and unconsciously.

Bargaining with God is the biggie. "If you'll just take me out of this situation, God, I'll do so-and-so for you." In a sense it is childish. If so, we are all children, for we never quite abandon that childhood trait of magical thinking.

We find that often when codependents go through grieving in childhood and adolescence, they form some strange bargains with themselves—cutting contracts, if you will—and usually not consciously. An example is Marlene, whose father was convicted of indecent exposure on one occasion and on another caught in a raid on a house of prostitution. The kids in school all knew about it. "Hey! Marlene's father got busted." "Yeah, did you hear why?" "Yeah. Wonder what it's like around home with him."

What it was like was not dramatic. Marlene's father never actively abused her. She was his little girl and the prostitutes and mistresses his big girls. He kept magazines in a locked cabinet; she knew that. He might wander around the house naked when he was coming or going to the shower. But although there were no shocking acts or physically harmful encounters, the passive abuse and its secondary effects on her reputation at school were just as real.

As an adult child Marlene made two vows, one conscious and the other unconscious. Her conscious vow was that she would never marry a sexually addicted man like that and subject her own children to such pain and ridicule. The unconscious contract, a bargain she never knew she made with herself, said, "I will never be sexual."

Five years into her marriage, she and her husband appeared in our offices for marital counseling. They had been sexually dysfunctional for four-and-a-half years and he had reached a breaking point. Either they get it together or he was leaving.

In adolescence, kids very commonly feel so ashamed and guilty because of the turmoil Mom and Dad are going through (you'll recall that kids easily take on the blame for circumstances totally beyond their control) that they make elaborate bargains with God and with self. Magically, for they have no unmagical power, they would somehow lift the family pain. It's almost like a monastic vow. Marlene very nearly made just such a vow unconsciously.

Marlene had to work through all this. In counsel we led her from the exploration of stage one into the grieving process of stage five. There Marlene got hung up, precisely because she was an old hand at bargaining with God. Her new bargain was, "Release me from all this, God, and I'll be a good wife." She wanted the shortcut. She wanted an edge against the pain. She began baking bread and cleaning the house daily. She went into all sorts of housewifely behavior. The sexual dysfunction remained. It took a lot of talking to root out that hidden bargain with God.

Anytime we see ritualistic behavior we understand that these codependents have locked themselves at least in part into the magic/bargaining stage. An excellent example is Sam, a former hospital patient. The soap we use in the hospital and in most offices kills dangerous germs. It also leaves behind a fine film. During normal daily handwashing that film never accumulates enough to show. But Sam looked like he was wearing white gloves. He washed his hands sixty and seventy times a day. His magical thinking: "If I can just wash enough times I can magically wash away the problem. Everything will be okay *if only . . .*"

If only.

(Just as an aside, we've noted that compulsive hand washers are usually men. Eating disorders usually plague women.

We don't know why. We do know that especially with such disorders as bulimia and anorexia a huge amount of magic is involved. "If I can only . . ." The anorexic genuinely believes that if she can just get down to a certain weight the world, or specific persons, will love her. It doesn't happen, of course, when she reaches that weight, so she sets the goal downward again. "*This* time, it will work.")

As we have seen, magical thinking is a normal part of childhood. Kids are so egocentric that if little Rob puts his shoes on the wrong feet and a thunderstorm strikes, he easily twists it around in his head that the thunder came because he got his shoes on backwards. Adults keep the magic but change the formula. Bettors at a racetrack or bingo parlor provide ample evidence. "This is my lucky hat. That's my lucky number. If I clap three times before covering the middle space, my bingo card is likelier to win. Honest! It worked once."

The codependent, true to the type, carries it to extreme.

In fact, a full-blown codependent continually keeps inventory, trying to determine what went wrong with the magic. The wife of a sexually addicted womanizer asks, "What am I doing that makes him do this? What can I do to make him stop? If I just do (so-and-so and so-and-so), surely I can make him stop. I know it will work. It has to."

Hear the key words: "Make him." "If only." The wife-beater uses the same magical thinking in the other direction. "You made me hit you." "I wouldn't have to do this if only you . . ."

Saying goodbye is, at the end of it, an essential maturation step. Persons realize they are giving up the magic—rather, they realize at last that they never had it. It is a powerful and important symbolic act, this leaving Mom and Dad behind, because you also leave behind childhood, and with it the magic with which you endeavored to change the world.

What is left, if magic is snatched away? In this imperfect world where pain and loss are so common, grieving is a normal, God-given way to deal with the imperfection. If we have access to a healthy grieving process, or can restore ourselves to that, this rhythm will run through life. One then grieves big losses successfully and also the little annoyances. In the healthy situation we grieve and then let go of the everyday pain and frustrations that arise so persistently in life.

In codependents the rhythm frequently breaks down. When the codependent becomes hung up at some stage of the process, grief is unable to flow to its proper conclusion. When that occurs, the person never reaches the forgiveness, acceptance, and resolution grieving is supposed to produce. Just realizing what happened may be sufficient to root out the blockage. The codependent might discover, "Now that you mention it, I've been locked into the shock and denial for fifteen years!"

Through her relationship inventory, Marlene recognized the painful embarrassment of her childhood with a sexually addicted father but not the unconscious bargain—"I will never be sexual"—she had made with herself to assuage the pain and prevent further shame. In order to void the bargain she had to say her effective goodbye to the home and her parents and, in the process, the magic. The way was now cleared for her to grieve through her losses—the years of misery both as a child and as an adult.

Finally, bargaining frequently takes place directly with the therapist. Patients moan, "Isn't there a shortcut around this?" It's not just that they are seeking the easy way out. The job may look too hard to handle. One of our clients compares her therapy with going to the dentist: it isn't fun, but it's better than the consequences of neglecting to go.

5. Sadness. We have reached the fifth step in this six-step grief process, sadness. Sadness absolutely overwhelmed our Walter Morgan, who wept and wailed uncontrollably for his sad, lost yesterdays. Usually, however, sadness comes upon us in manageable chunks over an extended period of time—days or weeks; in the cases of some who are strongly codependent, months or years. Sadness is normal. Sadness is ordinary. Sadness is the appropriate response to sad events. Better still, sadness can be comfortably dealt with, with tears. Best of all, sadness is not endless. Unlike chronic depression or repetition compulsions, or oftentimes, anger itself, sadness comes, is recognized, and goes.

6. *Forgiveness, Resolution, and Acceptance*. The final step in the grief process, the goal from the beginning, is
that blessed last step; forgiveness, resolution, and acceptance. Scripture translations phrase it perfectly: the peace
that passes understanding. When you reach this stage, the
roller coaster is on its way back up.

Be aware that what has happened so far is largely "a-
logical"; it neither contradicts nor serves logic. We have gone
beyond logic and reason (incidentally, something very hard for
Walter Morgan to do) into the innermost chambers of the soul.
We are tapping the deepest emotional wells, wells provided by
God for just this purpose. To complete the healing process we
must step from the chambers of the logical mind into the dark
sanctum of the emotions. It is right there that thought begins,
no matter how logical we fancy ourselves to be. Our patients
often have difficulty suspending their logical desire for retribution so they can forgive.

"Forgiveness?" Bessie Barnett looked her counselor
straight in the eye and said, "I understand now what happened
to me. I have grieved the process through as you directed.
You've been telling me how well I've gotten through this, and I
believe you. I feel much better about myself and I see now how
to avoid the kind of mistakes I kept making in the past.

"But my logical self tells me those people in my past don't
deserve to be forgiven. If they treated me that way through
some misguided sense of love, of course I could forgive them.
If they did something and didn't realize what they were doing,
all right. But they knew. They *knew* how much they were hurting me."

Bessie came from a severely dysfunctional home in which
the father, who didn't like children, ended up siring four. He
slapped them around. He griped about them to his friends
and denigrated them to their faces. His favorite response to
the question, "How many children do you have?" was, "Oh,
shoot, I dunno. Three or four; something like that." He neglected no opportunity to let them know they were unwanted.

Bessie's mother married because she had to. Those were
the days when a pregnant girl came to term in wedlock. Period. Besides, in that rural area, girls simply did not consider a

life beyond marriage and family. Bessie's ma dreamed of becoming a singer—country-western or blues, she didn't care—but then Bessie and her sisters destroyed the dream. Ma didn't bother to hide her constant disappointment and bitterness.

Typically Bessie married into a codependent relationship. She lived thirty-three years with a miser of a husband who allowed her ten dollars a week spending money and considered himself generous. He died leaving her with a huge bank account and a powerful desire to commit suicide. It was therapy or death.

She crossed her arms and her eyes were blazing. "Maybe someday I can forget. No way can I forgive."

Only when Bessie puts her logic behind her will she be able to break out of the place where she is stuck and take this final all-important step to healing.

Lest you protest, "I can't do that any more than Bessie can," recall that utter dependence upon logic as such is a relatively recent mindset. Oh, sure, the Greeks developed logic, including the logical mathematics that form the foundation of our scientific society. But it remained pretty much the realm of the intellectuals. The Arabic scientists carried it to new levels in math and astronomy, as did the Mayas and Aztecs in the New World. The general public in these societies, though, did not depend on pure logic. Neither did Europeans then, even during the Renaissance when true scientific thought came into flower. Only in the last few hundred years, since the French Revolution, have reasoning and logic come to dominate the mindset of mainstream Western civilization.

If such be so, what did logic supplant? Emotional responses. The "thoughts" of the heart. In our society, "In my heart of hearts I believe . . ." is pooh-poohed as childish nonsense. We are taught to carefully avoid the messages of the heart and espouse only the messages of the head. Consider bereavement. If a new widow maintains a stiff upper lip and deports herself with dignity, her friends support her. If during her bereavement she consistently falls apart—actually the appropriate, cleansing response to her tragedy—her friends counsel, "Now, now—you're being too emotional. You must be brave."

Or, uncomfortable, they simply back away from her completely.

Two hundred years ago, a bereavement called for a highly emotional response, and if the widow or widower maintained a brave or stoic front, the depth of their love came into serious question. Our utter dependence on reason and cool logic is a recent cultural phenomenon, and it is likely to get in the way of your recovery if you let it.

In Bessie's case, her cause for unforgiveness was, on the surface, logical. In fact, it would seem illogical to forgive deliberate hurt. Conversely, if the persons who caused her grief were innocent of malicious intent, it would be logical for her to look past the ignorance and forgive.

Bessie has two hurdles to leap. *First, she must sideline her reasoning mind and work from the heart.*

"I don't know how," she says. "I'm fifty-two years old, so I pretty much missed the women's lib thing where you aren't allowed to be emotional, but think of all the stuff you hear growing up. 'Be reasonable.' 'That's not logical.' 'Don't let your heart rule your head or you'll marry badly.' How do I turn it off now?"

"You mentioned to us before that you believe in God. Do you believe in the Bible?"

"Sure."

"According to God's Word, cold, calculating reason isn't His way."

A thousand years before Christ, God instructed "Trust in the Lord with all your heart and lean not on your own understanding."[2] Jesus Himself adjured, "I tell you the truth, unless you change and become like little children, you will never enter the kingdom of heaven."[3] How heavily does logic weigh in a little child's thoughts?

The head is the surface level of thinking; the heart is the depth. People are like a piece of furniture made of oak and veneered in costly wood. The veneer is very nice, and adds value, and looks lovely, but it's the oak that provides the sturdiness and strength.

Bessie snorted, and her eyes twinkled. "Now you're calling me a wooden-head." And she was smiling.

In our clinical practice we daily hear stories about grievances and atrocities that are literally unforgivable. Fathers do
unspeakable things to their daughters. Wives and mothers
wantonly lash out, wreaking emotional pain and havoc. Parents
deliberately snub capable children who do not measure up to
their false expectations. Men and women in violent rages bat-
ter the people they love most, physically and emotionally.

We are hopelessly human, and that is never truer than here.
Humanly speaking, neither mind nor heart is strong enough to
forgive some of these unforgivable acts. And yet true and honest forgiveness must be generated in order to make peace
with the past. Frustrating, at first appearance.

Can Bessie put her logic aside and get in touch with her
feelings? Can she forgive at the heart level regardless what her
upstart logical mind would tell her? Yes. And so can you. It is
built right into you, this ability to respond not to the head but to
the heart. But you will need expert help from God, and perhaps from man. God is the ultimate forgiver; man can point the
way.

Be wary, however, of a common danger in this final step of
the grieving process to which Christians are particularly vulnerable. That is forgiving without emotional integrity. It happens when the Christian quite sincerely declares, "I see the
past now, and acknowledge what happened" (step one of the
grieving process). "I turn it over to God and forgive it" (last
step). "There. That's done. The book is closed."

That jump from the first step to the last is a dandy bypass
around the painful parts of the grieving process. Although it
sounds scriptural and is certainly spiritually well-intended, it
won't work. The pain has not been dealt with. The infected
wound deep inside has not been cleansed, a very real and apt
allusion.

The grief process is built into us, which is reason enough to
suggest that it is the way God planned for us to deal with loss,
emotional turmoil, and pain. When we abort that process, we
end up forgiving (and no doubt quite sincerely) in an atmo-
sphere of emotional dishonesty. Even though we voice forgiveness, there remains a deep reservoir of anger and resentment.

The forgiveness lacks the integrity of reflecting all the facets of being human.

Emotional integrity was Bessie's other hurdle.

Bessie breezed through the first four stages of our ten-stage model for recovery. She handled the grief process well right down to this final step. By patiently working at awareness of what had happened to her and of her own emotions, and by conscientiously saying her goodbyes to her family of origin, Bessie built a foundation of emotional integrity. Now, when she said something like "I understand," or "I forgive you," she could say it from the heart, because there was no residual bitterness or anger belying the words on her lips.

And when she said "I cannot forgive," that carried the weight of emotional integrity as well.

When persons, and Christians especially, insist on serving the spiritual dimension to the exclusion of the physical, emotional, and other dimensions, they are being dishonest, untrue to who and what they are. Only part of them is offering forgiveness. God made us an integrated whole and therefore expects us to act from that whole. "Now may the God of peace Himself sanctify you completely," says Paul, "and may *your whole [being] spirit, soul, and body be preserved blameless* at the coming of our Lord Jesus Christ."[4]

Consider how our emotions influence our physical dimension. Stress jacks blood pressure. Fear and apprehension cause what might politely be called disruptions of the lower gastrointestinal tract. Repressed anger and bitterness may reduce resistance to infection, even some cancers. Emotions affect our spiritual dimension, to the point of reducing our concept of God Himself to codependent terms.

This interlinkage between all our dimensions is why it is so important to build a solid foundation of emotional integrity. Upon that we can make such powerful statements as "I forgive you" that echo to the very core. From a complete person comes complete forgiveness.

John and Gladys Jordan had a whole lot of people to forgive, starting with each other at the top of the list. As well-organized as always, John the contractor made an actual list, starting with

Gladys's name and ending with his own. Items 2 and 3 were his father and mother. From his relationship inventory came dozens of names. Many had wronged him. But he listed also those persons who had "righted" him. For each person on this second list, he specifically thanked God.

Gladys did not share John's methodical ways. She made no list as such. She dealt with each person who came to mind at the time that person came to mind. She prayed to God about each of them, and then she wrote them notes. Some were two-page letters. Most were simply, "Dear X, I forgive you for [   ]. Love, Gladys Hayes Jordan." These letters remained in her notebook, for to mail some of them would have caused more harm than good. The only one she mailed was her three-page letter to John, in which she also reaffirmed her love. He wept when he read it.

Bessie was neither a list maker nor a note writer. In fact, she claimed she wasn't even very good at praying. "Help me," she said. "How can I do what I cannot?"

"Let's say that you are strong enough to lift a hundred pound weight, but your grandson can only manage twenty-five. Can your grandson lift a hundred pounds if you help him?"

"Sure. But what . . .?" Her eyes lit up, but we elaborated anyway.

"God can handle any weight of forgiveness. How about you lifting what you can and letting Him take the rest?"

"How?"

" ' "Vengeance is mine," says the Lord. "I shall requite." ' You've heard that passage before."

"I don't want to take vengeance. I just can't forgive."

"A barrier to forgiveness is the hope, however vague, of getting back at the people who wronged you. Making them pay."

"Well, yes. When you think about it, that's true."

"God doesn't want you taking care of that aspect. He's reserved it for Himself. Agreed?"

"Agreed."

"Now let's read Psalm 4, verses 4 and 5."

Bessie broke her Bible open in the middle and thumbed

backwards to the place. "Be angry, and do not sin." She frowned.

"Mmm. Offer the sacrifices of righteousness, and put your trust in the LORD." She closed the book. "Sacrifices. Giving up things." She studied the cover of her Bible silently. Her face loosened into the humorous little smile that was so much Bessie. "Sacrifice. He doesn't want me slaughtering any sheep here, right?"

"Right."

"Just my anger?"

"And bitterness and hatred."

Bessie's hatreds did not present themselves quietly to be sacrificed; they struggled bitterly to stay alive. She prevailed, though, by placing one person at a time in her thoughts and making a mental picture of herself and God lifting that person above her anger. She forgave with the same emotional integrity with which she had said "I cannot."

You may use the same mental device Bessie used—forming a picture of what you need to do—to help you and God together work the necessary forgiveness. You may think of some other way: form an imaginary meeting between you and that person, write a story, or discuss the matter with God. In the depths of our most heinous grief and in the depths, too, of our most difficult forgiveness, only God suffices.

Acceptance and resolution go hand in hand with forgiveness; in a sense, the three cannot be separated. To accept the issues is to admit that things were as they were and that their effects are not irreversible. To resolve them is to reverse the effects.

We can, in fact, use *resolution* in both its meanings. There is the New Year's resolution: "From now on I resolve to . . ." And then there's the resolution a novelist, for example, uses to bring a plot to a satisfactory conclusion. We will be resolving the plot of our lives satisfactorily.

The resolution at this point is not complete by any means. Rather than turning the car around and driving down the road from whence we came, we are, at this stage, simply getting the car turned around. Stages six through ten of our recovery process will carry us down the road to completion, putting our resolution here to practical use.

Bessie could handle both acceptance and resolution. They weren't a problem. She had come to terms with her past and was no longer enslaved by it. Her car was turned around, and she was ready to move on down the road to stage six.

CHAPTER SEVENTEEN

Seeing Yourself in a New Light

James Portland was a clockmaker, a real, old-fashioned clockmaker, but he was only thirty-three. He decided to learn the exacting, tedious trade because no one else in his generation was mastering the dying art of repairing classic clocks and watches. He took pure delight in restoring some battered old windup timepiece to its former perfection. Most clocks he could calibrate to an accuracy within half a minute a week. His particular fondness was for the Seth Thomas parlor clocks and for cuckoo clocks.

James Portland's wife, Claire, claimed the cuckoo clocks said it all, because James was nuts. He was a demanding, perfectionistic, rageaholic neatnik who exploded if she failed to dust the tops of the door jambs. That is, he once was. Even Claire admitted that after seven months in therapy for co-dependency James had mellowed considerably. He was bringing himself under control. The change was dramatic enough that Claire consented to enter treatment for her own codependency problems.

STAGE SIX: NEW SELF-PERCEPTIONS

When the unclean spirit has gone out of a man, he (the spirit) passes through waterless places seeking rest, but he finds none. Then he says, "I'll return to my house from which I came." And when he comes he finds it empty, swept, and put in order. Then he goes and brings with him seven other spirits more evil than himself, and they enter and dwell there. And the last state of that man becomes worse than the first.

"Nature abhors a vacuum" is a cold, impersonal way of saying the same thing.

Stages one through five of the recovery process brought you into touch with your feelings, perhaps for the first time. They provided avenues to catharsis and renewal. Now, in stages six through ten, we'll clean out some more unhealthy rubbish, then fill the resulting void left by damaged and damaging thoughts and concepts. If that void is left empty, if the vacuum remains, it will fill itself with attitudes and thoughts that will almost certainly be negative and detrimental, for codependents think in negative and detrimental ways. You have discovered what you are not. Now let us explore what you are.

WHO AM I?

James stood at the built-in bookcase in our back office, studying the clock on the shelf. "This is the real thing, you know, and an antique. I can't date it without taking it apart, but I can tell you it was made prior to 1863. You'll notice on the label pasted to the back it says Plymouth Hollow. Plymouth Hollow was changed to Thomason in 1863."

"What makes it tick?"

James smiled. "Its spring provides the power. You wind the spring up tight. The spring wants to unwind all at once, of course. But the escapement holds it back, letting it unwind one little notch at a time. The notches measure out the unwinding just so, and it keeps time. You adjust the rate of unwinding to slow it or speed it up."

"What makes you tick?"

"Same thing, about." James sat down. He was still smiling, and the smile itself was something new for him. To call him "sullen" when first he came to us would have been a charitable gesture. "I was so messed up my escapement wasn't connected to the power train. The spring went whang-o however it pleased. Power with no discipline. Now I'm connected inside, for the first time ever. I'm in control. It's a great feeling."

"Glad you feel good. What do you think happens next?"

"Fine-tune the ticking until I'm in correct adjustment."

"How?"

"I don't know. That's why I'm here."

"You say you feel good. How do you feel about yourself?"

"I don't know that, either."

At this stage you will be working to find new internal messages about who and what you are. We sometimes call them "existential messages," not because they have anything in common with the philosophy called existentialism (they do not) but because they are messages you give yourself about your very existence.

If you grew up in a dysfunctional home, you inevitably carry an assortment of negative, distorted messages:

- "I am unloved."
- "I am unlovable . . . even in the eyes of God."
- "I'm responsible for everyone else's hurt and pain."
- "I'm not worthy, so I need to earn my way into salvation and grace, grace both in my family and in the greater family of God."
- "I must work myself to death if I am to deserve inclusion in the family of man or of God."
- "I do not deserve this success I'm having."

So many negative messages emerge from a dysfunctional childhood.

We inventoried those messages informally in stages one through five, glancing at them and skipping on. The treatment was rather diffuse. Now is the time to deliberately take a formal inventory of them. Were you to enter our counsel we would examine them in the light of the new information you've garnered about yourself. And we would ask you to write them out.

An Inventory of Old Perceptions. The object of listing your old perceptions of yourself, your messages, is quite simply to become aware of them. But to sit down and begin writing is next to impossible. So in a notebook or tablet, write some statements to get you started. At the top of one page write, "All men are . . ." Give yourself a page or two, then at the top of a new page write, "All women are . . ." Continue thus, allowing plenty of blank space. "God is . . ." "All people are . . ." "A home should be . . . ," etc.

Now, in some quiet moment, sit back, relax, and as spontaneously as possible, put down whatever comes to mind. This is what is sometimes called free association. Think tanks call it brainstorming. No idea is too fanciful, no item of recall is rejected.

All women are . . .

unfair
hurtful
pretty
bossy

All men are . . .

jerks
poor listeners
hung up on themselves
worth cultivating
protective

As your lists build, you will begin to discover not what makes men and women what they are, but what *you* are. Those old negative messages of self-perception begin to surface. If the first words you think of concerning God are "judgmental," "harsh," "not to be trusted," that says a lot about the "I" messages inside you. The lists might even reveal pockets of bitterness you will have to go back and root out.

For example, James Portland made a list: All fathers should be . . .

demanding
precise

strict
right, whether they're right or not

James never realized how miserably relentless he was in his pursuit of life until he read his own list.
Here's Jerry Braley's list: Life is . . .

full of toys
meant to be enjoyed
rewards you if you work
empty
bitter
too heavy to carry sometimes

Jerry realized graphically how material possessions simply were not filling the void. His happiness was all on the outside.

WHO DO I WANT TO BE?

Now the fun part. Make a contrasting list. What are some new, positive, healthy, balanced messages you can give yourself? Like the other lists, they will concern yourself, God, the universe, the opposite sex, other people—everything. Most codependents need help here. Right away you'll find yourself drawing blanks. As a former codependent you're simply not accustomed to thinking positively about yourself. For this you may wish to tap into other people.

In our hospital treatment programs we ask patients to go around to other patients on their floor and solicit ideas. Were you in treatment, your counselor might say, "This weekend go from room to room and pick up new messages from the patients who know you. Ask them what they see as a positive quality in you. Build a list of what others see in you."

Come Monday morning, the patient is likely to say, "Boy, this is exciting! I went around to ten people on the floor and got more than ten good, positive, affirming things about me!" The shock and delight comes in learning that there are so many positive things about a person whose self-esteem was formerly on the empty end of the gauge.

An excellent source of positive messages can be found in the Psalms in Scripture. When either the psalmist or all Israel did wrong, God was there anyway, lending an ear. The psalmist—and you—enjoys the infinite worth of being loved by God. Read, for example, Psalm 57, written when David fled his father-in-law, Saul, and hid in a cave. The world was against him; God was not. Read Psalm 18 and Psalm 139 as if they were written to you personally, and you'll begin to perceive the value God has placed upon you.

New Messages. A severely dysfunctional adult child desperately needs a sense of value. That person may require a message as basic as "I have permission to live." Prior negative messages were so vicious and penetrating that that simple thought, taken for granted by most people, becomes a welcome revelation.

Sometimes these new perceptions take an interesting twist. Jill Braley, once so bitterly critical and demanding, identified one of her hurtful old messages as "If I don't intervene, the person I love will mess up." We thought her new message might be something like "If I don't intervene, the person I love will probably get along all right." She changed it to "It's all right if that person messes up. I love the person anyway." What a wonderful new attitude!

John Jordan simply reviewed all the attributes of his father, kept for his own identity three that he thought were good, and substituted one word for all the others: tolerant. Instead of *demanding*, he determined to be *tolerant*. Instead of *perfectionistic, tolerant*. And on and on.

We have found that some codependents, addicts in particular, have been living out a death-style, not a life-style. Many addictions are, quite simply, slow suicide, and are finally recognized as such by the addicts themselves. For these people a new message might affirm their right to live. "I have a right to life. There is sanctity in life, including mine."

Louise, the anorexic nursing student, had a hard time convincing herself she could be just as lovable at a hundred and thirty pounds as at ninety, and the people who loved her wouldn't worry about her so much. Her head understood, but her heart clung viciously to the old messages.

Louise, like you and me, could think the messages out and accept them at the conscious level. But as you know, the conscious level is not where we make decisions. You need help incorporating the bold new messages about yourself. That help is at hand. The One who knows your deepest levels better than you do is waiting for you to ask His assistance. Don't hesitate to ask God in conversational prayer to plant your new messages deep.

Many codependents have spent a life trying so hard to keep everyone else happy, they've never realized they themselves have a right to some degree of happiness. Life is not going to be all roses, of course. But the legally protected right to the pursuit of happiness is a commendable goal reached, or nearly reached, much more often than the codependent might guess. Our book *Happiness Is a Choice* addressed this aspect in detail.

You might discover your right to genuine intimacy—not the pseudointimacy of codependency where two persons encroach so upon each other that their circles overlap, but the true intimacy of souls in unison. "I deserve to have some of that healthy intimacy if I find it."

"I can own my sexuality." Many codependents divorce themselves from their sexuality, especially during that magical thinking mess, and must reaffirm its appropriateness.

"I can own my anger and grief." New losses will come into life, from things as minor as traffic tangled on the freeway to the death of a spouse. You may have to give yourself a new message that "My feelings are legitimate and it's okay to have them." That's a brand new thought for a lot of codependents. With that message in place, sources of pain can trigger the grieving process spontaneously.

Some devoted Christians may have to give themselves permission to be comfortably successful. We find a large number of patients engaging in a lifetime pattern of self-sabotage on the assumption that no rich man at all can get through the eye of the needle.

Lastly and ultimately, work out new messages for yourself, not just with God's help but about God Himself. Previously you may have seen Him only in codependent terms and related to Him as a "harsh taskmaster" or a "demanding Lord who does not give out forgiveness freely."

If you suspect that you are relating to God in a codependent way, we suggest that you try a free association exercise. This is how we helped Bessie Barnett. Her exercise in free association, the jumping-off point from which she could build some new self-perceptive messages for herself, revealed much about her attitude toward God. Some of her notes:

God is . . .

- unloving in the human sense of the word *love*
- ready to pounce on moral errors
- two thousand years away from me
- a figment of somebody's imagination
- laughing at us

We asked her, "This picture of God is not what people you know and respect think of Him. Who's right, do you think?"

"If you want an honest answer, I think I am."

"How many of the attributes you've listed for God could be applied to your father?"

Bessie is a stout farm wife out of the old tradition. She's a no-nonsense sort of lady, not given to emotional outbursts. Now tears glistened as the truth struck home. Her weeping eyes said *all of them* although she spoke no word. She paused a minute or two to regain her composure. "He's not at all like my father, is He?"

"Not a bit. In fact, let's make a list of opposites."

God is . . .

- loving beyond our comprehension
- forgiving
- with us
- a very present help
- in sympathy with us

Bessie could not in a million years have forgiven her parents by tapping only her own strength. With her truncated attitude toward God she could not have asked Him to help. But when the truth about God dawned, when she went back to Scripture with her mind and heart cleared of the old negative messages, His strength, majesty, and love came through.

It didn't happen overnight. Bessie had to become acquainted with the real God first. Since childhood she had called herself a Christian. Two weeks after this written exercise she became one. Once she saw His grace and mercy (both terms until then alien), she could at last relate to Him on a one-on-one basis.

Just as James Portland would not be able to repair and adjust a clock if he didn't thoroughly understand how it works, so he could not make refinements in his life until he understood the cogged wheels within him. And some of the workings are delicate indeed.

"These new messages about myself . . ." he said. "I realize the old messages aren't good. But how do I convince myself deep down that the new ones are better?"

"You listed the attributes of fathers—do you remember that list?"

"I have it right here." James whipped out his sheaf of papers and leafed through them. "Demanding, precise, strict, right whether they're right or not."

"Is that the happy father of a happy child?"

"Happy? No. Effective, maybe."

"If the father and child are miserable, is that effective?"

"No, I guess not. The child may learn by rote what to do, but you can program a robot for that."

"Robots aren't happy and unhappy."

"I was unhappy. Angry and sad. You're saying we can't get away from the human element. Therefore the effective father deals with it effectively."

"Couldn't have said it better. Or more precisely."

"If I took the opposites on this list, I'd have a new self-image, but I'm not sure I'd like me as well. Lenient instead of demanding? What about when the kids slack off and just plain get lazy? Sloppy instead of precise? No."

"Adopt parts of both lists. There is great value in being precise, but not when others suffer emotional pain for the sake of precision. There are instances when being demanding is useful and appropriate, but not as a constant thing. To be demanding is to expect perfection. Neither children nor adults are perfect."

"So I don't have to eliminate my old self-perceptions. Just limit them."

"Greatly limit them, and temper them with the new. Our God is a very present help in Psalm 46 and a consuming fire in Hebrews 12. Same person, complex attributes. You're complex, too."

"Lots of cogged wheels up there." James tapped his forehead and grinned. "So I'll go around all day reminding myself I won't scream at Claire and the kids."

"Better yet, remember that your old perception of self doesn't need help being remembered. It comes automatically. Your new perceptions of self are pretty frail yet. They'll need to be brought to mind often."

James looked thoughtful. "About old clocks—the more you can maintain the integrity of an old timepiece by keeping the old parts rather than replacing them with new, the more valuable the antique remains."

"The old line about 'This is the hatchet George Washington used, but it's had six new handles and two new heads.'"

"Exactly. So you try to mend the old. But there comes a time when the old parts just don't work anymore. They have to be replaced or the clock won't function. I can see it's best if I replace certain parts completely. And refurbish the others. This self-perception is pretty difficult."

"But worth it."

"But worth it. Yes. My whole career involves bringing new life to old clocks. It's about time I did the same for me."

At the end of stage six—in fact, during stage seven—Bessie went back and reworked stage five. She forgave her parents more completely, more openheartedly, with her new strength derived from her new relationship to God.

Bessie Barnett illustrates another important facet of this recovery process. Patients often bounce back and forth from stage to stage as new elements enter their lives. It is not often a simple and orderly continuum. But it is a continuum, and the stages must be completed one way or another.

Patients who have gone through more than one major form of abuse may have to grieve through each one as a distinct unit. Physical and sexual abuses and abandonment each etch their own scars. Such persons, as perhaps will you yourself, cycle through the grief process, then on to new self-perceptive messages that emerge from the cleansing. If you find this happening to you, rejoice. It's natural and healing.

CHAPTER
EIGHTEEN

New Experiences and Reparenting

Pretend you are a seven-year-old calling a respected older friend on the phone. You're excited because you just received your first bicycle for your birthday. Now you want this friend to explain over the phone how to ride it.

Your friend can explain the positioning of the feet on the pedals, the desirable distance of the seat above the sprocket. He can tell you which brake caliper works which wheel. He can even go into the theory of gravity if he wishes but all to no avail. You must get on the bike before you can begin to learn to ride it.

Let's increase the difficulty. Pretend you want to learn how to walk a tightrope. Your friend doesn't know anything about walking a tightrope. Now how do you get help?

All the new self-perceptive messages in the world aren't going to improve your life so long as they remain on paper. They must be applied. And yet many of them—perhaps all of them—are brand new to you, outside your range of experience. How do you get on the bike successfully? How do you walk a tightrope you've never experienced before?

STAGE SEVEN: NEW EXPERIENCES

Computer and typing classes provide hands-on instruction. Chemistry, biology, and physics courses include laboratory time. The budding scientists read all about dissections and chemical reactions and experiments with springs and pulleys, but until they get into the lab and try these things out, it's all simply theory. Facts about the reaction of hydrogen with sulfur fade when the course is gone. Smelling hydrogen sulfide once lasts a lifetime!

In stage seven we are going to live out what we accomplished when we made those new decisions about ourselves in stage six. We're going to climb on the bicycle, attempt the tightrope. Quite possibly a scuffed knee will result, but it will be worth it. At last we can choose to trust when we wish. We can choose to love or not, and we can learn that depending on God is safe and rewarding.

We don't ask our patients to jump in with both feet. The journey of a thousand miles begins with one step. An extreme example is how you might deal with a phobia. Let us say you have an ingrained horror of furry animals. Since the world is full of furry animals, you want to shed the terror. The therapist will start by talking. That's all, just talking. You can talk about furry animals, discuss what it would be like to touch one, maybe study picture books and become better acquainted intellectually with them. Eventually you will get closer. Then one day you will touch one. When you are finally able to hold a kitten and discover that the world keeps turning and nothing horrible happens, you are ready for graduation. We recommend doing the same here, too. You sneak up on the discomfort these new self-perceptive messages tend to give, and by degrees allay it.

An artist claimed everyone will have fifteen minutes of fame in his life. Lena Wallace's fifteen minutes were front-page news after her abusive husband battered their only child, his stepson, to death. When he went to jail, Lena went to college. She also went into therapy for severe codependency problems.

Lena was a striking woman, tall and stately, her hair so blue-black it glistened, her skin the color of coffee with cream. With her usual efficiency she had brought her life under control in every area save one: Lena could not force herself to trust anyone.

It wasn't surprising. Her father had abandoned her mother. Her first husband had abandoned her and later died on the streets of Washington, D.C. And then her second husband killed her son. . . . She worked through the grief, the acceptance, the forgiveness. Her new message was, "Some people are trustworthy." She knew she must build a trusting nature. Still she could not.

In counsel we advised Lena that if she were to build trust she must start by making herself vulnerable in limited ways. *New inner messages require new experiences to affirm them,* if the heart is to accept them. We knew that as she began to trust, to live out the positive message she provided for herself, she would discover she didn't fall off the end of the earth after all. She probably wouldn't even get hurt, at least not seriously. Beginning was the trick.

She started with the people in her therapy group. Joe was a hulking macho guy with the same problem Lena had. He opened the door by saying out loud, "I need to trust people more."

"Okay," others responded. "Trust us enough to tell us about some area of deep insecurity or fears you never voiced before."

Joe let that challenge cook a couple minutes and then agreed, "Yeah, I'll take the risk." He opened up some self-doubts he had harbored for years, concerning his image and even his ability to impress women beyond the shallowest level of appearance.

As Lena watched the group respect Joe's fears enough to accept them without ridicule, she decided to take the plunge. She described her own deep-seated doubts, and entrusted her feelings for the first time in her life to someone besides her counselor. It was her first small step toward trusting the outside world.

Lena needed the group in order to solve a specific problem. In fact, following the guidelines of Hebrews 3:13—to exhort (or encourage) one another daily—we use seven-day-a-week groups at the hospital to just that end. An intimate group can see what one or two cannot.

Codependents in general also need willing ears and hearts around them in order to put their new "I" messages to work. These supporters serve two functions. One is simply to listen, perhaps help with a particular problem, as Lena's group did. The other function is to provide accountability. Every lab needs a lab assistant to oversee the operation. Otherwise the students would not know if their experiments were turning out correctly, would not know when they were doing something dangerous. Where do you find such help?

THE VALUE OF GROUP SUPPORT

Books and tapes can lead you through steps to self-awareness and healing, but only so far. There is great therapeutic value in finding a flesh-and-blood support group with whom you can interact. Unlike a family, in which membership is involuntary, these groups are a gathering of persons with like needs. As you get to know them and they you, you can begin taking healthy risks. Talk about pain and someone understands. Talk about changes you are trying to make and someone else probably is also.

Participants in sheltered support groups commonly report the joy of being able to take off the armor without getting hurt. The shock waves of dysfunctional family life built a shell. Now they crack the shell and find that the world isn't as punishing as the family was. Vulnerable people can make it, too.

If you are a member of a close church family, you may well find support among your fellow Christians. The various "anonymous" groups—Alcoholics Anonymous, Debtors Anonymous, Al-Anon, Alateen, and others—provide trustworthy support groups of concerned persons. Emotions Anonymous can even serve you if you're geographically or physically isolated from nearby groups. They link you up via mail with others with whom you can share problems and experiences—a support group by correspondence.

We caution you most strenuously that you be extremely discerning as you seek support. Two major dynamics are working against you. One is that your codependent radar may still be working just fine. If so, rather than find a healthy person with whom to bond and interact, you are quite likely to link into persons with problems as deep as yours—unresolved issues that will skew their view of you and your problems.

The other dynamic is that the helping professions are magnets for codependents, and not everyone now working in sociology, psychology, or the ministry has resolved his or her own problems. Patients come through our clinic who were dreadfully shamed by pastors or counselors suffering unresolved codependent issues of their own. As these individuals lived out their own abusive parents' roles, they offered not nurturance but condemnation or even added abuse.

BUILDING HEALTHY NEW BOUNDARIES

The final work, however, regardless of your support or lack of it, must be done by you yourself. And perhaps the most onerous task faces the person who must build new boundaries in a formerly codependent relationship. The difficulty is compounded if that other person has not dealt with unresolved issues of codependency.

If you are shouldering just that task, you'll be glad to hear that resetting boundaries does not tear your life apart. The first moments might get pretty rocky, but improvement should follow.

Codependents are not good at asking for things they need. As they descend ever deeper into their codependency and depression, they become more and more efficient at resentment. At first they ask, are refused, and resent the refusal. Then they cease asking, assume the refusal (the destructive internal message, "I'll never get what I want, so why bother?"), and move directly to resentment. Eventually, they don't even think to ask. They simply and immediately resent the fact they never get what they want.

To develop the new experience: "Sometimes I get what I want when I ask," we may have two clients in a relationship sit down facing each other. Each asks the other: "What do you need?" and "What are you willing to give?"

In the case of Gladys Jordan, who had such difficulty believing John would hear, the usual steps would be:

- Gladys asks regarding a need she wants met.
- John replies with a way he will (or will not, possibly) meet it.
- John then asks.
- Gladys replies.

We injected ourselves at several points in order to show them how better to hear each other:

Gladys described to John a need she wanted filled.

"John, I want you to be home in the evening, from supper on, two nights a week and all day Sunday."

We asked John, "What criticism do you hear in this request?"

"She thinks I'd rather be anywhere else than home. That's saying that the home I provide isn't good enough to stay in," John said.

We asked Gladys to clearly state her lack of critical intent.

"No! That's not what I meant at all. He provides a lovely home, and he's never there to appreciate it."

We asked John to recast what Gladys just said in his own words.

"Request and all?"

"Request and rebuttal. All of it," we said.

"Well, uh—for one thing, this is a lot harder than you think it ought to be. Let's see. She asked me to stay home two nights a week and all day Sunday; except for church, I assume. And she says it's a lovely home; she just wants me in it."

We asked Gladys, "Is this what you asked for?"

"Yes. That he stay home sometimes and not work constantly."

We asked John to describe how he would try to meet her need.

"Two nights. But I get to pick the nights and they don't always have to be the same from week to week. Maybe a

Wednesday and Thursday one week and a Tuesday and Wednesday the next. Something like that?"

Gladys: "If this works it'll be a miracle right up there on a level with the loaves and fishes."

John: "If this works, I'll donate the lunch."

Once they saw how to break the old patterns of nonhearing, primarily by repeating each other's thoughts, they could substitute the new and better pattern of truly listening. The strident shouts of their ghosts of the past diminished to an ineffectual murmur.

The eventual goal for the codependent is to trust beyond just a few persons. To request and accept help from the church, a community group, detached relatives—that involves a high degree of trust and confidence. Does God answer? The theory is "of course." The practice too often is, "I'm afraid to ask for fear He will ignore me." So twisted is the codependent's life, the ultimately trustworthy person, God, is often the last one to be trusted.

John and Gladys were particularly cooperative in their mutual development of trust and giving. Not always is that the case. Let us use you as an example. You are a wife trying to reset boundaries in what was a codependent relationship with your husband. Let us also assume he is not at the point of recovery that you are. He has been demanding and dictatorial in his control of purse strings. Now you, the wife, want to alter that specific situation. You want an active part in determining finances. As it stands now, you know nothing about your present financial status or what it would be were he to die. That's a very dangerous position to be in these days. For another reason, just as important, you want this marriage to be not a king/vassal arrangement but a partnership.

Based on what has happened in the past, here is what you can expect in advance if you are from an overly legalistic approach to God's Word. When you take your stand, your husband may instantly quote Scripture supporting his absolute rule. Then he may put you on a guilt trip. In the past, either or both of those responses would silence you.

The conversation might go something like this: You voice

your position. "I want to be involved in our financial manage-
ment. I want us to work as a team for reasons I've talked about
before. I don't want you to dictate every element of my financial life while I sit in ignorance."

"God's Word says I'm to be the head of this household. You
know the passages as well as I do by now."

"But we've never mentioned Priscilla, Dorcas, Lydia, and
the wife of Proverbs 31," you might respond. "And we could
talk about the women who financially supported Jesus and His
disciples. We haven't discussed them yet."

"You remember what happened the one time I let you have a
credit card, and you know what a disaster that was."

"That was a long time ago. I've changed. My life is under
control better and I'm more responsible now. I'm asking for
another chance."

Do you see the flow? There need be no adamant demand, no
confrontation. You have set new boundaries. You are maintaining your integrity as a person. The boundaries may seem
threatening, at first, to a man accustomed to holding all the
cards. You may not achieve your goals, even though they would
better serve you and your marriage than the present system
does. It is the boundaries that are important, your view of
yourself.

Frequently we encounter this argument from a spouse or
other significant person: "I'm depressed because you made
me depressed." The codependent spouse, overlapping this
person so completely, would instantly accept that. Now, safe
within a new boundary, the spouse can honestly respond, "I
understand your depression and I hurt for you. I'm sorry. But I
won't take responsibility for it anymore. I offer my love and
support, but not responsibility for your feelings. They are your
province."

Love has become a choice, not a demand.

STAGE EIGHT: REPARENTING

We find that most adult children need some reparenting as
part of their recovery. This can come from healthy family
members, a support group, therapy group, or therapist, or a

healthy church community. What would such surrogate parents do? What healthy parents do the world over: nurture, affirm, and guide. Three persons in your life will now become parents to you and assume the nurturing and monitoring function—yourself, another person or persons chosen for the role, and God.

THE OTHER PERSON

The other person will become a bridge parent until you develop the parent within you and develop a firmer relationship with God, so let's choose that other person first. Think for a few minutes who in your life right now can be a positive source of nurturance. Alcoholics Anonymous and similar groups use a system called sponsorship. The sponsor becomes a parental substitute, a wise eye to oversee you and guide you. The sponsor has been there before. He or she knows the road ahead.

The sponsor or reparent will serve in these ways:

- As a sounding board and nonprofessional counselor. A listener.
- As a friend. If you are seriously codependent, you can use one.
- As a daily contact. Contact might be a sixty-second discussion of the weather. Contact is the key.
- As a source of unconditional, nonjudgmental support. Very rarely can a family member fill this requirement. You need someone outside.
- As a gentle but firm confronter. When you're headed for trouble, your reparent will warn you. It takes real love.
- As a helper and confidante when you must recycle through the ten stages to cover unfinished business and new pain.
- As a healthy third party in your codependent relationship with another. Your reparent can take some of the pressure off with healthy distractions.

If your reparent is also recovering from codependency, he or she should be farther down the road than you are. We recommend your reparent should be of the same sex.

Just lately Brad, the exercyclist, gave up Joan again. Brad has great difficulty trusting men, for his father was not only an abusive dad but also an abusive coach. His father put him into a punishing regimen, preparing him for stardom as a collegiate (and perhaps Olympic) wrestler. Dad criticized mercilessly as Brad was training and fooled around with women on the side.

Brad's recovery is still in question; he's still making good—and bad—choices. Fortunately, Brad is in a good support group now. Unfortunately, he is still criticizing himself mercilessly inside. Fortunately he has not one, but two, sponsors. Unfortunately, they're both young women. Brad swears the relationships are platonic, but what a volatile mix. A clear-headed sponsor or reparent would tell Brad it's foolish to invite such intimate emotional contact when his own emotional relationship is so rocky.

When finding candidates to serve as surrogate parents, be sensitive to the appearance of any kind of abuse, either passive or active, in your relationship with this person. You've examined abuse thoroughly in your own life and now try to recognize it when you see it in others. If you find any sign of abuses in the relationship, set your boundaries up quickly and strongly.

We all read in the papers about sex therapists who seduce their patients, and counselors who browbeat their clients. You need to keep safety in mind, just as you did when seeking out a support group. You want to make certain your codependent radar isn't linking you up with new abusive parents.

Reparents can help fill the vacuum inside. They can give your love tanks a boost even if they can't fill them completely. They can reaffirm your new decisions about yourself.

YOURSELF

The second surrogate parent will be yourself. Growing up in a dysfunctional family, you already learned how to be your own negative parent. You criticize yourself, belittle and boss yourself. You'd hate it if someone treated a child of yours the way you treat that lost child within.

Develop a new, positive voice within yourself using the stage six technique you already know, replacing old internal messages with new ones. Some of our clients literally talk to themselves, the parent within addressing the child within. And sometimes, when the parent comes on in a negative way, the child within warns the parent to shun the old messages.

Just when you thought it was safe to get away from someone nagging you to eat your vegetables and get more rest, we tell you to internalize the parent. List the messages your parents gave you, all of them that you can remember. What were the unspoken messages, such as "You're no good" or "You can succeed if you work at it"? Put down all you can. Then choose the positive messages your parents gave you and consciously reject the negative ones.

And eat your vegetables.

GOD, THE FATHER

The final, ultimate parent refers to Himself as the Father. God. We mentioned that a major purpose of a functional family is to prepare its members for the greater membership in the family of God. You are to take a big step beyond the original family and adopt God as an actual parent. It's the future. Look again at the criteria of a reparent discussed above. Think how splendidly God can fulfill every item. His unconditional love makes Him the best friend and counselor you can have. Your other reparents can fill the love tank somewhat. God can fill it to the top.

One way to see Him as your Father is to seek out in Scripture the advice a parent would give a child. You'll be amazed how much is there, for instance, in Deuteronomy 5 and in Ephesians 5 and 6. Insert your name, as if God is speaking to you where it is appropriate. Another is to focus on a problem or need and discuss it with God in informal prayer. A third is to read *Healing the Child Within* by Charles L. Whitfield and *Becoming Your Own Parent* by Dennis Wholey, and apply them to your relationship with God.[1]

As you develop the parent inside, you will no longer look to persons outside to assume the parent role. For Sean McCurdy, this was the greatest step in his recovery. You will find it immensely helpful in yours.

CHAPTER
NINETEEN

Accountability and Maintenance

John Jordan sprawled flaccid in his chair and idly scratched his chin. "Seems to me, it'll be very easy to slip back into how we used to be. I mean, Gladys and I have been waging war for thirty years. That's a long, long time to build bad habits."

"You're right! This business of listening to each other is brand new for you. For a while yet it won't be as comfortable as the old ways were."

He nodded, with that mischief-on-the-hoof grin of his. "And I just bet you have some advice for us on the tip of your tongue."

"But of course. Tell me how you'd build a mid-priced single dwelling in, let's say, suburban Plano."

"Well, it pays to take a few legal steps first—establish ownership of the land, financial accountability. I almost never get stuck because I make certain up front that I'm not going to. As for the house itself, first pour the slab. . . ."

"The foundation."

"The foundation. Then, you know." He shrugged. "Framing and studs, joists and rafters, siding . . . finish the wiring, plumbing, and interior according to specs."

"And after you've built the house, you're done with it. Get your money and go home."

"Well, yeah, sort of." John almost looked a bit embarrassed. "Sometimes when I'm in the neighborhood of one of my biggies—there are some homes around I take a special pride in having built—I'll go a couple blocks out of my way and drive past it just to see how it's doing. See how the landscaping's holding up, whether they're maintaining it well. With a fine home, you don't just say, 'There. It's built. Now I can relax and ignore it.' Any little problem that starts, you take care of it right away. Then the home stays fine."

"That's exactly how you and Gladys will keep your new marriage running smoothly. Check every now and then to make certain the maintenance is being kept up."

STAGE NINE: RELATIONSHIP ACCOUNTABILITY

With this stage again you need the help of an outside person or persons. Your group may help, your reparent, perhaps a trusted friend not otherwise involved in your recovery. The object of this stage is to spot trouble early on and make a course correction before a problem develops. To do that you will maintain an ongoing inventory of present relationships.

THE INVENTORY

You should be pretty good at inventories now, and this one is almost like the detailed relationship inventory you did in stage two. That one, though, was historical, at least in part—relationships past as well as present. This one's contemporary. It will contain all your present friends and acquaintances and how you relate to them.

The inventory will do two things for you. It will reveal any codependent patterns as they emerge, and it will help you avoid the pitfalls of painful relationships at a time when you're very vulnerable. If you allow yourself to be held accountable by a trusted confidante, you will be much less likely to engage in a codependent relationship. The confidante will not be blind, as you will be, to your own motives.

That will be one of your biggest problems from now on, this blindness to self. Self-deception, denial, all the old defense mechanisms are waiting in the wings, ready to come into play.

You used them for years and they're comfortable. Even David, the apple of God's eye, could not see the enormity of his sin against Bathsheba and her husband. His advisor, Nathan, told a parable about a stolen lamb and ended it with the ringing condemnation, "You are the man." Not until that moment did David realize, "I have sinned against the Lord!"[1]

THE ADVISOR

Accountability works in this way. Our old friend Brad showed his relationship inventory of present friends and acquaintances to a trusted counselor, Jake. The inventory mentioned a woman, Susie.

"So who's Susie?" asked Jake.

"Works at the deli downtown. She just left a terribly abusive relationship with a real creep."

"Doesn't sound good," Jake warned Brad. "She could be another Joan. You might be getting yourself into a victim-rescuer situation, and that's the last thing you need. She needs solace and support, but not from you. You better rethink that relationship before you get in too deeply. Wait another six months before you see Susie. See what changes have occurred in both of you."

GUIDELINES

In AA, sponsors adjure their charges to avoid entering any serious new relationship the first year into recovery. "Concentrate on staying clean," they say, "and on growing emotionally and spiritually. You've been through a very hard time and it's still not easy. Don't load another ton on the old mule."

This is the same wisdom given persons whose spouses have died or divorced. "Marriage on the rebound," the old wives used to call it.

The wise ex-codependent will heed the words of an observer from the outside, who can see the picture better. In summary, you want to find a healthy Christian friend (or perhaps a support group), someone off whom you can bounce details of how you're doing, especially in regard to relationships.

But you can keep an eye on your relationship inventory also, monitoring for possible trouble. We offer these guidelines against which you may measure new relationships and changing old ones. You don't want to fall back into old habits and attitudes of codependency, and as John Jordan observed, it's so easy to do.

If You Are Dating. Never date someone who is emotionally or morally unavailable. That means no one committed in any way to another person. Anyone married, of course, is totally off-limits. So, too, should be the person who has recently divorced, the person who has trouble saying goodbye to the past and the people in it, the person who is obviously very much interested in someone else. To most people this guideline is obvious.

At the first sign of significant abuse, consider ending your involvement immediately. By now you know what the major abuses are. You have too much self-worth to subject yourself to them. Remember, too, that in the early stages of dating, both parties are usually on their best behavior. If you see smoke when dating, fire will surely follow.

At the clinic our single patients try to date persons in their codependency group meetings. We immediately warn them, "Whoa! Certainly you might find someone who's been working with the program a long time and has advanced far down the road. But look how the odds are stacked against you."

"Everybody in my singles group at church is dull," protest some patients. "Immature."

"Well, look there first anyway, at least until you're sturdier on your own two feet."

If You Are Widowed or Divorced. All the guidelines applying to singles apply to you as well. In addition:

For the first three to twelve months following a death or break-up you are extremely vulnerable. Codependency multiplies that vulnerability. Codependents are so hungry for affection and affirmation, 90 percent will jump into a new relationship almost immediately. That almost invariably leads to disaster and pain. We recommend a long wait, until you are emotionally stable again, before you even consider developing new other-sex relationships.

If You Are in a Committed Marriage. The largest part of

your ongoing inventory will deal with your spouse, and rightly so. We suggest you keep a close eye on these areas:

Authority and control, particularly of finances. Are you maintaining a partnership in marriage? Are you sharing control, with a head of the household and a responsible lieutenant? Are you both comfortable with the way you are sharing authority?

Needs and wants. Are you meeting each other's needs comfortably?

The sexual relationship. First, there is no outside sexual interest for either of you, right? Good. Is the sexual aspect of your relationship subject to control struggles or signs of addiction in either of you? Did the bedroom door slam recently, and if so, why? Are you both satisfied with the degree and frequency of contact? If there is dissatisfaction, have you sat down to talk about it?

Stock market syndrome. This, remember, is the "I'm happy if you're happy, and if you're not, I'm not" attitude. Is either of you coming to depend too much upon the other's emotional state of the moment?

To All Persons Recovering from Codependency. These items are more or less universal for all persons and can be applied to most circumstances. Use them as an informal yardstick to measure the quality of your ongoing relationships.

- No physical or verbal abuse by anyone.
- No immoral or unethical behavior. This means you will not lie to cover for another person, nor expect that person to stretch ethical standards to protect you. Codependents can go to unbelievable lengths (and then rationalize it in unbelievable ways) to protect persons in a close codependent relationship.
- No alcohol or chemical abuse by family members, particularly on the premises.
- Nothing illegal. From drug dealing and drunk driving to ignoring parking tickets—serious codependents tend to kiss off a lot of illegal activity, or simply fail to see it. That must not be.
- No more rescuing. Having identified rescuing behavior

pertinent to your circumstances, you are here pledging not to indulge in it any more. No, not even "Just this one little time."
- No being taken advantage of, unless I decide God would prefer I do it. Confusing? We trust not. How often does the codependent, with low self-esteem to start with, get suckered into helping someone, or bailing someone out (figuratively; even sometimes literally)? Here you must examine carefully the line between good Christian service and letting yourself be a doormat.

The guide in this situation is always Jesus Christ. He quoted His Father when He said, "Love your neighbor as yourself" (Matthew 19:19). That was *not* "Love your neighbor instead of yourself." It was not "Do anything for your neighbor whether it's necessary or in their best interests or not." Such unconditional love for people is always a choice!

A case in point is Gladys Jordan. She ended up with a neighbor's kids several times a week. The neighbor always had a need: "I have to run to the store." "If I don't get away awhile I'll scream." "I have to get the kitchen waxed before Dan comes home and the kids are tracking all over." "I'm taking a casserole over to Gertie, the shut-in, and the kids make her nervous." Gladys didn't mind at first. After all, this was a church member and sister in Christ. But with time, Gladys began to resent it. The resentment festered, as Gladys kept silence. Her internal discussion with herself went back and forth. *You're supposed to help your neighbor. Meet your sister's need. I'm being taken for a sucker. She's using me. Her needs are legitimate.* The crosscurrents tore at Gladys's conscience.

She brought the matter up during a session. We asked her these questions:

"Are you baby-sitting as a service to Jesus Christ, or are you baby-sitting because you're afraid she'll be angry if you don't? In other words, what are your motives? Does what you are doing fill an urgent need, or is it merely a convenience? Does she have other possible resources, or are you the only game in town?"

Gladys decided her motives were not altruistic service to

God but fear of what others would think. She served more a convenience than a need, and the woman did indeed have other less convenient resources, some of which cost money, some of which did not. From that Gladys decided to limit her service to matters of urgency and to perform it specifically as a gift to the Lord. But how was she to know an urgent need from a convenience? She sat down with the woman and made her own wishes known for the first time in that relationship. She would give X number of hours weekly to baby-sitting, and that was all. The woman could choose what hours and what needs would be met. It took several months for the woman to realize Gladys was firm in her resolve and would remain firm. Gladys feels much happier now about her service, and the woman is getting along fine.

Finally, as Gladys eventually did, weigh all your relationships before God. What are you doing for Him? What are you doing that is ostensibly for Him but isn't really? Are your existing relationships helping you grow spiritually?

You're pedaling the bicycle now. You're up on that tightrope and doing all right. A mentor remains beside you to steady you when you waver.

There is one final stage, maintenance, but it is a continuous process rather than a stop along the way. It is with maintenance that you most need God's support and nurturance, for human mentors, however trustworthy and mature, cannot see you all the way to the end.

STAGE TEN: MAINTENANCE

John Jordan sat on the patio under the chinaberry tree, sipping lemonade. His upper arms, bulging from under his rolled-up sleeves, were thicker than the tree trunk. When John and Gladys first visited us they positioned their chairs nearly six feet apart. The chairs touched now, their arms in gentle contact. Gladys looked ten years younger.

John waved a finger. "You know—about this inventory business. If anybody knows about inventories it's a small contractor. I tried it out in some of the other areas of my relationships, too. The kids I hire for entry-level jobs, the plumbers and roofers I subcontract. Do you know how many of them I chalked off as grumps and gripers and criticizers in the past?"

"All of them?"

"Close. Very close. And the couple of guys I didn't think grumbled are dead between the ears. I'm learning to listen to them. It's not easy, but it's paying me back in dollars and cents. You can't beat that for a bottom line."

"How about you, Gladys? You look good."

"I'm feeling so much better lately about so many things."

"Think you'll stay away from your old codependent ways of not listening and of hearing wrongly?"

John grinned. "We're keeping our eyes and ears open. Keeping our guard up about that, you might say."

Keeping his guard up. John Jordan nailed it right on the head.

MAINTENANCE NEEDS

Pico Martinez owns a '57 T-Bird in baby blue. That's his Saturday night car when he and his wife go out on the town. He also owns a CJ5 Jeep in red, orange, and yellow—his Sunday afternoon squirrel-around-in-the-foothills-with-the-kids vehicle. His shiny black Roadrunner he drives to work.

Three cars for one guy? He shrugs and grins. "Seven days in a week, eh? I got four to go."

Pico was employed as a mechanic at age twelve, quit school at fifteen, and went into adult education at eighteen. He earned his high school diploma and continued to an engineering degree, supporting himself and his family by day as an ace mechanic and studying at night. These days he doesn't just fix cars. He designs them.

Ask Pico about auto maintenance and he'll bend your ear for twenty minutes. "Most of what goes wrong with a car goes wrong because of neglect. These are delicate instruments and deserve daily care."

"Daily?"

"You bet! Every time you use it, 'fore you take it out, look for puddles, wet spots on the insides of the tires . . . any signs of leaks or problems. I painted my garage floor white, so anything shows up. Check the coolant if you don't have a sealed radiator, even the wiper fluid. All that stuff. Just go down an automatic checklist, like an airplane pilot would."

"It's really worth the effort?"

"In dollar cost as well as breakdown prevention, yes. Then every three months you change the oil and filter, check the carburetor and air filter . . . keep it clean inside and out. Keep a little spiral notebook in the glove box so you can write down when the next lube is due, when to pull a wheel on schedule and check brake linings . . . whatever."

Pico almost never has car trouble. His neighbors sniff and say he's just lucky. Pico says luck has nothing to do with it.

As a recovering codependent, you will want to put Pico's practical philosophy of preventive maintenance to work in your life. But varying degrees of codependency will call for varying degrees of maintenance. If your codependency thermometer registered on the low side, your maintenance won't entail all the meetings and the constant attention we'll describe here. Occasional tune-ups will do the trick. If you are struggling back from severe codependency problems, you'll want to go the max, helping yourself improve and avoiding slipping back in every way possible.

Maintenance affirms that recovery from codependency is not a once-and-for-all thing. Like cars, you are a complex machine requiring frequent adjustments and tuning. By keeping a watchful eye on your day-to-day living, you can enjoy the fruits of your recovery. Consider yourself as being under a strict maintenance contract.

We recommend three categories of maintenance. The daily routine comprises the first. Use of support groups forms the second. The third might be called recycling, as the vicissitudes and memories in your life send you through the ten stages as needed.

DAILY MAINTENANCE NEEDS

Daily maintenance should include a time for prayer in addition to the pauses for prayer during the day when things come up requiring them. You should set aside a quiet time for both meditation and for study. Scripture is very helpful in learning what God is like and what He wants for you. As you read, keep your mind's eye alert for His promises of parental love.

If you were previously enslaved to a strong addiction, compulsion, or obsession, do a brief daily inventory. Are the old ways creeping back?

If you are battling severe codependency, you may want to make contact with an advisor or support group a daily matter.

PERIODIC MAINTENANCE CHECKS

Every three months, just as Pico checks his brake linings, you need to do an inventory to compare with your earlier relationship- and self-inventories. Do you see improvement? Regression? Is it all just sitting there unchanged?

Persons who had to deal with particular problems should keep a close watch on their specific needs. Sean McCurdy must maintain an ongoing inventory of his relationships, particularly with employers. Because he understands what was happening, he can watch for problems and nip them in the bud. Incidentally, he's been with the same employer nearly a year now and is himself a mid-level sales manager. Jerry Braley is still trying to convince his son to enter therapy. He just might do it, too, because the improvement in the quality of Jerry's life and Jill's offers strong encouragement to Bill. To maintain their progress, both Jerry and Jill attend Emotions Anonymous meetings several times a month. Jill's rageaholism and eating disorder are under complete control now.

USING SUPPORT GROUPS

To some, the phrase "support groups" sounds like something only weak or nutty people need. It might even sound a bit frightening. After all, you have no idea what to expect. What might you find if you walk into such a group?

From the beginning, your anonymity is honored. No one uses a last name. "Hi, I'm Sam," is the most you ever learn of an identity. The chairs usually form a circle, although if many are present they may be arranged in concentric circles or in rows. Sit anywhere you wish.

You will be encouraged by the warmth and friendliness.

These people have been around the block and they share a great deal of pain and victory. You feel an intensity here and a strong sense of purpose. You may introduce yourself if you wish. It's not required. You'll not be expected to speak. Whatever participation you choose to make is voluntary. Arrive and leave in a cloud of mystery, if you want.

The people present will talk about their pain and their progress. They will tell how they use the twelve steps of their particular group. The details may be helpful to you or not. Some meetings will be more valuable to you than others in that way, but the overall feeling you will come away with is, *I'm not alone. These people are finding help, and I can, too.*

Appendix A offers lists of national organizations and support groups to whom you can turn for your own recovery and maintenance needs. They can tell you about help available locally, whatever your area. Several Christian recovery groups, like Overcomers Outreach and Substance Abusers Victorious (SAVE), have chapters throughout the country.

For many maintenance tasks, a long-term support group is invaluable. Such support groups and some church groups will serve you well over the long run.

CYCLING BACK THROUGH THE STAGES

We might call this aspect "cleanup." Periodically review the ten stages of recovery and recycle back to this stage or that as needed. Life throws some mean curve balls. Accidents, tragedies, minor annoyances clutter up what we would prefer to be a nice, trim, hassle-free life. These bumps in the road call for a recycling to stage five grieving, perhaps, or a reexamination of your self-perceptive messages. Pockets of pain we didn't know existed erupt suddenly. They must be dealt with. Old memories surface; they must be treated, not reburied. It is so easy to slip back into the old codependent tricks of denying pain, burying it, letting it fester.

Bessie Barnett is going to remember her childhood, and the pain of it will surge up now and again despite her sincere forgiveness, resolution, and acceptance. As part of her maintenance she'll remind herself of the division of labor between herself and God; she renews the forgiveness if necessary, her assigned task, and He will take care of the justice and retribution which is His province.

As you work through the healing you will find yourself cycling back to one stage or another as required, sometimes repeatedly. That's normal. You understand the healing process; now use it to maintain your new, healthy sense of self.

GOD'S ROLE IN YOUR RECOVERY

And now the warning: so long as you maintain on your own strength, you might get somewhere. But to succeed and succeed well, you need a strength beyond your own. Consider that codependency is multigenerational. You must break the bondage of the past with all its accumulated destructiveness. If you suffered a severe addiction, your very body is fighting you. Your chemistry has been altered, and not for the better. Obsessions cling. Compulsions refuse to stay dead; they resurface as some new repetitive activity, potentially more damaging than was the first. Old codependent patterns of thinking tarnish relationships with others and with God.

The founders of Alcoholics Anonymous saw an almost universal bitterness toward God in the people they sought to help. And yet, God was the only hope for these people. How could these men and women be drawn to call upon a God they wanted nothing to do with? A dilemma indeed.

Fortunately for the millions whom AA has benefited, God already had that base covered. Romans 8:26 assures us that "Likewise the Spirit also helps in our weaknesses. For we do not know what we should pray for as we ought, but the Spirit Himself makes intercession for us with groanings which cannot be uttered." The founders used the phrases *a Power greater than ourselves* and *God as we understood him*. That phrasing stops short of meeting core spiritual needs since He is not "as we understood him" but as He has revealed Himself. Yet the principle God has always employed is that people who need Him can reach out to Him from wherever they are spiritually and be heard.

Without spiritual growth, recovery is stunted. Persons in

the anonymous programs almost universally agree that a spiritual lack underlies the symptoms of addictions, compulsions, and obsessions. To quote the Big Book of Alcoholics Anonymous, "We are not cured of alcoholism. What we really have is a daily reprieve contingent on the maintenance of our spiritual condition."

GOD'S ROLE IN YOUR LIFE

Sean McCurdy needed a loving father. God becomes the ultimate loving Father.

Louise's love tank was on empty. God alone can fill the tank as no other human resource can.

John and Gladys required a mediator, a third person in their marriage. God mediates all healthy relationships.

Bessie Barnett needed the assurance that the suffering in her childhood was acknowledged and handled justly. God promises to do that.

Walter Morgan, the former pastor, found within himself an enormous burden of pain. Pain is the touchstone to spiritual progress; God can lift that burden.

In a word, God can serve every need. You have probably heard that your whole life. One commonly used slogan is, "Let go and let God." However, as we apply this principle according to the prophet Isaiah's reminder, "Those who wait on the Lord shall renew their strength," we see this not as passivity but active dependence.[2] Waiting on the Lord does not preclude your taking responsibility or appropriate action. It does involve not running ahead of His timing.

Now is the time to apply it to your specific situation. What is your need? How do you think God might serve it? That may not be what He actually chooses for you. How else might He serve it? God reserves for Himself limitless options. Be attuned to the possibility of more than one response from Him.

Spiritual Progression. W. C. Fields made famous the quote, "Everyone has to believe something. I believe I'll have another drink." In all its meanings, flippant and profound, it speaks so sadly to the lost world of the addict and the obsessive compulsive. A system of belief is universal in humankind, and everything the addict truly believes (whatever lip service might be made to God or to some philosophy) is encompassed in his or her addiction.

With this book we have led you from an understanding of the mechanics and dangers of codependency through the ten stages that lead to recovery. Every book has a theme; that is, an underlying message; and the theme of this one is control. Who is directing the shots? Who is making the choices? As you have seen, control or the lack of it is central in the lifestyle of the codependent.

Your spiritual progression travels four mileposts. The first is the addictions, compulsions, and obsessions. We defined codependency as addiction to places, behaviors, and things. Addictions by their nature control you; fool yourself if you will, but you never control them.

At the next milepost, you break the addiction's control and get reacquainted with your *self*. Your self is now in the driver's seat—an uncomfortable place to be, at first.

At the next, you reach out into relationships with others. You make yourself vulnerable, trust, and are trusted. This is the beginning of a working, personal relationship with God. You share control of your life with others.

Finally, in a personal relationship to a personal God, you learn to trust Him, then progressively turn control over to Him. This is the term *spiritual surrender* in action.

The various secular schools of psychology stop at the third milepost. You must travel that fourth mile to find completion, for the key to overcoming codependency is a relationship with God established the only way He has declared He wants it established—through Jesus Christ.

Spiritual Surrender. "I have no idea how to surrender to God." Lena pursed her lips.

"What is holding you back?"

"I don't know. Ignorance, I suppose. I don't know what to do. And maybe lack of trust has something to do with it. Maybe if I could see Him—if He were something you could reach out and touch somehow."

"Like Mrs. Horner?"

"Who?"

"Mrs. Horner, one of our former patients. She's been blind since the age of fifteen. She has never seen her husband or her children."

"That's so sad!"

"In a sense, yes. And yet, Mrs. Horner relates to her family very warmly and well. She knows what the kids are going to do before they even think of it."

Lena nodded. "I see your point. You don't have to see to relate. So how do I begin?"

"Did you ever trust Jesus Christ or acknowledge Him as your savior?"

"Years ago. But I don't think that's the same thing."

"It's not. It's an essential start, not an end. Alright, what do you need?"

Lena smiled. "Money, power, prestige." The smile faded. "I'm being facetious, of course. What I need most is a friend."

"In John 15:14, Jesus says, '"You are my friends."' And then goes on to say, '"you did not choose Me. I *chose* you."' We paused a moment to allow Lena to reflect on this. Then we asked, "What else do you need?"

"A father. The reparenting business calls upon God as the ultimate Father; I understand that with my head. But my heart is still an orphan."

"Sometime look up the word *father* in a concordance and see how often it refers to God. Why, just in the book of John it appears over a hundred times. As you read Scripture, the truth will be drummed into you; here is the ultimate father."

"So He serves my needs. That's not surrendering to Him."

"When you asked His help in resisting your addictions, did He do it?"

"I tried a zillion times before—on my own will power, you know?—and I was never able to lick it. I couldn't have done it without Him."

"And when you asked Him to help while you were assembling your relationship inventory, what happened?"

"Things I never guessed kept popping right out of me. I'm sure I had divine help with that."

"There you are. That's the key."

"What's the key?"

"When you accept His friendship, you are surrendering that part of you. When you admit you can't master your addictions without Him, you are surrendering that control to Him. Surrender is not tossing the whole chunk at His feet. It's giving Him every aspect of your life, aspect by aspect, an area at a time. You're much farther along that road than you would imagine."

Lena was radiant. "I'm much farther along the road than *you* imagine! Six months ago I couldn't trust anybody. I couldn't even trust my boss to mail my paycheck. I picked it up at the desk. Now I see that I'm trusting God in many areas where, it used to be, I didn't even trust myself."

"There you are. You're living out Philippians 2:13, 'For it is God who works in you both to will and to do for His good pleasure.' Trust is the glove on the hand of surrender."

"*Two*-thirteen? Wait . . ." Lena thumbed through her Bible. "Here's the one I know, two chapters over—4:13. 'I can do all things through Christ who strengthens me.' That's my verse."

"That's surrender."

If you are severely codependent, like the alcoholic you will never be free of your illness. You can, however, keep it in arrest, not through your own strength but through the strength of God. Your strength and will power are not sufficient to keep in chains all those ghosts of the past that would control you.

You cannot trust your head, for your most important decisions—choosing love, choosing a lifestyle, choosing God— are framed beyond reason. And yet, you cannot trust your heart, for there the ghosts reside.

Lena, who had such bitter trouble trusting anyone at all, found the seat of trust, God. We encourage you, as we encouraged Lena, specifically to do two things in your relationship with God: Depend utterly upon Him, drawing from Him and from healthy human relationships He opens to you all the love you need for your love tank. And take the initiative in both serving Him and bettering yourself. Seek help for problems. Seek ways to do things God needs done—not for the praise of men but for His glory. The patients who derive the most pleasure from life (as do we ourselves) are those who plainly and actively enjoy their relationship with our Lord.

With His love encompassing you, you need no longer tie yourself in the codependent knots of an unhealthy relationship, grasping, enmeshing, suffocating and being suffocated. "The truth shall make you free," said Jesus in John 8:32. Free! Free to enjoy, free to choose. And one of the choices is love.

APPENDIX A
A Personal
Perspective

Codependency is not a simple concept. We humans are susceptible to codependency because of our sinful tendency to use defense mechanisms to fool ourselves. In codependent relationships, deceitful games are played. In addition, important Christian principles are often taken out of context and abused. For example, "Wives, submit to your husbands" is a biblical principle; but, taken out of context, the husband can avoid his responsibility to be loving while using his leadership role as a club to try to keep his wife in an unhealthy codependent relationship.

God wants us to have healthy relationships with a balance between being dependent and independent. He wants us to avoid addictions of any kind, including that of unhealthy codependency. Paul described this balance in Galatians 6:2–5 when he told us to bear one another's "over-burdens," yet reminded us that every man shall carry his own load in terms of personal responsibility.

The most effective means for overcoming codependent relationships is to establish a relationship with Christ Himself. This is done merely by realizing that "all have sinned and fall short of the glory of God";[1] that there is a penalty for sin,[2] yet sin's penalty has been paid through Christ's death in our place.[3] Because of this, we can receive forgiveness, meaning in life, enablement to overcome sin and even addictions, and a home in heaven forever merely by trusting Christ.[4]

If you have never entered this relationship with Christ, then I would like to personally extend to you an invitation to accept Christ as your personal Savior and Friend. When we do, we are free to develop healthy relationships with others because of the relationship we have with Christ.

Frank Minirth, M.D.
President of The Minirth-Meier Clinic

APPENDIX B
Support Groups and Other Sources of Help

These recovery resources for codependents can serve you well in two ways. They are, of themselves, an important source of help. Also, the volunteers or employees know about other related resources in your area. Use them and their advice to tailor a program of help to your specific needs.

The support groups welcome you without prejudice. However, groups addressing sexual addictions must necessarily be very careful about who is sitting there listening. They will screen you thoroughly. If your need is real they want nothing more than to help you. You will appreciate the security their screening provides.

You can reach these groups, some of them recently formed, by consulting the white pages of your phone directory. If what you need doesn't seem to be there, call a related organization; they will be able to help you contact the group. Or, search through the phone directory of a larger city nearby. Ask a local librarian or call one of the big libraries in major cities. Most county library systems and many city libraries have a reference number, often an 800 number. Reference specialists at those numbers probably have just the information you need literally at their fingertips.

Alcoholics Anonymous
P.O. Box 459, Grand Central
Station
New York, NY 10163
(212) 686-1100

Al-Anon/Alateen Family
Group Headquarters Inc.
P.O. Box 182, Madison
Square Station
New York, NY 10159
1-800-356-9996
(212) 302-7240

Debtors Anonymous
314 W. 53rd St.
New York, NY 10019
(212) 969-0710

Emotions Anonymous
P.O. Box 4245
St Paul, MN 55104
(612) 647-9712
(international)
(612) 738-9099 (Twin Cities)

Gamblers Anonymous
P.O. Box 17173
Los Angeles, CA 90017
(213) 386-8789

Narcotics Anonymous,
World Service Office
16155 Wyandotte St.
Van Nuys, CA 91406
(818) 780-3951

Codependents Anonymous
P.O. Box 33577
Phoenix, AZ 85087-3577
(602) 944-0141

National Association for
Children of Alcoholics
31582 Coast Highway
Suite B
South Laguna, CA 92677
(714) 499-3889

Overcomers Outreach
2290 W. Whittier Blvd.
Suite D
La Habra, CA 90631
(213) 697-3994
(Alcoholics and Adult
Children Claiming Christ's
Promises and Accepting
His Healing)

Overeaters Anonymous,
World Service Office
2190 190th St.
Torrance, CA 90504
(213) 542-8363

National Clearinghouse for
Alcohol Information
P.O. Box 1908
Rockville, MD 20850

Adult Children of Alcoholics,
Central Service Board
P.O. Box 35623
Los Angeles, CA 90035
(213) 464-4423

Incest Survivors Anonymous
P.O. Box 5613
Long Beach, CA 90800

Be advised these organizations exist also. Seek them out locally.

Adult Children Anonymous
Al-Atot
Alcoholics Victorious
  (Christian recovery
  support group)
Bulimics/Anorexics
  Anonymous
Child Abusers Anonymous
Cocaine Anonymous
Codependents of Sex
  Addicts
Parents Anonymous
Pills Anonymous
Sex Addicts Anonymous
Sexaholics Anonymous
Sex and Love Addicts
  Anonymous
Shoplifters Anonymous
Smokers Anonymous
Spenders Anonymous
Victims of Incest Can
  Emerge
Workaholics Anonymous

NOTES

Chapter 7
1. See Joshua 6.
2. See 2 Kings 5.
3. Jeremiah 17:9.

Chapter 10
1. Robin Norwood, *Women Who Love Too Much: A Closer Look at Relationship Addiction and Recovery* (Los Angeles: Jeremy P. Tarcher, Inc., 1986).

Chapter 12
1. The roles were first described by Sharon Wegsheider in *Another Chance: Help and Hope for Alcoholic Families* (Palo Alto, CA: Science and Behavior).
2. Matthew 25:21.
3. Matthew 7:9-11.

Chapter 16
1. Ephesians 4:26.
2. Proverbs 3:5.
3. Matthew 18:3, *NIV*.
4. 1 Thessalonians 5:23.

Chapter 18
1. Charles L. Whitfield, *Healing the Child Within* (Deerfield Beach, FL: Health Communications, 1987). Dennis Wholey, *Becoming Your Own Parent* (New York: Doubleday, 1988).

Chapter 19
1. See 2 Samuel 11 and 12.
2. Isaiah 40:31.

Appendix A
1. Romans 3:23.
2. See Romans 6:23.
3. See Romans 5:8.
4. See John 1:12.

ABOUT THE AUTHORS

Dr. Robert Hemfelt, Ed.D., is a psychologist who specializes in the treatment of chemical dependencies, codependency, and compulsivity disorders. Before joining the Minirth-Meier Clinic, he was an addictions specialist with a Fortune 500 corporation and, before that, the supervisor of therapeutic services for the Substance Abuse Study Clinic of the Texas Research Institute of Mental Sciences.

Dr. Frank Minirth is a diplomate of the American Board of Psychiatry and Neurology and received an M.D. degree from the University of Arkansas College of Medicine.

Dr. Paul Meier received an M.S. degree in cardiovascular physiology at Michigan State University and an M.D. degree from the University of Arkansas College of Medicine. He completed his psychiatric residency at Duke University.

Dr. Minirth and Dr. Meier founded the Minirth-Meier Clinic in Dallas, Texas, one of the largest psychiatric clinics in the world, with associated clinics in Chicago; Los Angeles, Newport Beach, Orange, Laguna Hills, and Palm Springs, California; Little Rock, Arkansas, Longview, Fort Worth, Sherman, San Antonio, and Austin, Texas; and Washington, D.C.

Both Dr. Minirth and Dr. Meier have received degrees from Dallas Theological Seminary. They have also co-authored more than thirty books, including *Happiness Is a Choice, Worry-Free Living, Love Hunger, How to Beat Burnout,* and *Beyond Burnout.*

THE MINIRTH-MEIER CLINIC OFFICES

National Headquarters
MINIRTH-MEIER CLINIC, P.A.
2100 N. Collins Blvd.
Richardson, Texas 75080
(214)669-1733
1-800-229-3000
OUTPATIENT SERVICES
DAY TREATMENT CENTER
HOSPITAL PROGRAMS

MINIRTH-MEIER TUNNELL & WILSON CLINIC
Centre Creek Office Plaza, Suite 200
1812 Centre Creek Drive
Austin, Texas 78754
(512)339-7511
1-800-444-5751
OUTPATIENT SERVICES
DAY TREATMENT CENTER
HOSPITAL PROGRAMS

MINIRTH-MEIER CLINIC WEST
260 Newport Center Drive, Suite 430
Newport Beach, California 92660
(714)760-3112
1-800-877-4673

OUTPATIENT SERVICES
DAY TREATMENT CENTER
HOSPITAL PROGRAMS

MINIRTH-MEIER CLINIC, P.C.
The Grove, Suite 1510
2100 Manchester Road
Wheaton, Illinois 60187
(708)653-1717
1-800-848-8872
1-800-545-1819
OUTPATIENT SERVICES
DAY TREATMENT CENTER
HOSPITAL PROGRAMS
NATIONAL COMMUNICATIONS DIVISION

MINIRTH-MEIER-RICE CLINIC, P.A.
Koger Center in the Shannon Building
10801 Executive Center Drive, Suite 305
Little Rock, Arkansas 72211
(501)225-0576
1-800-488-4769
OUTPATIENT SERVICES
HOSPITAL PROGRAM

MINIRTH-MEIER BYRD CLINIC, P.A.
4300 Fair Lakes Court, Suite 200
Fairfax, Virginia 22033-4231
(703)968-3556
1-800-486-HOPE(4673)

OUTPATIENT SERVICES
DAY TREATMENT CENTER
HOSPITAL PROGRAMS

For general information about other Minirth-Meier Clinic branch offices, counseling services, educational resources and hospital programs, call toll-free 1-800-545-1819.

National Headquarters: (214)669-1733   1-800-229-3000